The
JEWISH
100

The JEWISH 100

A Ranking of the Most Influential Jews of All Time

Michael Shapiro

A Citadel Press Book

Published by Carol Publishing Group

Carol Publishing Group Edition, 1996

A Citadel Press Book
Published by Carol Publishing Group
Citadel Press is a registered trademark of Carol Communications, Inc.

Editorial, sales and distribution, rights and permissions inquiries should be
addressed to Carol Publishing Group, 120 Enterprise Avenue, Secaucus, N.J.
07094

In Canada: Canadian Manda Group, One Atlantic Avenue, Suite 105,
Toronto, Ontario M6K 3E7

Carol Publishing Group books may be purchased in bulk at special discounts
for sales promotion, fund-raising, or educational purposes. Special editions
can be created to specifications. For details, contact: Special Sales
Department, 120 Enterprise Avenue, Secaucus, N.J. 07094

Manufactured in the United States of America
10   9   8   7   6   5   4   3   2   1

Library of Congress Cataloging-in-Publication Data

Shapiro, Michael
    The Jewish 100 : a ranking of the most influential Jews of all
time / Michael Shapiro.
        p.   cm.
    "A Citadel Press book."
    ISBN 0-8065-1814-6
    1. Jews—Biography.   I. Title.   II. Title: Jewish one hundred.
DS115.S465   1996
920'.0092924—dc20   96–27332
[B]   CIP

To Barnett, Annie, Esther, and Uncle Charlie
Sam and Jean
Theresa, Benjamin, Gregory, and Nathaniel
I owe you my life and all my love

. . . but your name shall be Abraham; for the father of many nations have I made you. And I will make you exceedingly fruitful, and I will make nations from you, and kings shall come out of you. And I will establish My covenant between Myself and you and your seed after you throughout their generations for an everlasting covenant, to be a God unto you and to your seed after you . . .

—Genesis 17:5

CONTENTS

INTRODUCTION

From Abraham to the death of Simon Bar Kokhba in the tragic revolt against the Romans of 135 C.E., the Jewish people exerted an influence on world civilization more profound and lasting than any other ancient culture. Surely other peoples added their own richness to humanity: Babylonian government, Chinese invention, Egyptian architecture, Greek philosophy, literature, and democracy, Hindu mysticism, Roman imperialism—all contributed much to the forces of history.

Yet the Jews were a people capable of producing Moses and Jesus of Nazareth and inspiring the Prophet of Islam. The beliefs of Christians and Muslims in one God comes directly from the Jewish S'hma ("Hear, O Israel, the LORD our GOD, the LORD is One!"). Those words, first uttered in a desert almost devoid of life, blossomed into the faiths of countless billions.

When the Romans massacred Bar Kokhba and his rebels, the survivors were either sold into slavery or dispersed into the empire. Except for the flowering of Jewish expression in pre-Inquisition Spain, no Jew, until Baruch de Spinoza in the seventeenth century, was permitted to leave any mark on western civilization. Almost 1,600 years were spent in seclusion and bare survival. Jews did not participate to any noticeable degree in the Italian Renaissance or the Elizabethan Age. Nonetheless, during these centuries of hiding and Diaspora, a succession of rabbis of genius and an observant people kept the Jewish religion and culture intact.

Only when leaders such as Moses Mendelssohn and the Rothschilds pulled themselves and their people out of the ghetto that was their lot in Europe (and with the special help of Napoleon) did Jewry again participate in the development of a world community. The period from the Enlightenment in the late

1700s through the present day has witnessed the third greatest period of Jewish culture and influence.

This book ranks the 100 most influential Jews of all time. In their areas of human endeavor each of them worked a special influence on mankind. They changed the way we live and think. Even the few who touched only the souls and minds of Jews are important to us because of their defining presence on Jewish identity.

Some of the Jewish 100 modified their Judaism into something new. Saul of Tarsus became Paul, disciple of a man he claimed was the Jewish Messiah. Spinoza applied a logic that carried him straight out of Judaism. Karl Marx imposed an almost biblical sense of history to prove the imperative of his political ideal. Whether their modifications improved life will always generate discussion and argument. Their special examples prove why examining the influence of the Jewish 100 is so compelling.

Another source of debate is the relative weight given to different spheres of human involvement. Figures from the Bible are not necessarily more influential than some contemporary people. Neither is entertainment always less crucial to humanity than religion or science.

Some of the Jewish 100 have had the benefit of thousands of years to work their unique influence. The weight of centuries would seem to favor the ancients over the moderns. However, it would be unfair to belittle the accomplishments of an Albert Einstein because a King David preceded him by three thousand years. Einstein will remain influential into the next millennium as mankind either suffers nuclear conflagration or hooks onto the speed of light to blast far into space.

This overview of the Jewish 100 is not designed to be a reference book. Most of the lives of the Jewish 100 are very adequately described in encyclopedias and learned biographies. Rather, in the Talmudic tradition of presentation and analysis, the Jewish 100 have been ranked and examined in their order of influence on the world, not just on Jews. The rankings are open for discussion. Not all the Jewish 100 were great and good men (though most were), but all altered conventions or directed society into what they viewed as righteousness, seeking to improve life not only for their minority but for all of God's children.

The
JEWISH
100

1

Moses

(Thirteenth century B.C.E.)

He was a prince in Egypt, then a killer, an outcast, a shepherd, a liberator of slaves, a receiver of God's laws, a judge, a conqueror, a prophet. Snatched from the Nile, he was raised by Pharaoh's sister, attended by an Israelite woman (actually his mother). Only a slave brought up as royalty could have had the courage and know-how to lead the oppressed in such a revolt. The Jews' flight from Egypt was, remarkably, the one successful rebellion of an enslaved people in ancient times. The Exodus, that singular event in history, transformed nomads into a power that changed earthly life forever.

The Exodus, rather than the Creation, defined the Jewish people. The laws given by God directly to Moses in the desert became known as the Sinai covenant, with the Ten Commandments, or Decalogue, its core. Simple justice and respect for life were established in Sinai as the controlling forces of humanity.

In the ancient Egyptian language, Moses, or Mosheh, means "born of" or "is born"; the Hebrew *masheh* translates as "drawn of." Whatever the origins (which seem to combine the strongest strains of ancient Egyptian and Hebraic cultures), Moses' life story dominates the Bible. He was the most exemplary of the Hebrew prophets and the most influential Jew in all history. As either a model or a real man, he brought to human life a concern for the downtrodden, an idealism, a hope, a system of laws by which people can survive each other, whether lost in the wilderness for forty years or seated in the courts of great palaces of stone and marble. Through Moses, God directed mankind. Yet Moses spoke sluggishly, relying on his brother Aaron for eloquent speech.

"I am what I am," God declared to Moses. The God of Moses and the Israelites is *one* god; Moses, however, was a man with faults like other men, never a minor god (unlike the pharaohs of Egypt and emperors of Rome, who fancied themselves gods). Monotheism, the belief in one god, displaced forever the primitive worship of gods in the guise of animals. Each person's experience of God must be personal, *that* person's experience. God can only be comprehended in the abstract, not through graven images. Distinct from the deathly imagery of the Egyptian gods, the God of Moses is always the God of life, affirmation, existence, of what is and what is next. The Hebrew word for God, YHWH, means "to be."

The Lord's prophet, Moses, the political leader, remains a vital symbol in the righteous fight against persecution. In our times, the biblical exhortation "Let my people go!" became the clarion call of the American civil rights movement, and was later sounded for Soviet refuseniks.

Moses always fought injustice. As a young Egyptian prince, he slew a brutal overseer and buried him in a shallow grave. As a noble, Moses could have ordered the overseer to halt his abuse of a slave. Instead, in a blind rage, Moses felled the overseer. It is as if Moses wished to be uncovered as an imposter. He also stopped two Hebrews from fighting, defended his soon-to-be Midian wife and her sisters from marauding shepherds, and led a rebellion against a great, oppressive, and suffocating power.

His every act has rich, symbolic meaning: After killing the overseer, he fled into the desert, began a family with Zipporah and her wise father, sheik Jethro, and purged his soul of Egyptian customs. Moses knew that his murder of the overseer was produced by an uncontrollable rage against Egyptian tyranny. Slavery and the worship of animals had made Jewish life in Egypt an abomination. All human life, whether slave or pharaoh, must be held sacred. God directed Moses to free the slaves from their bondage so that they might pray to Him.

Although Moses pleaded with his cousin to let the Israelites go, and despite fearful plagues, Pharaoh's heart turned to stone; his silence brought repeated pestilence and sure death on Egypt. Whether the plagues and the drowning of Egyptian charioteers in the Red Sea are viewed today as magic or gospel, the events are based in history. The Egyptians did drown Hebrew babies in the Nile as a vicious method of controlling a swelling slave population, and the Red Sea was really a sea of reeds, a swamp in which chariot wheels could easily become mired.

The rabbis of later generations directed the observant not to rejoice at these miracles. Rather, the lesson of the Exodus is one of compassion: Do not hate the Egyptians, as you were once strangers in their land. At the Passover seder, the spilling of a few drops of wine reminds observant Jews that their joy in salvation is diminished—the cup of happiness is not full—when others suffer or are despised. This remarkable conciliatory response to the pain of the defeated defines not only Judaism but all western civilization.

The burning bush also sears a new meaning into suffering humanity. No longer are animal gods to be worshipped. The golden calf and all who bow down to it are condemned and destroyed in Old Testament fury. A burning bush that is not consumed manifests God's omnipotent control over nature. (The burning bush has also been seen as a symbol of Jewish survival and of the visionary wisdom of Moses.)

The laws given in the desert, the Sinai covenant, are known today as Mosaic law. Although more ancient codes have been discovered in the ruins of Mesopotamia (especially the Code of

Hammurabi) and while Jewish law has much the same structure and diction of other laws of antiquity, Judaism was the first system of human beliefs that respected human life. Most ancient governments valued property over people. Crimes against property were punishable by death. Murderers, on the other hand, could compensate the relatives of their victims by paying them or by sacrificing a valuable slave. Jewish law is consumed with caring for morality and social values. There has been nothing in history quite like it.

Moses, the prophet and giver of laws, is revered by Christians and Muslims, albeit in slightly different ways. After Abraham, of course, Moses is viewed as the second most important figure. Many events in the New Testament seem modeled on Moses' life and work. Jesus' young life parallels that of Moses. An evil king threatens to kill newborns, the prophet flees into exile in the desert, only to return to "free" his people. When the prophet is absent from his people, he is despised among men, his preaching forgotten. The Sermon on the Mount is meant to enrich the covenant given at Sinai. Jesus is depicted as a "second Moses." Both Moses and Jesus are referred to as "redeemer." For Saint Paul, the faith of Moses is a religion of law, while that of the Christians rests in the grace of God in the Christ. For Christians, however, Jesus is the son of God, while for Jews, Moses remains a man, an ambassador of God's laws.

For Islam, Moses, like Muhammad, received God's revelation through a book. Both are recipients of God's laws. Muhammad, too, must flee into the desert to Medina, but he returns in triumph, leading to his blessed death and ascent into Heaven. What distinguishes Islam from Judaism and Christianity is the Muslim belief that Muhammad is the final *seal* of all biblical prophecy, proclaiming the word of God in its purest state.

Moses, unlike Buddha or Confucius, was not an inward-looking mystic. For Moses, perfect life is not found adrift in the sea of the infinite. Judaism and the religions it gave rise to, Christianity and Islam, call their followers to interact with God through everyday behavior controlled by His laws. Moses, like Jesus and Muhammad, not only has visions of God, but speaks directly to Him. Mankind must likewise dream of heavenly grace while living together in a community governed by ethics and morality.

2

Jesus of Nazareth

(ca. 4 B.C.E.–ca. 30 C.E.)

In any ranking of the most influential Jews in history, Jesus of Nazareth must be listed near the top. If history is carefully examined, with an open mind and cold logic, the true effect of his *ethos* must be viewed, however, as less influential than Moses'. The traditions established by Moses defined the Jewish people and formed the basis of the three great monotheistic religions: Judaism, Christianity, and Islam.

Any person, Jew, Christian, or Muslim, must recognize that many of Jesus' teachings contain essential truths and exhibit the highest standards of ethical behavior. The bright light of his vision has illuminated innumerable souls and inspired the creation of many of the greatest artistic masterworks. Yet so many in the world have failed, century after century, to obey his good and wise moral teachings. The meek have not inherited the earth. From the savagery and destruction of the Crusades through the "ethnic cleansing" of today, humankind has repeatedly failed this son of man. People of all faiths continue to show that they need the guidance of Mosaic law to survive each other.

There have been countless and notable exceptions to the murderous misuse of Jesus' name by the wicked. The abolition of slavery during the American Civil War, the saving of Jewish lives by righteous Gentiles during the Holocaust despite indescribable risk, and the caring for the sick by saintly women such as mothers Teresa in Calcutta and Hale in Harlem, are recent examples (from untold many).

Jesus' example of pacifism has had a vast and supremely beneficial influence on the faithful of all religions. His lesson of turning one's cheek was the first example of pacifism in western history and surely one of its most important civilizing teachings. Regrettably, there remain instances in life when aggression can only be halted with arms. Christian pacifism was wholly ineffective against the Nazi terror. Jesus' spirit of nonviolence, however, has returned in recent times in the work of Dr. Martin Luther King Jr. (also influenced by the example of the Hindu Mahatma Gandhi). However, nonviolent resistence to tyranny is only possible in the rare circumstance when a society is fundamentally just.

If Jesus' message of peace had been followed, Europe would not have been continually ravaged over the centuries by vicious religious and cultural wars: Crusaders on their way to battle in the Holy Land massacring defenseless Jews as easy practice for the slaughter of Muslims, Spaniards expelling or burning infidels in an Inquisition of organized hate or raping the New World of its people and natural riches, Catholic France battling Protestant England, Napoleonic wars of conquest and domination, mass annihilation of millions of innocents by post-Christians Hitler and Stalin, Irish maiming Irish, Croats killing Serbs killing Bosnians.

Only the most narrow-minded would deny that Jesus would have been repulsed by these thousands of years of carnage (especially the near destruction of his people in the Holocaust). The sins committed in his name by churches, governments, and individuals must be separated from his legacy of love and charity. His essential message was not to separate but to bring people together. A crucial mission of the contemporary church must be to recognize how easily his revelations can be turned by the false prophets of bigotry into unmitigated hate.

How would Jesus have reacted to the dozens of creeds founded in his name? When he made Simon and Andrew into "fishers of men," could Jesus have imagined not only the Eastern Orthodox, Catholic, and Protestant churches, but the infinite, ever-changing, denominations? Surely, the ability of Christianity to adapt to disparate cultures (think of a Catholic mass in Boston versus one in East Africa) allowed it to spread and to multiply the faithful. Jesus' dreams of brotherhood and an afterlife in Paradise proved universally acceptable to peoples of diverse cultures and backgrounds. The largely insular and national religion of Judaism became through his changes to it and personal example (as molded by Saint Paul, the Apostle to the Gentiles) a path of instant and easy conversion for multitudes.

Examining Jesus' life and thoughts raises many unanswered questions. He is often impossible to pin down, an enigma. His use of parables, wondrous tales, homespun stories, to make a point, render him incapable of encapsulation. However, he seemed always to cast doubt on assumptions.

During a time of brutal Roman oppression and zealous opposition, Jesus urged his fellow Jews not to revolt, but to render to Caesar what was Caesar's. Did he foresee the destruction of the Temple in Jerusalem and the dispersion of Palestinian Jewry, or was his "prediction" created by later Christian theologians to justify the rise of their religion and to show allegiance to Rome during the Judean revolts?

Jesus' views on personal possessions are well-known. He urged that people sell what they own and give to the poor. In this, Jesus was squarely in the tradition of Jewish charitable giving (or tsedakah). Yet, over history, how many Christian kings or papal rulers have given up their treasure for the downtrodden?

The basic ethical principles of Christianity were first enunciated by Jesus. With a charismatic presence, vibrant mind, and skillful way with words, Saint Paul interpreted Jesus' teachings and developed them into a religion. Although it is unclear what Christianity would have been without Paul, it would not have survived so vigorously without his proselytizing and theology.

The ability of Jesus to undermine conventional wisdom made him controversial in his time. His teachings retain their freshness and controversy today. They are often easy and difficult to understand at the same time. In the tradition of the great rabbi and Pharisee Hillel (who may have been his teacher), Jesus quoted Scripture for emphasis. He was also influenced by the Essenes, a monastic Jewish group of believers in rites of purification, sacred priestly garments and ritual, devotion to the poor, and worship away from the pomp of the great Temple centered in Jerusalem. Jesus surely thought of himself as a reformer, seeking in the tradition of the Jewish baptist and Essene sects to purify religious practice.

It is difficult, however, to find the true man in the New Testament. The Gospels were written many years after his death, serve institutional purposes, are inconsistent with each other, and cannot be viewed as reliable sources of his life. Was his name Joshua, Y'shua, Yehoshua? We cannot be sure of any of this. There are often cited references to him in the works of ancient writers—Josephus, Tacitus, Suetonius—but are these accretions added by medieval translators? Enough ancient shards have been retrieved from the desert sands to confirm Jesus' existence. So, why have so many in the world over and over again forgotten his lessons? Myths have overwhelmed truths.

Indeed, his preaching of the Golden Rule accentuates his concern for mankind. This concern is derived directly from Jewish tradition. Before Jesus, Rabbi Hillel stated that the Golden Rule was the fundamental principle of Judaism. Of course, prior to Hillel, Confucius and ancient Hindu poetry contain the identical principle, and it was found later in the sayings of Muhammad. There can be no monopoly on virtue.

Jesus' mission was one of tolerance and peace. Whether or not he was divine must of course be viewed as a matter of faith. Jews and Muslims believe that no man can be divine. Only God is God. The Pauline assertion that Jesus was the Messiah and the later declaration by the Nicean Council in the fourth century that he was godly have divided Jews, Christians, and Muslims from much common ground.

Jesus most likely saw himself a part of a long line of Jewish prophets, teachers, and holy men. He surely would have found comfort in the transformation of so many disparate peoples the world over into monotheistic observers daily seeking the guidance of what are essentially Judaic visions and insights.

3

Albert Einstein

(1879–1955)

The most influential person of modern times was the German-born physicist Albert Einstein. Moses, the lawgiver, defined the Jewish people and, in essence, established civilization. Jesus of Nazareth exposed countless millions to a faith beyond themselves. At the dawn of the first technological century, Einstein revealed the inexhaustible power of matter. His famous equation, $E = mc^2$, became synonymous with the concept that energy and mass are equivalent. His theories, expressed in elegant formulas and eloquent prose, are highly complex, and were, when first uttered, wholly revolutionary and controversial. Unlike the ideas of Sir Isaac Newton, which are relatively easy to understand, Einstein's theories are very difficult. Einstein felt, however, that any student who had been through basic physics could understand his special theory of relativity.

His life is forever linked with three of the defining events of the twentieth century—the eruption of Nazi hate and terror, the rise of Zionism and the creation of the State of Israel, and the development of nuclear weapons and power. The juxtaposition of mankind's most destructive and most creative tendencies made the 1900s and much of Einstein's life a period of torment and exaltation, blackest night and blinding light. Einstein is important not only for his scientific accomplishments (and he did alter accepted norms), but also for his involvement in the dynamic social events of his time.

Einstein was born in the small town of Ulm in Bavaria. His father was an unsuccessful owner of an electrochemical concern. The family moved frequently during Einstein's youth to accommodate his father's repeated attempts to improve business. The young Einstein was apparently slow to talk. He attributed his failure to mature as the prime reason behind a wholly original view of the world. Albert had a secular education, attending Luitpold Gymnasium in Munich and developing a lifelong repugnance for rigid, Teutonic authority and inflexible thinking. For him, militarism had no place in a free community of ideas.

After his family moved to Italy, Einstein followed. Repulsed by the increase of German nationalism, he renounced his citizenship. A stateless person, Einstein moved to Switzerland, eager to study at the famed Polytechnic Institute in Zurich. Rejected on his first application (the headmaster acknowledged his superiority in mathematics and science, but noted decided weakness in other subjects), Einstein, the most brilliant person after Newton, spent a year in preparatory school in a small Swiss village. Only in 1896 was he accepted at the institute. After graduation in 1900, Einstein, having become a Swiss citizen and unable to secure a teaching post at the institute, accepted a post as a patent clerk in Berne.

His work in the patent office as a civil servant provided free time to pursue his research. His coworkers marveled how Einstein in one hour could accomplish as much as the average worker in a full day. In 1905, Einstein had published in the

Annalen der Physik, a prominent scientific journal of the day, three extraordinary papers. The first quantified the so-called Brownian motion of molecules (affecting the future of scientific methods of measurement). The second paper concerned the "photo-electric effect," which was to lay the theoretical foundation for the later invention of television. His third subject, a "special theory of relativity," would change the way we view the world.

Einstein postulated that physical laws do not change when observers move in relation to one another. His conception of the relativity of motion proved that space and time are not absolute, but are affected by the relationships of movement and mass.

His first paper on relativity did not contain his famous equation. $E = mc^2$ appeared, almost as an afterthought, in a supplementary paper Einstein submitted the summer after the special relativity theory first appeared. After altering conventional explanations of the physical world, Einstein took the next logical (for him) step. He examined the differences between mass at rest and mass in motion, and the consequences of transforming matter into pure energy. Forty years before Hiroshima, Einstein had revealed the core of energy beneath all material bodies.

Einstein at blackboard.

Einstein did not, like Bohr, Fermi, Szilard, Oppenheimer, and Teller, involve himself directly in researching nuclear fission. Their work and that of others just "proved his point."

Einstein's first theory had changed the way the world was viewed and also displayed how little mankind knew. Picasso's cubism, Joyce's stream-of-consciousness writing, and Schoenberg's atomization of harmony and melody occurred at about the same time, paralleling aesthetically Einstein's radiant discovery.

After the publication of the paper on special relativity, Einstein taught briefly at the universities in Zurich and Prague, returning to teach at the Polytechnic Institute in 1912. On the recommendation of the distinguished German physicist Max Planck, Einstein was named professor at the Prussian Academy in Berlin. While remaining a Swiss, Einstein resumed his German citizenship (he would renounce it again when the Nazis seized power). During the First World War, he was one of only a few notable pacifists in a jingoistic Germany. Amid the fires of death and trench warfare, Einstein announced in 1916 his general theory of relativity. This theory applied relativity to all movement, uniform and irregular. He noted the relationships of gravitational fields with large masses. Applying non-Euclidean geometry to concepts of four-dimensional space, Einstein was the first to note that the light of the heavens was "bent" by the gravity of the sun.

When his theory of the "curvature of light" was proven by scientists observing a solar eclipse in 1919, Einstein became world-famous almost overnight. Although his modest temperament was ill-suited for fame, Einstein used his notoriety for worthwhile goals. A celebrated symbol of a new scientific age after the ravages of world war, Einstein preached for peace on behalf of the League of Nations, urged the use of science to benefit, not destroy, mankind, and on the urging of Chaim Weizmann, ardently supported Zionist goals.

During the 1920s, while the importance of his scientific activities diminished, Einstein's celebrity grew. He encouraged other younger scientists to discover practical applications of his theories. His public debates with Niels Bohr raised the awareness of what was again, albeit only for a short time before the Nazis, an international scientific community.

When Hitler came to power in 1933, Einstein resigned his professorship in Berlin and accepted a position at the Institute

for Advanced Study in Princeton, New Jersey. He never returned
to Germany, and became an American citizen.

Recognizing the German nuclear threat and encouraged by
Leo Szilard, Einstein wrote a now-famous letter to President
Franklin Roosevelt noting the need for intensive atomic research.
Einstein's letter is widely credited with inspiring America's secret
development of the atomic bomb which led, of course, to the end
of the war with Japan and the modern age. Einstein later voiced
his opposition to the use of the bomb. During the 1950s he also
vigorously opposed the totalitarian tactics of Senator Joseph
McCarthy, advising scientists not to testify before the House Un-
American Activities Committee.

Before he died in 1955, Einstein was hard at work on a
"unified field theory." He had hoped to explain in one thought
the interplay of gravity and electro-magnetic theory. His work on
a unified theory has been continued by scientists such as Stephen
Hawking and others.

More than any other scientist, Einstein ushered in our
science-driven world. No other person so represents the power
and importance of scientific accomplishment. Although nations
still remain obsessed with grabbing as much power as possible,
their peoples consider scientific progress the swiftest route to
their own material well-being. Einstein's great influence lies not
only in his pathbreaking theories, but also in his spiritual
example. He reportedly noted that God does not play dice. There
must be a purpose under Heaven. Future generations will do well
to remember Einstein's warning that scientists should not lose
their souls in a coldly logical quest, but serve the interests of
humanity.

4

Sigmund Freud

(1856–1939)

On any list of the most influential Jews of not only recent history but of all time, Sigmund Freud must rank near the top. Freud was (in Paul Johnson's words in *A History of the Jews*) "the greatest of all Jewish innovators." There is much truth to Johnson's characterization. Freud's colleague and personal propagandist Ernest Jones (in his three-volume biography of the Viennese psychoanalyst) also noted the huge influence the founder of psychoanalysis had on many fields. To name but a few, Jones identified Freud's impact on clinical psychiatry, biology, anthropology, sociology, religion, the occult, art, literature, psychology, education, and criminology. There are few figures in history who have had so wide (and controversial) an effect.

Freud is commonly known as the father of psychoanalytic theory and practice. He was not the first psychologist, yet he is the first person people discuss when they think about the diseases of the mind. Many of his theories were attacked when first introduced, and many are still disputed, others derided as imaginative but useless. Freud's importance rests securely, however, in the quality of his thought, not just for the provocative nature of many of his theories. His ideas changed the way people think about the unconscious. Before him, most people thought hysteria was caused by demons.

Because of Freud, people are now more understanding about mental illness. Prior to his discoveries, the mentally ill were thrown into insane asylums without hope of recovery. Despite lingering prejudice (and fear), many recognize psychological disorders today as simply another sickness, curable through therapy. Selecting the correct method of therapy has stirred the greatest controversy. Many scientists have questioned the medical basis of Freud's theories. They are uncomfortable both with his psychoanalytic methods (which often take a long time to work) and with Freud's basic assumptions. Still, his ideas continue to work their influence.

Freud was born in the town of Freiberg, Moravia, then a district of the Austro-Hungarian Empire. His earliest memories were of a prosperous home. When Sigmund was four years old, however, his father lost his wool merchant business and the family moved to Vienna and into a period of great poverty. Freud would never forget the feelings of privation he suffered in his youth.

His family were not practicing Jews. Despite a fascination and respect for Jewish history and the character of his people, Freud was never observant. Yet he refused to convert, finding in his Jewish roots a strength to be different.

When he entered the University of Vienna, Freud was shocked to encounter the anti-Semitism of both students and faculty. Their racial hatred, sometimes muted, sometimes overt, both sensitized and energized him. He recalled later with some bitterness a story his father told him when he was ten. The young Jakob Freud was once walking well-dressed through the streets of Vienna, and suddenly his new fur cap was knocked off his head by a Christian thug shouting, "Jew! Get off the pavement." Jakob walked quietly into the street, picked up his hat, and went away without protest. Sigmund was outraged by his father's humiliation, referring to the story in traumatic terms. Freud's rage over the incident fueled his desire to fight for his beliefs.

A top student, Freud studied medicine with a particular fascination for the physical sciences. Not sure what he wanted to do, other than somehow study the human condition, he worked first as a researcher at a physiological institute, then, desperate to earn a better living, joined the staff of Vienna General Hospital. While working in the clinics of the hospital, Freud continued to conduct research. During this period he tinkered with the use of narcotics such as cocaine, becoming addicted, then suffering withdrawal. With his career sullied by rumors of his addiction, Freud left the hospital for studies with Jean Charcot, a prominent French neurologist in Paris. During this period he wrote over twenty articles on the nervous system.

When he returned to Vienna, reacting to the need to support his new wife, Martha Bernays, Freud set up a private practice as a neuropathologist. He began to work with another Jewish doctor, Josef Breuer, fourteen years his senior, who was conducting experiments in the treatment of hysteria through hypnosis. Together they attempted to treat a young woman by trying to purge her of her worst memories. In their classic text *Studies in Hysteria*, published in 1895, Breuer and Freud dubbed her "Anna O." (Her real name was Bertha Pappenheim, and she would later do much to establish early German social welfare organizations.) Their cathartic method was a primitive precursor of later psychoanalytic techniques, but they attempted to show "Anna O." that her repression of feelings and hysterical state were the result of a defense mechanism hiding the truth from herself.

Working from Breuer's lead, Freud began to develop theories of sexuality that the older physician could not accept. Their friendship ended bitterly. This was to be the first of several important friendships Freud would enjoy, then angrily end over philosophical disagreements (Wilhelm Fliess, Carl Jung, and Alfred Adler, to name the three most famous). Freud acted like a biblical prophet when his ideas were questioned, surrounding himself with followers like a Hasidic rebbe uttering Talmudic wisdom to disciples hanging on every word.

In 1900 Freud published arguably his greatest book, certainly his most influential. *The Interpretation of Dreams* revealed that people act without being fully conscious of their desires. By analyzing dreams, unconscious thoughts hidden from awareness can be uncovered and deciphered. Freud proposed new theories about what causes the way people feel and act. Regression, repression, displacement, transfers of emotional reactions, were all psychological states he first acknowledged. Freud made us think differently about the way we view ourselves and the words we use to describe those thoughts.

With Sigmund Freud, a whole new vocabulary entered common language. Slips of the tongue ("Freudian slips"), infantile sexuality, sexual drive, reaction formations, the id, the ego, the superego, libido, Oedipus complex, inhibitions, phallic symbols, death wish, pleasure-pain principle, gratification, reality principle, attraction and repulsion, sublimation, anxiety avoidance, behavior modification, metapsychology—are all terms he coined in a treasury of psychological writings.

He often used the lives of great men to prove his psychoanalytic theories. In particular, Freud was fascinated with the lives of Moses, Leonardo da Vinci, and William Shakespeare. Freud posited the theory that Moses was really an Egyptian and the true founder of Judaism (not Abraham). According to Freud, Moses took an Egyptian theory of monotheism and preached it to Jewish slaves. In a great confusion the Jews murdered Moses, carrying with them to this day an unconscious, never-ending guilt. Jews and non-Jews vilified Freud for his Moses tale, ignoring its implications for humanity.

Freud was not only a pathbreaking scientist, but a great literary stylist. A revolutionary thinker, he was quite conservative in his artistic tastes, his personal habits rigid (strict schedules caring for patients, conducting research, walking, meeting with his beloved B'nai B'rith) and comfortably middle-class. Assimilated though he was, Freud was a proud and defiant Jew, never capitulating to the Nazis after the Anschluss. On exiting Vienna in 1938 for London, in great pain from the jaw cancer that would kill him a year later and forced to make a positive public statement about his treatment by the Nazis, Freud wrote, "*Ich kann die Gestapo jedermann auf das beste empfehlen*" ("I can highly recommend the Gestapo to all"). Freud's own life proved the dual nature of the psychological man.

5

Abraham

(ca. 20th–19th century B.C.E.; according to the Bible, 1813–1638 B.C.E.)

Father of three great Semitic religions, Judaism, Christianity, and Islam, ancestor of the Hebrew and Arabic peoples, seminal prophet, model of holy obedience, believer in and recipient of a personal, eternal covenant with his single, eternal God, Abraham is surely one of the most influential men in the history of the world.

Until the eighteenth and nineteenth centuries, most people assumed that he really existed. The stories of the Bible were accepted with faith, no questions asked. Then philosophers such as Georg Hegel began to rationalize the lives of the Patriarchs, imposing contemporary concepts on age-old tales. Later, archaeological digs at Abraham's birthplace, the city of Ur on the banks of the Euphrates River near the Persian Gulf, and the discovery in recent years of ancient tablets corroborating many of the names of his relatives, friends, and enemies, appeared to confirm his history. Time-worn ruins exposed to light after thousands of years confirm that Abraham lived in a sophisticated society, not with primitive Middle Bronze Age men. Cities were ruled by monarchs tied to other rulers for trade and security. Never out of sight from a city's gates were its planting fields, the lives of its inhabitants nurtured by the fruits of the soil. God's gift of the Promised Land to his people has a special meaning when one remembers how close to the earth Abraham and his brethren truly were.

He was a leader or sheik of a group of nomads or outcasts called the Habiru (later the Hebrews). The Habiru, a group of non—city dwellers, wandered from place to place, settling for short periods, yanking up their roots to move on when it suited their purpose. Not a part of settled society, the Habiru were viewed with distrust, but also with a hard-won respect. Unlike the more pastoral Bedouin, whose movement was tied to the grazing of their animals and their agriculture, the Habiru served as mercenaries and traders. Their wanderlust did not lead them to build cities, but wherever they roamed, they kept their language, literature, and beliefs. Their religion was portable—thus Abraham, the first wandering Jew.

Indeed, the Bible records his remarkable moving around the Middle East, from his birthplace near the Persian Gulf, through the land of Canaan, past drought, to the harvests of Egypt and back. Along the way Abraham negotiated treaties with local kings, acted as a hired soldier, and purchased burial plots from the Hittites, noting carefully that he was a stranger and sojourner among them.

As the pilgrim Abraham made his progress across deserts and mountains, he did not immediately become the great prophet of legend. His wanderings exposed him to personal danger and hardship. As a kind of early Moses, his mettle was tested. First called Abram (probably an Amorite name), he was transformed by his experiences and faith into a new man, Abraham. While the Canaanites prayed to their old god El for a plentiful harvest and long life, Abraham expanded such worship into a special new relationship. The concept of a land promised forever to one people, a special covenant with the children of Abraham, was novel, and is unique to the Jewish religion. Yet this covenant may be revoked if God's laws are not carefully followed. Heavenly grace and favor are won only after an anxious existence. Abraham's tale first made plain the delicate nature of Jewish life through the ages.

The patriarch's deepest faith was challenged when he was instructed to carry his son Isaac (delivered from the womb of his elderly and barren wife, Sarah, long after her child-rearing years) to the top of a mountain to sacrifice. Isaac too, in his passive acceptance of his fate, is an ideal symbol. God can take back all that has been given, the covenant as a lease, not a perpetual gift. When Abraham was restrained from sacrificing his son, an essential lesson was taught mankind: human life is sacred and adored by God. Indeed, recent archaeological digs in Israel have uncovered jars from Abraham's time containing remains of little children who apparently were killed by the Canaanites in ghastly ancient rituals. The story of Abraham and Isaac showed humanity how to believe and to trust.

Illustration by Jan Van der Straet, *Abraham and Isaac.*

To the Jews, Abraham is their ancestor, the father of Isaac, whose son Jacob was also called Israel. Descended from Shem, Noah's son, Abraham was a S(h)emite and that rare model of strict obedience to divine law. He exhibits pity and concern for the evil of Sodom and Gomorrah, bargaining with God over how many good men still remain in those decadent towns. His faith in God is unshakeable. He is willing to sacrifice his Isaac at his Lord's direction. Abraham receives God's promise of a Promised Land and a people infinitely numbered.

For the Christians, the promises given by God to Abraham are fulfilled in Jesus. Abraham and Jesus both possessed a simple faith which motivated their actions. The renunciation of the "Son of God" by the "Father" is analogous to the "sacrifice" of Isaac by Abraham. Both Abraham and Jesus were transformed absolutely by their absolute faith. While Abraham received the covenant for his people, Jesus was said to have transmitted God's love for all to share.

Muslims share the same devotion to Abraham as Jews and Christians. As the actual father of Ishmael, the father of the Arabs, Abraham establishes Mecca as the one true sanctuary of God. Abraham's flight from Ur is also an archetype for the Prophet's flight from Mecca. Abraham is a prime example of Islamic virtue, the man who lives by God's laws, is righteous and pleasing to his Supreme Judge; his receipt from God of the original unveiling of divine truth is best expressed for Muslims in the blessed Koran without what they have viewed as the distortions of Judaism and Christianity.

Abraham's central place as the father of the three great Semitic religions, the source of monotheism throughout the world, demands that his descendants try finally to make peace with one another. All three religions share the same early language, the same belief in the one God of Abraham and the prophecy that there is a purpose under Heaven to what happens in the world, and that without ethical behavior man is bereft of his divine origin.

6

Saul of Tarsus
(Saint Paul)

(4–64 C. E.)

Ηe was a Jew, born at Tarsus in Cilicia (now Turkey), raised in Jerusalem, the great Rabbi Gamaliel's pupil, called Pharisee of the Pharisees, a tentmaker, zealous all his life for God. Known through the centuries as Saint Paul, apostle to the Gentile world; without this remarkable Jewish man, it is unlikely that Christianity would have become a worldwide religion.

As this is a book about influence, not greatness, and people are ordered here in relation to the power of their influence, Paul must rank near Moses and Jesus as the most influential Jewish religious figure of all time. Paul, however, would not have existed were it not for Jesus of Nazareth. Jesus was surely the greater man, his followers assert, the greatest spirit the world has ever known. Paul, however, may have been more influential in shaping his present and the future. For all the good and sorrow it would bring to the world, the universal religion of Christianity could not have been created out of Messianic Judaism without the unique genius of Saul of Tarsus.

During his lifetime, the grandiose Second Temple was built by Herod the Great in Jerusalem. At the same time, developing out of the compelling logic of its precepts and to some degree marked by overwhelming Roman persecution, Judaism became not a faith only of Temple rituals and sacrifices, but a religion of interior thoughts. Great rabbis such as Hillel, Shammai, Gamaliel (and later, Akiba and Johanan ben Zakkai), stressed the overwhelming importance and, more crucially, the meaning of the law, a temple of belief grounded in the Torah, not in a great edifice.

Paul's huge leap was to guide non-Jews into Jewish monotheism without demanding they be circumcised or observe dietary laws or countless regulations of virtuous behavior. Paul indeed quotes the Torah in his Epistles some six dozen times, to deny the references each time. Only through faith in a man Paul considered the Messiah would salvation be reached.

Paul recognized that without belief in the Resurrection and in the history and divinity of Jesus, Christianity unravels. For Paul, Jesus' death was a crucial event in world history. With the Resurrection, death itself is overcome. "Grave, where is thy triumph? Death, where is thy sting?" Rather than the appeasement of God in countless Temple sacrifices of birds and sheep, the "Lamb of God" died on the cross to set his children free. The sacrifice of one life for all, in Paul's view, was a singular and essential act of atonement for humanity.

Like some of the early Jewish Christians, he was obsessed with the death on the Cross. Paul was much less concerned about the actual events of Jesus' life. Many of the early Jewish Christians did not know how to deal with Jesus' awful death. The Romans reserved death-by crucifixion, a shameful, horrifying form of execution, for those they considered the worst criminals, for rebellious slaves and terrorists against Rome.

Paul's obsession with the Crucifixion arises directly from his novel theory of original sin. In contrast to the basic optimism of Judaism (that good works, virtue, morality, and righteousness count; God can be seen in all the minutiae of life, therefore most facets of daily living require regulation to ensure order and a religious spirit), Paul's view was largely pessimistic. Jewish law, he argued, cannot be wholly followed. We are imperfect. We cannot obey every rule, every moment. The law's very presence establishes how truly sinful people are. Jesus, unlike Paul, clearly stated that the law must be obeyed. For Paul, faith in Jesus supplanted the need for the law.

The aggregate sin of mankind is so overwhelming that one unique person had to pay for it. Paul saw Jesus' death on the Cross as the cost of man's sin. Indeed, in a literate attempt to explain Pauline theology, A.N. Wilson and others have dubbed Paul's new religion "Cross-tianity."

With the Resurrection, Paul was convinced that hope everlasting had brightened a dark world. Through Jesus' love and forgiveness, sin was forgotten and heavenly grace opened the eternal kingdom to the weakest slave. The meek and the strong, rich and poor, girl and boy, can commune with God only through Jesus.

Paul was the product of a wealthy, cosmopolitan, hellenized background. He spoke and wrote in Greek and was a Roman citizen. At first a strictly religious Jew, zealous in his defense of his faith, and a confessed persecutor of Christians, on a journey to Damascus he abruptly shifted to a belief in Jesus as the Messiah or Christ. Saul became Paul. His conversion to Christianity in a blaze of blinding light remains controversial. Recent studies of the early Jewish Christian church reveal that Paul opposed the Jerusalem church (led by Jesus' brother James) in the most vehement terms. He viewed it as just another sect, though following "the Way," too obsessed with traditional Jewish ritual, believing in Jesus only as a great prophet, and not open to Gentile converts.

This Pharisee of the first century was the greatest publicist and interpreter in human history. We know him from his own writings. In notable addition to the historian Josephus, Paul's

Epistles are the only extant written record of a first-century Pharisee we now possess. Like many of the other Pharisees of his era (contrary to biased custom, the Pharisees were devout men and the founders of Talmudic Judaism), he was a pious and God-filled man. But Paul was obsessed with the idea of Jesus.

Of course, the Christian religion is the result of the work and ideas of two men, Jesus and Paul. However, it was Paul who combined his hellenic background and Diaspora Judaism (much more liberal in personal habits and not tied to worship in the Temple in Jerusalem) with the messianic solution, to create a new theology, a new religion—and to gather sufficient followers to ensure its survival. Paul was the first to understand that belief in Jesus of Nazareth had a cosmic importance. The changes basic to Jesus' teachings demanded a break with Jewish practice (Paul's conflict with the Jerusalem church of James may have contributed to this schism). While Jesus lived in a wholly Jewish country, preaching and seeking to influence Jews only, Paul proselytized in a largely Gentile empire. Most Jews would not naturally recognize any man as divine, but in the Gentile world men (especially royalty) were continually being made gods. It was easier therefore for non-Jews to commune with God through the symbol of a perfectly good man.

Perhaps Paul's idea of grace was his most persuasive lesson. God, Paul argued, forgave everyone out of an infinite and divine love of humanity, without regard for morals or evil acts. To the downtrodden masses living without hope under Roman tyranny, such an idea, tied to life eternal in God's kingdom, proved irresistible. Paul, the first Christian theologian and credited by many historians as the "creator" of a religion, expressed in his own dynamic prose a way for an ancient monotheistic religion to become a universal practice. He changed not only biblical law and history, but provided an alternative concept and purpose for people. For Paul, Jews were not the only people chosen specially for God's grace.

The writings of Paul had a profound influence on his contemporaries in establishing early Christianity, as well as on generations of important figures such as Augustine, Aquinas, Luther, and Calvin. When Christian theologians have sought answers to essential questions, they have frequently turned to Paul's letters for inspiration.

It is also clear that without Gentile acceptance of the Christian faith (a faith grounded in Jewish virtues and traditions) the future history of the world would have been radically different. Without Paul there would have been no shift to government-endorsed Christianity under the Emperor Constantine, no Church centered in Rome (the site of Peter's and Paul's deaths), no Greek culture tinted with Judeo-Christian ethics, no Crusades, no Catholic-Protestant European wars—in fact, no Christian religion.

7

Karl Marx

(1818–1883)

During the late 1980s, Communists ceased to dictate the affairs of Eastern Europe and Russia. Even China and Vietnam, once rigidly extreme examples of Marxism, adopted capitalist methods. Despite the retreat of much of the world from his teachings, Karl Heinrich Marx, a German Jew, descended on both sides from generations of rabbis, remains the most influential political philosopher in Jewish and indeed *world* history.

Marx was born in Trier, a small town in the Rhineland. His father, Heinrich was a prosperous lawyer, his uncle the town's rabbi. Seeking to improve his position by denying his heritage and over the rabbi's objections, Heinrich converted his immediate family, including six-year-old Karl, to the Lutheran Church. Instead of the yeshiva, Karl went to a secular gymnasium. The conversion of Karl Marx would have the gravest consequences on the future of much of the world.

Marx was educated at universities in Bonn, Berlin, and Jena (the last, more a degree market than a school). He was particularly drawn to the philosophic teachings of G.W.F. Hegel. Marx first thought he would become a poet, then a philosopher, and finally a journalist. He met another young Jewish thinker, Moses Hess, who had founded the *Rhenish Gazette*. Hess initially used his journal to criticize the reactionary policies of the Prussian government. Marx overwhelmed Hess, taking on editorial control, attacking the local government, and after fifteen months was stripped of his German citizenship and deported to France for criticizing Berlin's alliance with Moscow.

With his newly wed twenty-nine-year-old wife, Jenny von Westphalen (whom he married after seven years of courtship, the death of her objecting father, a baron, and wearing down her widowed mother), Marx settled in the Paris of Balzac, Chopin, and Sand and gained the acquaintance of another German expatriate, poet Heinrich Heine. During this period, Marx also met the Russian anarchist Mikhail Bakunin and the French radical author Pierre Joseph Proudhon.

However, Marx's most fortunate encounter was with Friedrich Engels, the impressionable son of a wealthy German textile manufacturer. Engels was a curious mixture of capitalist factory owner and revolutionary. Marx was impressed by Engels's writings on the English working class and his ability to express himself clearly and simply. For nearly the next forty years, Engels would largely support his friend (often to his own detriment). Other than an occasional newspaper job, Marx never worked for a living, preferring to spend his days studying and writing articles and manifestos (all eagerly edited by Engels). To this day it is often impossible in Marxist literature to distinguish the ideas of Marx from the style of Engels.

Expelled again, this time from Paris to Brussels, Marx, living on Engels' support, wrote his first important work, *The Poverty of Philosophy*, in 1847. One year later, Marx and Engels published their most important joint work, *The Communist Manifesto*. Only days after its publication (and having nothing to do with its radical ideas), workers in France and Germany rebelled against political oppression. It was as if Marx and Engels had predicted their revolt. Yet Marx's class war was not on the revolutionaries' minds, but rather progressive, liberal politics. During these unstable years, Marx predicted (almost forty times) that the era of class struggle would foster rebellion. He was mostly wrong about the near future but brutally accurate about the next century.

Throughout his life, Marx bitterly opposed the tsarist regime in Russia, identifying it as the most oppressive in the world. Ironically, Marxism would be responsible for Stalin's massacre of millions of landed peasants and the frigid death of the Gulag.

Much more than his friend, the lyrical poet Heine, Karl Marx became a virulently self-hating Jew. His vicious temperament (whether a product of his miserable life or equally difficult self), loathing for Jewish culture, warping of his people's history, and fiercely analytical mind, combined to form one of the most influential economic and political systems of any age (Marx's well-known anti-Semitism strangely did not discourage young Jews of future generations from leaving behind their heritage to follow his example). Marx viewed his ideas as rooted in and compelled by history. It was imperative to him that people understand his interpretation of history and act accordingly. For him, his ideas were a new Gospel—Marxism as Torah and Talmud uttered by its only prophet.

> A specter is wandering over Europe now—the specter of Communism.
>
> The workers have nothing to lose but their chains.
>
> Workers, everywhere, UNITE!

Drawn to the revolutionary fires of 1848, Marx returned to Germany. He began to publish and distribute a new *Rhenish Gazette*, was quickly arrested and tried for sedition, and won an acquittal by his own eloquent defense. Although they lost in the courts, the authorities found another, more effective way of silencing Marx. He was expelled forever from his homeland as a subversive alien.

Refused admittance to France and Belgium, Marx and family traveled to England. For most of the rest of his life, Marx lived in abject poverty in London's slums. Several of his children died in young childhood. Marx chose to work only on his research and writings, spending hours in the British Museum compiling statistics to justify his philosophic claims. A small allowance from Engels, some journalistic work for the *New York Tribune* of Charles A. Dana, and the remains of an inheritance from his wife's mother sustained the family.

Marx's personal fury over his wretched condition exploded in *Das Kapital* ("Capital"), a huge and severe indictment of the economics of his contemporary society. The volume was to be the first in a series of tomes which Engels completed from Marx's voluminous notes after his death.

Marx's only effort to organize in the spirit of his beliefs was an involvement in the First International of the 1860s. Marx was placed on the council of this loose confederation of workers. He proceeded with bulldog perseverance first to dominate and then, when he could not get his complete way, to destroy the organization. (To his credit, during these years, and despite a racist bent, Marx loudly supported the North in the American Civil War, trumpeting with the fervor of an abolitionist the delivery of African-Americans from slavery.)

In 1870, Prussia savagely defeated France. Marx supported the leftist revolutionaries of the Paris commune who attempted in vain during a period of political vacuum to seize control of France. In their frenzy, the commune leaders executed the archbishop of Paris and other prominent leaders. Establishment forces reacted with a massacre of their own, staining the medieval byways of old Paris blood red. For his support, Marx became internationally known as the infamous "Red Doctor." In the common psyche, communism became synonymous with deadly violence, an association which Lenin and Mao later proved true.

In his remaining years, Marx was viewed (mostly by much younger, idealistic followers) as the gray eminence of communism. After the quickly successive deaths of his beloved Jennys, wife and daughter, he raged no more. Marx was buried in Highgate Cemetery in London. His grave became almost a holy shrine to his believers.

Marx's work is an integral (and, for some, hateful) part of

mankind's intellect. From Marxism came the famous "isms" of Lenin, Trotsky, and Mao. Partly in reaction to his leftist creed came the fatal onslaught of the Fascists and Nazis.

Marx's concept of the exploitation of the workers by the bosses was, however, only part of economic life. Ideas of "surplus value," or excess left to owners after exploitation of workers, did not fully explain how output was affected, quality controlled, or worth created. Marx seemingly ignored the fact that people were worth something too. Spiritual, cultural, and intellectual capital *did* make a difference. His intense concentration on the causes and operations of systems failed to recognize the interplay of people making things happen. Initiative has never been induced by a five-year plan.

Marx's personal aloofness and arrogance also served as the prime example for future communist leaders. Lenin believed strongly that the masses had to be led by an elite; left alone, they would barely aspire to trade unionism. "Dictatorship of the proletariat" became a hollow phrase connoting terror, dull lives, conformity, class consciousness but no conscience, democratic republics without democracy. Marx's dream of a utopia far from his impoverished existence was a world under control. He forgot basic Jewish principles that man cannot avoid responsibility by retreating into regulated behavior. The world is too complex for so simplistic an answer.

8

Theodor Herzl

(1860–1904)

He was a fop, a boulevard dandy. He was said to have adored Wagnerian opera, fancy dress, cafe gossip, parading down the avenue. He was everything a fin de siècle gentleman should be, sporting a full but perfectly trimmed beard, writing fashionable plays, moody travel pieces, and feuilletons, enjoying the idle pleasures of a young man in peacetime Vienna. However, while reporting in the early 1890s as the Paris correspondent of a leading Viennese newspaper, he was transformed by the vicious anti-Semitic Dreyfus affair. More than a decade of creative and commercial writing culminated in 1896 with feverish work on a pamphlet proclaiming the necessity of a Jewish state. Though others before him had urged a return to Zion, it was Theodor Herzl's visionary article and political devotion in organizing a Zionist movement that led fifty years later to the creation of the State of Israel. Herzl's zeal also led to a debilitating heart condition which ended his life abruptly at age forty-four, leaving his ailing young widow alone with three small children.

Although Herzl is identified with Vienna, he was born and raised in Budapest. The Hungarian capital was at the edge of the Austrian empire, a border town rising during the 1800s into a great city. His father won and lost most of his fortune in business, alienating son Theodor from commercial pursuits and turning him to literary goals. His mother, devoted to German language, literature, and culture, exposed Herzl to the influences which marked his lifelong outlook and expectations.

After the death of his nineteen-year-old sister from typhoid fever, Herzl and his parents relocated in Vienna. At the urging of his parents, he began law studies at the university. He rapidly became more Viennese than the Viennese. Vienna was then fertile ground for the many young Jews who came to live and work in the city. Not far from the Herzls lived Arthur Schnitzler, the great novella writer, and Gustav Mahler, soon to become a leading conductor and one of the most important composers of the turn of the century. Although Herzl was at first militantly pro-German (as Freud, Schnitzler, and Mahler had also been), his experiences with anti-Semites in university clubs and with Jews who despised being Jewish (seeking to hide in German *Kultur*) began to affect him. For beneath the sweet veneer of Viennese *Gemütlichkeit*, or congeniality, sinister forces lay ready to leap out. These forces burst forth in the election of the popular Karl Lueger as mayor of Vienna. Lueger, a charismatic anti-Semite, inspired a young house painter named Hitler whose hand-to-mouth existence a few years later in Vienna would shape his passion for power and hatred of Jews. (Sigmund Freud recognized the power of these dark forces in man's subconscious, and his discoveries led to the establishment of modern psychoanalytic therapy.)

After working as a law clerk for a short, unhappy period, Herzl, supported by his father, devoted himself to writing.

Gradually his short, melancholy travel pieces and plays became fashionable. After a major success at the most prominent Viennese theater, Herzl felt emboldened to marry a young Jewish woman of considerable fortune. He learned soon thereafter, however, that during their courtship she had masked a deepening psychosis. Despite the births of his three beloved children (one of whom would die in Theresienstadt, a Nazi concentration camp), his wife's illness and Herzl's temperament contributed to a desperate and unhappy marriage.

Herzl was hired by the *Neue Freie Presse*, Vienna's most famous newspaper, first as a freelance travel writer and later as a foreign correspondent. Separated from (and later reconciled with) his wife and family, Herzl began in 1891 his Parisian assignment. It was the era of the belle epoque, the time of Toulouse-Lautrec, Debussy, Baudelaire, and Bernhardt. At first, Herzl was enthralled by the French capital. However, soon his adoration was quelled by the anti-Semitic Drumont and Mayer incidents culminating in that international scandal, the Dreyfus affair.

A notorious anti-Semite, Edouard Drumont, accused a prominent politician of being manipulated by the Jews. A series of duels between anti-Semites and Jewish military men followed, as officers' patriotism (and affiliation with the hated Germans!) was tested. Herzl reported in great detail on the Drumont trial as well as the well-attended funeral of the Jewish army officer Captain Armand Mayer, who had died in a duel brought on by a French chauvinism poisoned with hate.

The playwright Herzl began imagining grandiose plans to save world Jewry from these irrational forces. First, he would fight a duel with some prominent anti-Semite, like Lueger. Rather, he would make a grand alliance with the Pope to convert all the Jews in Christendom to Christianity.

In 1894, reality in the form of the Dreyfus affair brought Herzl to a clearer vision. Herzl, in fact, was present on the military ground when Dreyfus was shorn of his rank and sword in an infamous tableau of degradation and injustice.

Spurred to action by the Dreyfus affair, Herzl sought out the help of Baron Maurice de Hirsch, one of the wealthiest Jews in the world and a supporter of Jewish settlement in the New World. In an embarrassing interview with Hirsch, the nervous Herzl failed to set forth clearly his still unformed plans for the rescue of European Jewry by exodus to a new Zion. Commentators have since remarked that Herzl's failure with Hirsch was a great tragedy as the rich man had the desire and the means to implement the visions Herzl would later state so clearly.

Unfazed by his failure with Hirsch, Herzl went on to develop an exodus scheme partaking of Wagnerian pageantry. As he revealed his plan to learned colleagues, Herzl was greeted with shock, dismay, and fears for his sanity. Toning down the literary bent of his initial draft, Herzl reworked his plan into what would become a celebrated pamphlet, "The Jewish State: An Attempt at a Modern Solution of the Jewish Question." Jewry would request that the world provide a land large enough to house a nation. It did not matter where Zion would be. The Jewish people would approve the location offered if it met certain reasonable requirements. The state would be modern and progressive, incorporating all the latest and best ideas of civilized society. Herzl did not envision that Hebrew would be the nation's language. Rather, the first Jewish settlers would communicate in all of their languages until a national dialect emerged from the most practical tongue.

The pamphlet was initially printed in five hundred copies by a small Viennese bookseller. Within months the pamphlet had received worldwide attention and controversy, aided by virulent attacks by anti-Semitic politicians and press.

With the help of a merchant named David Wolffsohn, who after Herzl's death became the president of the Zionist movement, Herzl began to organize (a Zionist political organization), propagandize (by writing, editing, and publishing a Zionist weekly), and politick (meeting quixotically and unsuccessfully with important political leaders such as the grand vizier of Turkey and Kaiser Wilhelm). Baron de Hirsch died just as the movement began to gain momentum.

Herzl used the remaining years of his life in the service of his cause. He founded and wrote a weekly newspaper in German as the official organ of the movement. His ability to entrance his listeners with visions of Zion gained him many followers despite the opposition of some rabbis and their flocks. To show the world the serious nature of what was being discussed at each annual Zionist congress, Herzl insisted that formal dress be worn. Failing to secure the Turkish ruler's grant of Palestine as an autonomous

Jewish region, Herzl began to gain the attention of British authorities. In 1903, he was offered a charter by Great Britain for Jewish settlement in Uganda. Herzl was willing to accept Africa as the site of the new homeland, but met violent opposition at the Zionist congress. The conflict over this issue rapidly became bitter and led to Herzl's death of a heart attack in 1904 near Vienna.

His funeral was attended by countless thousands who descended on Vienna from all over Europe. The Viennese were shocked by the depth of Jewish reaction to Herzl's death. They remembered him only as a literary type who had some fanciful nationalist ideals. The anti-Semitic press, however, did not resist the opportunity to publish nasty rhymes which sought to dance on Herzl's grave.

In remote parts of Europe, however, old rabbis and young people felt the meaning of Herzl's message. Both Chaim Weizmann, later architect of the Balfour Declaration and first president of the State of Israel, and David Ben-Gurion, later to be its first prime minister and then growing up in a small town in Poland, responded in their individual ways with deep grief. Inspired by Herzl's visions, they were ready to lead the first pioneers to the soil of Palestine. Herzl predicted in 1897 that he had founded the Jewish state; his prediction came true just fifty years later.

Herzl's Zionism also in a way gave rise to a parallel Arab nationalism which has also sought a homeland grounded in history and myth. Herzl had foreseen conflict with the Arabs but asserted that Jews and Arabs could build together a greater society based on their best qualities. Herzl's influence on world history is still unfolding.

His remains were moved in 1949 to a hill just west of Jerusalem. On Mount Herzl he lies with his compatriot David Wolffsohn. A large military cemetery containing fallen heroes of Israel's tragic wars and Yad Vashem, the Holocaust memorial, are nearby. Like Moses, Herzl was driven by dreams of Zion. It would be left to others to lead the remnants of the faithful home.

9

Mary

(b. ca. 20 B. C. E.)

There are very few details of her life. What is known is in the Gospels, mostly picturesque references written by sages who lived more than a century after her death. We know of her, of course, due to the great life and death of her son. Yet Mary, daughter of Galilean parents, with the Hebrew name, Miriam, became the most influential woman and mother in human history.

In the art of the early church, she is depicted as a queen to Jesus, the emperor. The largely illiterate flock of the young church needed visual stimulus to aid in their prayer and to

Oil painting by Gerard David,
The Virgin Feeding the Child from a Bowl of Soup.

comprehend biblical stories. The Byzantine Church sought to move worshipers away from pagan ties. With the almost geometric increase of saints and martyrs vying for attention, and in direct conflict with the proscription against graven images in the Old Testament, the Church mass-produced icons of their faces, including otherworldly, often sorrowful portraits of Mary.

In the fifth and sixth centuries Christian religious leaders sublimated worship of hellenic and Egyptian gods (among others), retaining from these symbols their most loving features. The "cult of Mary" was awarded August 13 each year as the Feast of the Assumption, on the day formerly reserved for Isis and Artemis, pagan goddesses of fertility and the hunt.

Through the following centuries, the common people assigned to Mary the spirit of all motherhood. The special place in their hearts and aspirations for the Virgin influenced the development of Christianity and world culture simultaneously. After the terrors of the Dark Ages (reflected in what was a harsh religious environment), people sought a more humane environment in which to pray. In the twelfth and thirteenth centuries the idolatry of Mary, called "Mariology," made her the most beloved figure in history. No longer was the demanding God sternly casting damned souls into Hell. The Blessed Virgin would save her children, give them warmth, good health, hope. She had pity, a mother's compassion.

Mary became for many medieval Christians almost a part of the Trinity. Although a role for her in the Trinity was denied by theologians, her developing role as protector and intermediary with God transformed the Church into a more caring institution.

Church fathers from Augustine to Popes in recent times took special care in defining her place in the religious hierarchy. The Gospels stated that Jesus was "born of a woman." Some assigned this the Hebraic definition meaning that Jesus was a human being, truly a man. Without a human parent, his activity among men would be too supernatural. Others denied the virgin birth, asserting that they did so in the name of humanity. How could Jesus be human if not born as others were? This question of the guarantee of the Incarnation remains controversial. Like belief in Jesus as divine, it remains fundamentally a matter of faith.

Although textual variants in the Gospel of Matthew include lines that "Joseph begat Jesus," the greatest amount of Christian writings concerning Mary are about her virginity. It is the almost unanimous teaching of Catholicism that Mary conceived Jesus with her virginity intact.

That her virginity was unimpaired was tied to the Pauline concept of original sin. All people are inherently sinful, said Paul. The later Church (as late as the 1800s in official dogma) declared that she was immaculate. At the very moment of her conception she was freed from sin.

It was stated by theologians in the fourth century that Mary was the *theotokos,* the "God bearer." When Jesus was pronounced divine at that time by the Church, her title as the Mother of God followed logically. Her sacred purpose inspired icon painters in the Eastern Orthodox Church. Others viewed her as the symbol of humanity's redemption through nature. The minnesingers and troubadours of the Middle Ages sang praises to her perfect nobility. Through her, chivalry was born. During the fifteenth and sixteenth centuries, Italian Renaissance artists saw her as the exemplar of ideal beauty. "Ave Maria," full of grace, was sung with consoling warmth in Catholic churches. Much of the loveliness of Christian art was inspired by the physical beauty of woman, personified by Mary's image.

Mary became the Church's symbol of family and the central role of the mother. Christian visions of apocalypse and terror (inspired no doubt more from the plague of life in the Dark Ages than from religion) were transformed into dreams of mercy and compassion.

In modern times, the symbol of Mary, full of warmth and grace, has been altered by some philosophers, psychoanalysts, feminists, and entertainers. Recast as a female goddess figure, cited as the origin of the "whore/Madonna" syndrome of male oppression, or exploited by an Italian Catholic rock star into one of the most profitable (and debased) show business reputations, the myth of Mary, even if corrupted, retains remarkable powers.

10 *Baruch de Spinoza*

(1632–1677)

During the time of Rembrandt, there lived in Amsterdam a shy and courteous young man who studied rabbinical law and the Holy Scriptures, but who at the age of twenty-four so outraged his fellow Jews that he was violently chastised and excommunicated from his religion and community.

Baruch de Spinoza was the son of prosperous Portuguese immigrants who had fled the religious and political persecution of the Inquisition for the safety and freedom of Holland. These Portuguese Jews had concealed their religion in their homeland through conversion, but had still practiced Judaism secretly. Spinoza was able to witness firsthand the conflict between these newly arrived "Conversos" (or converts) and the Ashkenazic or Talmudic Jews who had resided in Amsterdam for centuries. Added to the turmoil was the availability in this free society of a secular education. Young Baruch not only learned the classics of literature and philosophy, but was able to study Latin and, horror of horrors, the New Testament taught to him by an ex-Jesuit priest.

While a young student he became a member of a group of radical thinkers and at the same time learned the craft of grinding optical lenses. By temperament he was slightly melancholic but remarkably even, never quick to respond in anger. He managed to subsist on a barely nutritious diet consisting mainly of buttered porridge and gruel flavored with raisins.

It is not entirely clear how the dispute with the Jewish community arose. However, he was accused of denying the existence of angels, the orientation of the Bible by God, and the immortality of the soul. The official excommunication document may still be read today; its virulence was obviously intended to leave him in unending torment. Spinoza was thrown out of his community and even threatened with assassination. Ironically, the Portuguese and Spanish refugees of Amsterdam, safe in their bourgeois existence, had conducted their own Inquisition.

Baruch ("blessed" in Hebrew) changed his name to the Latin equivalent, Benedictus, and after some wandering, finally settled in The Hague. Other than a small state pension and an annuity from an admiring friend, he supported himself through his lens craft. All other offers for help were quietly rejected, even a professorship at the prestigious university in Heidelberg. He preferred a scholar's life, austere, ascetic, the monk's habit of the poor workman. He died at age forty-four, alone, of a lung disease caused by his repeated breathing in of toxic dust from grinding glass.

Despite this life of virtual obscurity and sobriety, Spinoza is recognized as one of the central figures in the history of philosophy. Despite his excommunication, many philosophers correctly call him a "God-intoxicated man." Despite his denial of divinity as the original source of the Bible, Spinoza is commonly regarded as the first modern biblical critic. And despite his reverence for reason, his work has elicited a baneful irrationality from many important philosophers and writers who followed him.

Spinoza's philosophy was expressed in a theological and political study, the *Tractatus Theologico-Politicus* (the only book of his published while he lived) and the *Ethics*. He was surely influenced by the rational teachings of Maimonides, but was also marked by the antirationalism of the Jewish mystics or cabalists. This combination of reason and "unreason" carried his philosophical investigations out of Jewish tradition to a point of no return.

While Spinoza believed in resolving disputes through reason, he did not believe, as did Maimonides, that the Messiah would come through strict obedience to God's law. Rather, Spinoza urged that religious writings be cast aside as worthless and artificial. Only through pure intellect could man's passions be tamed. Spinoza then sought a prescription for what he perceived as the disease of the emotions. Sin was not due to evil but was caused by ignorance. Suffering was not an isolated event but was instead a part of an infinitely larger and uncaring whole. If man only accepted that he was part of an unchanging order of nature, of God (they were the same to Spinoza), then hatred and sorrow, worry and upset, anger and deceit, would vanish.

God is not only everything (pantheism), God is *in* every mode of life. Nothing is left to chance. There is no free will. If we would only realize this, we would be liberated. Albert Einstein, echoing Spinoza, is quoted as having said that "the Old One does not play dice."

In his *Ethics*, Spinoza used Euclidean geometry as essential proof of the inevitability of his philosophy. Not only has God predetermined everything, but Spinoza's use of geometric progressions makes his philosophy appear immutable and absolute.

Spinoza's approach to biblical analysis revolutionized the way people viewed religious tradition. His rational discussions of biblical tales in their historical context exposed the sometimes superstitious and complex commentaries of Talmudic teachings. Spinoza's cold-blooded observations led the way for Voltaire and others during the French Enlightenment of the eighteenth century to ridicule Christianity and what they considered its cartoon cousin, Judaism. Inadvertently, Spinoza gave anti-Semites an intellectual basis for attack. While revealing the Bible to be an inexact history, his method undermined permanently the foundations of organized religion and had a long-term and deadly effect on the Jewish community.

Contemporary philosophy rejects much of Spinoza while remaining in awe of him. Each new generation finds something of itself in his words. The German Romantic writers at the beginning of the 1800s imposed their own world on Spinoza; the great poet Goethe considered Spinoza essential to an understanding of the cosmos. In our century, the eminent British philosopher Bertrand Russell found weakness in Spinoza's ideas, preferring the twentieth-century scientific view that facts are never fully discovered by reasoning but rather by observation. Yet Russell adored Spinoza with an uncharacteristic ardor, urging that his philosophy be used to flee the insanity of modern life, so that we may never again be paralyzed by the bitterness of despair.

11

David

(fl. 1000 B. C. E.)

Shepherd, mercenary, bandit, lyric singer, ritual dancer, polygamist, slayer of Goliath, adulterer, conqueror, empire builder, father, king. Of all the over three dozen men and women who ruled the ancient kingdoms of Israel and Judah for more than four hundred years, David was surely the greatest figure. Revered by Christians as a forerunner of Jesus of Nazareth, cherished by Islam as a prime example of the virtuous qualities exhibited by the Prophet, David is to Jews, with all his human frailties, one of the most admired of all men. His name may be derived from the term *davidum* which signifies a military marshal.

Before David, Jewish history seems a tangle of petty tribal hostilities. His reign gave coherence and an international resonance to Jewish affairs. By David's example, God's covenant with the Jewish people, with every soul on Earth, was channeled into everyday life through a humane method of governing, constitutional monarchy, or what has been called by the eminent Paul Johnson "theocratic democracy."

David was never an Oriental-style monarch, dictating to his subjects absolutely. His actions were mostly limited by their will. A deeply religious man, he despised oppression and sought to ensure that justice would prevail. These concepts of freedom and responsibility exerted immense historical force, serving as models for constitutional government in America and Europe during the eighteenth and nineteenth centuries.

The development of David's personality has been repeatedly studied and discussed over the centuries. Much more popular than his predecessor, the brooding warrior Saul, and more capable than his beloved friend Jonathan, Saul's son, David, a model leader of fighting men, could not control his own family. Three sons, most prominently Absalom, died tragically, committing crimes of passion in open revolt against the established order.

David's liaison with Bathsheba, a married woman, had disastrous consequences. Viewing her taking a bath on her terrace, David was smitten, invited her to his palace, slept with her, and made her pregnant. He then arranged to cover up his act of adultery by ordering her husband back from the army to stay with Bathsheba. Instead, her husband slept in the palace, ignoring Bathsheba, providing no opportunity to legitimize her pregnancy. David completed the subterfuge by ordering her husband to be sent to the forefront of the battlefield and sure death. When confronted by the prophet Nathan and even though the supreme authority in his kingdom, David repented, asked forgiveness, displayed his humility before God (one might argue that David's deeds were punishable by death, but kings apparently are able to live by different rules while setting poetic examples for future generations to ponder). Bathsheba later gave birth to Solomon, David's scholarly successor.

To consolidate his power, David transformed a society of disputing tribes into a centralized national government. Like so

many successful leaders in history, he was highly skilled in
military affairs, trained by the Philistines in the use of their new
iron weapons. In the power vacuum left after Saul's death, David
subdued the marauding Philistines and other local groups,
seizing land which was reassigned to the tribes in exchange for
loyalty and a consolidated state.

David captured Jerusalem in a daring raid (penetrating its
fortifications through an underground water conduit), and established the city as the capital of his united kingdom. Jerusalem lay
at the crossroads of the northern region of Israel and southern
Judah, with nearby access to ancient trade routes.

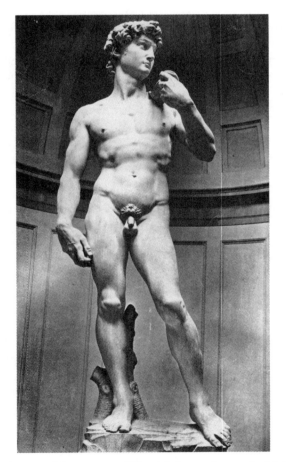

Michelangelo's marble statue of David from the early 16th century.

Seeking to display his obedience to God and vesting his reign in religious armor, David moved the ark of the covenant to Jerusalem and made plans to build a great temple for its home. Jerusalem became the "City of David," site of the Second Temple of Herod, Jesus' crucifixion, Roman massacres, the Prophet's ascent to the heavens, invasion by the Crusaders, Ottomans, and British (among many others), and today's Israeli Knesset. Jerusalem remains the center and heart of western religion and politics.

For Jews today, the golden age of David's rule established their national identity. The six-pointed star of David worn by Jewish people and featured on the Israeli flag symbolizes their home, eternal Zion. The inhabitants of the tiny state of Israel have long viewed themselves as a nation of Davids, clustered together in a hardy army ready at all times to defeat the Goliaths of the Middle East. The Jewish memory of David's era remains perfect, an ideal for modern Israelis.

Through the centuries before Jesus, Jews believed that the Messiah or "anointed one" would be a direct descendant of David. Jesus was indeed repeatedly called "son of David" during his life, and the authors of the Gospels take great pains at listing his genealogy. Like David, Jesus was said to have been born in Bethlehem. David as precursor of Jesus became a model for early Christian royalty. Charlemagne was dubbed the "new David." David's open relationship with the Prophet Nathan (who held David accountable for his sins) was used as precedent for the many Christian European kings during the Middle Ages and Renaissance desiring legitimacy through the sacred anointment of the Church. For the Renaissance artist Donatello, David is a slight Italianate boy with ideal, somewhat female shape, a new Apollo. Only in Michelangelo's enormous marble statue can we feel David's unique charisma, fortitude, courage, and humanity. David, singer of psalms, glorified his people and his good name through the poetry of enlightened rule.

12

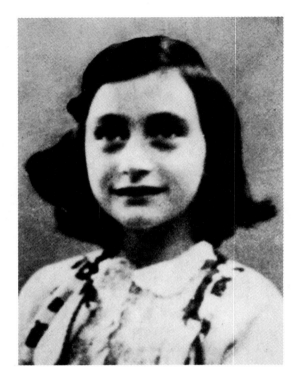

Anne Frank

(1929–1945)

It seems hardly possible to imagine the deaths of over six million people. Think of the town or city you live in. Unless you are in a great metropolis like New York or Tokyo, most likely the number of people living around you is much less than six million. Six million people may be greater than the total number of persons in your country, in your state, perhaps in your entire region. Still, you cannot imagine so many people, so many lives, and so many deaths. This is beyond your understanding.

Yet you do know Anne Frank. Her story is familiar from the well-known stage and film dramatizations. You remember her family and friends hidden in an attic, the Secret Annexe, in Amsterdam, helped by Christian friends, betrayed to the Nazis, followed by death in the concentration camps. You remember her childish hopes and fears, her teenage love, her spunk and lack of respect for certain elders, her great ability to write. You must surely cherish her memory.

For most people (prior to the remarkable testament of Steven Spielberg's *Schindler's List*), Anne Frank's diary is the only way to begin to comprehend the personal tragedy of the Holocaust.

Her diary begins on June 12, 1942. The first entries are those of a giddy young girl at home, gaily itemizing her birthday presents. Soon, however, she states the reason for her writing—she has no really close friend, she wants her diary to be her real friend, she will call her friend Kitty. She details in brief how her father, Otto, at thirty-six, married her mother, Edith, then twenty-five, and that her older sister, Margot, was born in 1926 in Frankfurt, Anne joining the family three years later. In 1933 the family escaped Nazi persecution for Holland. With the Nazi invasion of 1940, anti-Jewish laws are brutally enforced, Jews severely restricted in their activities. Despite the horrors around her she gossips about her girl friends in class, her test results, who's a good or bad student.

One sunny afternoon Anne is sitting outside on the veranda, lazily reading a book. The front doorbell rings. Her life suddenly changes. The SS has issued a warrant for her father's arrest, the family must flee. Mother is warning the Van Pels family. Mr. Van Pels is a coworker of Mr. Frank. Otto's Christian friends Miep and her new husband, Jan Gies, arrive to take away some personal belongings. Soon the family reaches Otto's office, climbs the stairs to a plain gray door. Behind the door are several rooms, you could never imagine there are so many rooms there, the Secret Annexe. A few days later Mr. and Mrs. Van Pels and their fifteen-year-old son Peter join the Franks. Peter brings his cat, Mouschi, with him. The Franks and the Van Pels settle in, while the streets around the Annexe echo with the sounds of transports of Jews being carted away to unknown destinations.

Anne writes in detail about their mundane life in hiding. Mr. Van Pels and she upset each other (he prefers Margot). Peter is boring, Anne thinks him a fool. The weather is nice. The Van

Photos of Anne Frank before she went into hiding in June 1942.

Pels quarrel while the Franks try to keep the peace. No one dares move around during the day; someone below might hear, get suspicious. Otto starts to read the plays of Goethe and Schiller to Anne every night. Great German culture is passed from one generation to another amid the greatest Teutonic barbarism. Anne clings to her father.

They all listen to the radio for news of the war. Appalling stories of Jewish persecution are told to them by Miep and their other Good Samaritan hosts. They decide that since "it is just as dangerous for seven as for eight," they will take in another boarder, a dentist named Friedrich Pfeffer. Anne must share her little room with the quiet dentist, who is very slow to understand her and can't seem to remember anything. Despite her new eccentric companion, she feels "wicked" sleeping in safety while her classmates are outside meeting some cruel fate.

Burglars strike below during the night. Anne notates carefully the behavior of all her companions in hiding. Taking literary license, she changes her name in the diary to Anne Robin, the Van Pels to the Van Daans. Dr. Pfeffer becomes Dr. Dussel, the cat is renamed Boche (meaning "German" in French). Anne experiments with language, dialogue. As 1943 progresses, she notices Peter's helpful contributions to their common plight. His parents have terrible rows, arguing over hocking Mrs. Van Pels' fur coat, over their lack of money. Anne composes an ode to her fountain pen, cremated by accident in the stove. She deeply regrets harm possibly inflicted on a friend in school. Where is that friend now? She prays that the girl will survive the war.

Anne sees herself in the mirror. Her face has changed, her mouth softened in appearance. If only Peter would notice! Politics and news of the imminent Allied invasion is mixed with her confused longings for spring. The year 1944 brings questions about her sexuality (why don't parents explain more to their children?), desires for her first kiss. More burglars attack their building and the police come as far as the swinging cupboard hiding the door to the Annexe; the hidden Jews are lucky not to be discovered.

Anne speaks directly to God. Why must the Jews be treated differently from other people? But she recognizes the strength of her people, that they will last despite the hate. She too will not be insignificant but will work for the world, for mankind. Shortly thereafter, the diary entries break off.

Just one month after the Allied invasion of Normandy, the Secret Annexe was raided by the Gruene Polizei. Everyone was sent to concentration camps along with two of their Christian friends. For most of August 1944 the Franks, Van Pels, and Dr. Pfeffer were all together in a Jewish transit camp. Anne and Peter were inseparable during this time. On the night of September 5–6 they arrived at the death camp, Auschwitz. The men and women were immediately separated. Mr. Van Pels was gassed immediately. Pfeffer was transferred to another concentration camp where he died shortly thereafter. Just after New Year's of 1945, Anne's mother died in Birkenau, the women's camp adjoining Auschwitz. With the approach of the Red Army, large groups of prisoners were moved on death marches in the bitter cold to Czechoslavakia and Germany. Mrs. Van Pels died on one of these marches sometime between April and May. Peter survived such a death march only to die just three days before the liberation of the Mauthausen concentration camp by the American Army. Margot and Anne were moved to the Bergen-Belsen camp where they survived under the most harsh conditions until their deaths from typhus sometime in late February or early March. It was said that Anne died a few days after Margot.

Otto Frank was the only occupant of the Secret Annexe to survive the war. He was in Auschwitz when it was liberated on January 27, 1945 by the Russians. After the war, Otto resumed his business and devoted himself to the memory of his youngest child, publishing her diary which was found in Anne's hiding place undisturbed. He died in Switzerland in 1980 with the knowledge that Anne's diary had been translated into dozens of languages and read by millions of people. In grade schools throughout the world, the diary is required reading. By the freshness of its language it retains the power it exhibited when first revealed.

Anne Frank's diary is a great work of world literature. Her story is powerful and meaningful not only because it tells a heroic story but also because it is so well written. Her warmth and simplicity of expression and her ability quickly and directly to relate her innermost emotions and thoughts mark her as a brilliant talent. That she used the convention of a young girl's private diary does not reduce her accomplishment.

She asks us important questions. What should we feel for her? Poignancy, anger, regret, deep loss, admiration, astonishment, amusement at her teenage fantasies, affection for her loving. We must always respect her courage, writing in constant fear of being discovered. Where was the rest of the world when humanity's brightest lights were being snuffed out? Her message is one we must never forget, that the most beautiful and good can be destroyed by the great evil of hate unless resisted with the strongest means. Anne's example should influence us never again to forget that it is always possible for a people to be singled out for destruction, and that the slaying of countless human beings via cold modern technology is just too easy.

In 1994, Anne Frank would have been sixty-five years old.

13 *The Prophets*
(Biblical times)

Religions develop not only through the interaction of like-minded believers, but often require the cleansing presence of great spirits to reduce into prophetic visions the clearest paths to righteousness. In the ancient world, these spiritual leaders were called Prophets.

They were mostly men who viewed mankind as defined only through its relationship with God. To the Prophets, history was the story of man's involvement with the Lord. Knowing the mind of God was a prerequisite to knowing one's own mind.

From a painting by Sargent of the Prophets:
Zephaniah, Joel, Obadiah, and Hosea.

Prophets seemed to be everywhere in biblical times.

After the Patriarchs, Matriarchs, and Moses, names like
Joshua, Deborah, Samuel, Nathan, Elijah, Isaiah, Jeremiah,
Ezekiel, Hosea, Joel, Amos, Obadiah, Micah, Nahum, Habakkuk,
Zephaniah, Haggai, Zechariah, and Malachi populate the Scrip-
tures. These extraordinary souls were markedly different from
the visionary holy men of the Buddhist or Hindu faiths or the
Christian saints who attempted to purify their lives in sanctity
and compassion.

The Prophets were angry, annoying, questioning, endlessly
debating, uneasy with man's plight, furious with his failures and
follies, disgusted with his ignorance of godly ways. During
periods of great crisis and disorder, they rose seemingly from
nowhere, demanding that the people act as God's chosen, to set
an exemplar of behavior for mankind. Their idea that Jews were
specially chosen to be a "light unto the nations" (in the words of
the later Isaiah) was later appropriated by both Christians and
Muslims for their own use and represents one of the central
organizational forces of civilization.

The Prophets also helped establish religion as a faith of ideas, not just practice. When people began to think of morality, of helping the poor, doing good, observing laws, rather than killing birds and lambs in rituals of sacrifice conducted by high priests, the Jewish religion could survive the destruction of a great Temple and dispersion into foreign lands. The Prophets' insistence on bettering man's behavior into righteousness made Judaism a religion that could move to any place. High priests became rabbis or teachers, prayers replaced ritual, one great Temple was replaced by countless synagogues, all served as models for Christian and Muslim piety in church and mosque. Jeremiah prophesied that Jerusalem would be destroyed by Babylon and for this was scorned by his people. Yet despite captivity in Babylonia, he asserted that God's covenant with Israel would be as promised to Abraham, unbroken and everlasting.

The Prophets such as Jeremiah preserved Judaism. When an idea is simple enough, simply right, it can be held onto, even in the face of terrible suffering. Ritual separated from morality is false, spawns cults. The Prophets defined Judaism as a religion of humane thought, peace, and justice. The spiritual voice of Jewish thinking was for all peoples to hear. The worst periods in western history have occurred when mankind has been deaf to Judaism's special message.

In Abraham Joshua Heschel's words, the Prophets expressed the "understanding of an understanding." They operated on many levels. They spoke of this world and of visions transcendent. In their attempt to reconcile man to God, the Prophets raged during periods of prosperity against temporal power, shouting against the total futility of it all. Only by believing in one God and God's law would man overcome his addiction to many gods and waging war. In the great words of Isaiah:

> And they shall beat their swords into plowshares
> And their spears into pruning hooks:
> Nations shall not take up
> Sword against nation;
> They shall never again know war.

14

Judas Iscariot

(ca. 4 B. C. E. –ca. 30 C. E.)

His very name arouses hatred. It is synonymous with treachery, deceit, greed. Think of the progression Judas Goat, Judas Kiss, Judah, Jude the Obscure, Judas, Judaism, Jew...

Some scholars, including the eminent Hyam Maccoby (in his *Judas Iscariot and the Myth of Jewish Evil*), believe that Judas the traitor did not exist. Paul himself makes no reference to Judas in the Epistles. It is possible that the character was created by the Pauline Church in Antioch for propaganda purposes. Especially after the destruction of the Temple in Jerusalem in 70 C.E. by Titus's troops, the Pauline Church sought to separate itself from the rebels in Judea and the Jewish Christians once led by Jesus' brother James. The Gospels were written during and after the Judean War. Roman centurions were made to appear more appealing than the Jewish masses. Borrowing instances of hellenic anti-Semitism, the authors of the Gospels assumed a pro-Roman stance, denying that Jesus was a rebel against Rome but asserting that he was an opponent of Judaism. To the anti-Semites, Jewish denial of Jesus' divinity established Jewish guilt in his death by crucifixion.

The foundation of Christian hate for the Jews was laid in the Gospel According to Saint John. Unlike the earlier Synoptic Gospels of Mark, Matthew, and Luke, John refers to Jesus as divine. Judas is set forth as fundamentally evil, terrifying, and avaricious. For such a divine figure as Jesus to fall, someone almost as divine must bring about his demise: the Black Christ, the Antichrist, Judas, with a full head of red hair, sporting a yellow robe, corrupt treasurer of the Apostles, money bag always in hand, ready (after haggling) to sell his Master for thirty pieces of silver. For those believing in John's words, Judas was allied with Satan, the fallen archangel. The foul lie of an unholy trinity of Judas-Satan-Jews became implanted in Christian consciousness from the earliest years of the Pauline Church.

Many pagan religions directly preceding Christianity shared a common theme of the godly figure sacrificed by a closest friend or brother. First by official synods of the Church and later by parish priests and passion plays, Christians were instructed that Judas had betrayed Jesus to the Jewish authorities with a kiss. The Church argued that those authorities then exerted political pressure on the Romans to crucify him. Betrayal by someone Jesus deemed most intimate made all Jews enemies of all men for all time. Through its preachings, the Church emphasized that Jewish resistance in recognizing the Christ symbolized the murder of Jesus over and over again by every Jew in every generation.

With increasing savagery, Jews were dubbed by Christians a Judas nation, a people basically evil, of negative spirituality and obscene materiality. In religious literature (Saint Jerome, Martin Luther), folklore (the Judas myth), drama (Passion, Easter, and morality plays, Shakespeare's Shylock and Iago), and literature (Dickens' Fagin), the Judas character became the emblem of the demon Jew. Jewish people were characterized as stinking (Jewish stench), grotesquely shaped and lecherous (with grossly enlarged sexual organs ready to rape), homeless (the Wandering Jew), sadistic vampires (the ritual killing of children for their blood), scapegoats (horns protruding from their foreheads), treacherous (Alfred Dreyfus), usurers (never bankers), Satanic (wearing pointed hats), and unclean (Judaism as a filthy sow sucked by Hebrew piglets).

Judas Iscariot's name is full of meanings. "Iscariot" is close to the Latin *sicarius* which means "dagger man." Judas is identified as an assassin, someone who sticks a knife in your back. He may have been a rebel against Rome like another apostle, Simon the Zealot. Judas is the one name among all of the Apostles that sounds like the name of the Jewish people. These relationships (especially the name Judas) were stressed by the Church to reveal what it viewed as the fundamentally Judaslike nature of Jews.

Whatever the connection between his name and his people, his role as the traitor selling his closest friend, confidant, master, for money, has endured as a potent and dangerous symbol. Modern movements of the left (Communists and Third World nationalists) and the right (Nazis and skinheads) with no professed ties to the Church, have utilized and institutionalized with horrible force the image of the Jew as traitor to the father- or motherland. For the Nazis and far rightists, the Jews were all Communists (see Trotsky!). For the Communists, every Jew was a capitalist (look at Rothschild!). In the post-Christian era of totalitarian regimes, ethical principles founded in New Testament beliefs have been cast aside. Jews are totally expendable in such an environment. In a religious vacuum the Judas tale continues to flourish.

Maccoby has urged that anti-Semitism, founded in the Judas myth, will disappear only when the Pauline concept of atonement is eschewed in favor of observance of Jesus' teachings when he was *alive*. So as long as the death of Jesus is viewed as the central event of Christianity, the psychological need for the traitor, the Jew Judas, will never disappear, even in possible post-Christian ages of assimilation and atheism.

15

Gustav Mahler

(1860–1911)

Whem my beloved conducting teacher, Carl Bamberger, was nine years old, he came home one day from school in Vienna to find his mother crying in the kitchen. Before her, spread out on the table, was the daily newspaper blaring the headline MAHLER IST TODT! ("Mahler is dead!"). When Carl in his early eighties recounted this story to me, Ronald Reagan was president of the United States and Zubin Mehta was conducting the New York Philharmonic.

Of all the figures in this book, the most influential on me and on countless other musicians and listeners was Gustav Mahler, surely one of the greatest and most original composers in the history of music and a leading force in the explosive Jewish and Viennese artistic movement in the twenty years before the First World War.

Mahler's large influence on Arnold Schoenberg will be recounted in that chapter. In addition to Schoenberg, Mahler exerted an immense force on composers Alban Berg, Anton von Webern, Kurt Weill, Dmitri Shostakovich, Benjamin Britten, and Leonard Bernstein and conductors Bruno Walter, Willem Mengelberg, and Otto Klemperer. Although some musicologists would claim that twentieth-century music belongs to the disciples of Schoenberg and Stravinsky, it was Mahler who with his very different contemporary, the French impressionist Claude Debussy, let loose the furies of chaos and dissonance, neoclassicism, symbolism, and glaring nationalism, which have since dominated musical composition.

Mahler composed nine symphonies (a tenth was left incomplete at his death), large orchestral song cycles (*Songs of a Wayfarer, The Youth's Magic Horn,* and *The Song of the Earth*), a cantata, and many individual art songs. He was also one of the best-known conductors and music directors of his era, working in opera houses in Budapest, Hamburg, Vienna, and New York as well as leading the Vienna and New York Philharmonic orchestras.

Mahler is the musical equivalent of Sigmund Freud. His symphonies use huge, complex orchestral forces to express often the most intimate, private thoughts. It is the music of an introvert expressed in a very public, almost naked manner. Fully aware of his musical heritage, Mahler used classical form as a beginning, then pushed, refined, and expanded musical shapes to satisfy his very personal, expressive desires. Unlike Debussy who employed impressions, repetitions, and symbols to express psychological states, Mahler's approach was more immediate. Painfully uncovering, achingly searching for his deepest wants and wishes, in expressions of almost suffocating lyricism and wild agitation, Mahler developed an almost therapeutic style of writing. Demons were exposed, and more often than not, after a grand and tiresome struggle, Gustav, the hero, prevailed in radiant triumph.

Mahler's background was humble, his father a small pub keeper of violent temperament. Five of his siblings died at young ages of diphtheria, another at twelve of heart disease; his elder brother Otto, a talented musician, jealous of Gustav's greater success, shot himself, and his eldest sister Leopoldine succumbed to a brain tumor after a short, unhappy marriage. His brother Alois behaved like a fool, imagining himself the friend of the crown prince or a powerful dragoon, veteran of foreign campaigns. Mahler's wife, Alma Schindler, would later remark that his brothers and sisters behaved in a way that could only be described as "Gustav Mahlerish." Mahler's music is often fantastical, exhibiting outlandish orchestral effects at the service of what sometimes seems an unconscious gone insane.

Raised in Bohemia, now a part of the Czech Republic, the young Mahler often heard local regimental marching bands whose instrumentation would play a strategic role in the style and content of his symphonies. He was also undoubtedly exposed to indigenous Bohemian folk songs and Jewish liturgy (his father was an active member of the local synagogue).

Mahler was not, like many of the great composers, a child prodigy. However, he showed a keen interest in chamber music, German Romantic poetry, and drama. Trained at the conservatory in Vienna, he shared lodgings with fellow student Hugo Wolf soon to be a preeminent song composer (before going mad and dying in an insane asylum at age forty-two), and became a disciple of the Austrian symphonist Anton Bruckner (who referred to Mahler—to his face—as "my little Jew").

Mahler secured positions as a journeyman conductor in rapid succession and with increasing prominence, culminating in his appointment in 1897 as opera director of the Hofoper in Vienna, Europe's leading theater. Anti-semitic Viennese society would not permit a Jew to direct its most important theater. To secure the position, Mahler chose to renounce his Judaism and convert to Roman Catholicism. It was a decision that tormented him for the rest of his life.

Mahler's years in Vienna coincided with the rise of the influential Secession art movement led by, among others, the painters Gustav Klimt and Carl Moll, architect Otto Wagner, and stage designer Alfred Roller. Mahler and Roller championed a series of productions of Mozart's operas which reestablished the composer's reputation as the greatest musical dramatist, not the classic trifle many then thought him to be. Mozart was revealed by Mahler (as Mendelssohn had "rediscovered" Bach) as Shakespeare's equal in unlocking the secrets of love, infidelity, sex, power, and the soul (fifty years later Leonard Bernstein would do the same for Mahler's reputation, establishing him as a symphonist the equal of Mozart, Haydn, Beethoven, and Brahms). Mahler also developed the revolutionary concept of a repertory company of acting singers. He worked with the leading composers of the period, giving local first performances of works by Leoncavallo, Puccini, and Richard Strauss.

Viennese musical politics in Mahler's day were treacherous (they remain so to this day), and he was forced out in 1907 after ten brilliant, innovative years. First, the Metropolitan Opera and then the New York Philharmonic offered him positions. He spent an unhappy four seasons in New York, ultimately losing out in a musical power struggle with a young musical tornado named Arturo Toscanini.

Mahler died in Vienna in 1911 of heart failure brought on by a streptococcal infection.

Apart from Mahler's important contributions to musical practice and performance during his lifetime (and as did Toscanini, Mahler raised the standards of music making in his time to high levels of professionalism), his music challenges the listener, the instrumentalist, and the composer to dig deeper into their emotions, intellect, and subconscious for revelation. Audiences did not wholly understand Mahler's works until quite recently. After his death, performances of his symphonies dwindled, kept mostly alive by his assistant, Bruno Walter. The Nazis banned his music (and murdered his niece in Auschwitz). Only after the Second World War in trailblazing performances by Jascha Horenstein and Bernstein did Mahler's time come.

Bernstein once remarked that Mahler's music anticipated and predicted the Holocaust. This melodramatic declaration has some truth to it, but one cannot fail to notice that Mahler always avoided artificial musical expression. He hid behind nothing. His music preserves the emotional quandaries of his era, when Austrian society, largely through its Jewish artists, reached an apex of civilized life before the mechanized slaughter by the National Socialists. More than any other composer, Mahler's innermost feelings and thoughts are laid plain to us. We are urged to swim in a chasm of swirling feelings, madly rushing past danger, to the refuge of a heavenly life.

16

Maimonides

(1135–1204)

From Moses to Moses, there was no one like Moses.

So reads the people's epitaph to the greatest Jewish philosopher
of all time, Rabbi Moses ben Maimon, known to pious Jews by the
acronym Rambam and to the world by the Greek name Maimonides. Born in Cordoba, Spain, buried in Tiberius in the Holy
Land, Maimonides experienced the turmoil of the Crusades;
perils at sea; the noble court of Saladin, the dynamic ruler of all
Arabia; challenges to rabbinical authority; and developing trends
in medieval medicine.

Until their discovery in the late 1800s, hundreds of thousands of documents from the Middle Ages lay hidden in a storeroom attached to a synagogue in Fostat, a suburb of Cairo, preserved by the perfectly dry Egyptian climate. From this documentation we can recreate much of Maimonides' life—often in his own words.

Maimonides lived a life of privilege sustained first by his family and then, in his late years, by the skill of his medical arts. The level of intellectual and political authority he achieved could only be reached in this time by someone of high birth, commercial wealth, and great scholarship. Many of Maimonides' ancestors were famed rabbis. His younger brother, David, successfully supported the family as an international trader. But it was Maimonides' encyclopedic mind and consummate understanding and memory of Jewish law that set him apart. In his teens and early twenties he wrote important religious treatises. Indeed, all through his life he exhibited the need to codify and explain, to guide the faithful to a rational understanding of the infinite.

Maimonides admired Aristotle above all ancient philosophers. The ancient Greek philosopher had written texts on logic as a means of understanding the world. With his unique knowledge of Jewish law and tradition, Maimonides applied Aristotelian logic to religious thought. Rambam asserted that one's imagination could be used to lift the mind and spirit away from the restraints of thinking, ultimately toward divine prophecy. After his death, Maimonides' philosophy influenced important Christian thinkers such as Thomas Aquinas, Albertus Magnus, and Gottfried Wilhelm Leibniz (who also interpreted and synthesized Aristotelian logic for religious purposes) and remarkably the excommunicated Jew, Baruch de Spinoza. Although beloved by most Jews as their greatest philosopher, ironically Maimonides has had less effect on Jewish life than, for example, the French commentator Rashi or the Hasidic and mystical movements.

Maimonides represents one of the first great flowerings of human thought after the long drought of the Dark Ages. In his day the Arab world stretched from Babylonia through North Africa into Spain. Christian Europe did not provide the peace necessary for Jews to practice and develop their religion. Muslim rule, on the other hand, when not dominated by extremists, was more tolerant, permitting heathen Jews to be Jews, quietly. Maimonides fled Spain to escape the persecution of the Almohads who gave Jews the impossible choice of conversion to Islam or death. After dangerous voyages to Morocco and Palestine, Maimonides settled in Fostat. His brother, David, supported the scholarly Moses by developing a flourishing trading business. The trading range of the Jewish merchants was astounding, extending even as far as Malaysia and Sumatra. During the late 1100s, Saladin liberated Jerusalem from the marauding Crusaders, displaying a restraint not shown by the Christians years before. When the Crusaders in 1099 had freed the Holy City from those they considered infidels, the Christian soldiers herded all the Jewish inhabitants into a square and murdered them in cold blood.

When Maimonides was in his early forties, David was lost at sea, far away on a trading expedition. Maimonides was shattered. He never truly got over his brother's death. For the rest of his life Rambam greatly mourned his separation from his Spanish home of Cordoba, the "Bride of Andalusia," and David's death. Maimonides' early years had been spent in quiet contemplation, compiling important texts on Jewish law, codifying and analyzing divine instruction. His remaining days, however, were incredibly active. To support his family, the learned Maimonides began to practice the art of medicine, aided by his ability to retain scientific teachings and to empathize with people. After the ancient Greek physician Galen, Maimonides' influence on medical practices would extend across centuries.

The influence of his brother's death, greater public responsibilities, and increasing controversies over the meaning of holy law motivated Rambam to compose in elegant Arabic his great *Guide to the Perplexed*. The *Guide* was not intended for the average reader. Maimonides asserted that a simple understanding of Jewish law does not bring one closest to God without metaphysics or what we call today philosophy. Only if man is possessed by that higher knowledge will the age of the Messiah come. Maimonides was driven by the popular prophecy that during the early 1200s the misery of the Dark Ages would usher in the Messianic age. To prepare for that supreme moment, one had to have faith, and faith was only achievable through thinking. Knowing is more important than doing. Logic can fail us, as we are incapable of taking reason to its infinite resolution, but it is better for man's being to be operative within its realm.

Maimonides was disturbed that Jewish tradition had no one system for teaching its laws and no real concern for classical philosophy. He therefore sought to filter Judaic thinking through Aristotle to assert that man's soul is exactly equal to the sum of his knowledge. Our thinking is not a random thing but rather our existence. The sum total of our knowledge is our essential being. Our total knowledge, our inherent reason, brings us closer to holy perfection, to oneness with God. Faith can only be achieved through thought.

Maimonides' rise to political power as a leader and judge as well as the era's most acclaimed and desired physician brought him endless days and nights of work in service to his community and sovereign. In his final years he became a figure of international importance. Maimonides declined the offer of the "Frankish king" (some think it was Richard, the Lion Heart, king of England) to leave Egypt and return to a European court. Rambam declined the offer, preferring to remain in Africa to guide his people to physical and spiritual health.

Despite his public dedication to the commonweal, Maimonides' rise to political power and his blend of classical logic with Jewish law angered many prominent rabbis. He became a target. His sources were questioned, his focus on thought ridiculed. After his death even his tomb was desecrated by those who viewed a literal interpretation of religion law as mandatory.

Although observant people to this day are more aware of rules of behavior prescribed by teachings such as the Talmud and religious parables, Maimonides guides us still to a higher path. He understood that how we think and what we know is what we are—and what we can be.

17 *Niels Bohr*

(1885–1962)

I believe that, without Bohr, we would still today
know very little about atomic theory.
                                    —Albert Einstein

Niels Henrik David Bohr, son of a Christian father and Jewish
mother, was, next to Albert Einstein, the most influential physicist of the twentieth century. Bohr is universally thought of as the
father of modern quantum theory. He was awarded the Nobel
Prize in 1922 "for his series in the investigation of the structure of
atoms and of the radiation emanating from them."

Bohr was the founder of the Institute for Theoretical Physics in Copenhagen (now known as the Bohr Institute) and acted as a guiding light to three generations of physicists. His theories on the surface tensions of liquids (resulting later in the liquid drop model of the nucleus), spectra, energy loss of alpha particles, periodic system, complementarity principle, quantum electrodynamics, measurement of electromagnetic fields, compound nucleus in nuclear reactions, fission, and superconductivity, are the basis of modern nuclear science.

Bohr's most famous and imaginative theory on the constitution of atoms and molecules, expressed in his essay dubbed the "Trilogy," although largely refuted today, remains physics' most recognized symbol. Celebrated worldwide on dozens of stamps and other memorabilia, the Bohr atom resembles a solar system with electrons in orbit around a central nucleus. The Bohr atom has also symbolized the use of atomic energy by nations united in peace.

In war, however, Bohr contributed his knowledge of the atom to develop the most destructive weapon yet devised by man. During the Second World War he worked at Los Alamos on the Manhattan Project, assisting the American effort in creating the bomb. Even before Hiroshima, Bohr realized the awesome and horrific effect of this force of mass destruction. In 1950, fearful of the improper use of nuclear energy for the wrong political purposes, Bohr in an open letter petitioned the United Nations in what was to become the most personal manifesto of his ideals. Of course, the great powers ignored his pleas, entering into an arms race that lasted over forty years.

Bohr, the philosopher of peace and almost godlike atomic power, came from a liberal and intellectual background. He was born in Copenhagen. His father was a respected physiologist and university professor. Niels's gentle, caring nature was derived, it was said, from his Jewish mother, Ellen Adler. He and his brother Harald (later a well-regarded mathematician) were when young star soccer players, sports heroes throughout Denmark (Harald played on the 1908 Danish Olympic team).

After studies at the University of Copenhagen and work on the surface tensions of liquids and the electron theory of metals, Bohr traveled to England. Studies at Cambridge's Cavendish Laboratory under J.J. Thomson were disappointing. But the trip proved worthwhile when Bohr journeyed to Manchester and at the university met Ernest Rutherford, the great physicist and professor. Until his death in 1937, Rutherford was almost a second father to Bohr.

Professor Rutherford's ideas about the structure of atoms and his discovery of the nucleus laid the foundation upon which Bohr built his own atomic theory (stated in the Trilogy). The Rutherford model set forth a theory, in Bohr's words, that "atoms consist of a positively charged nucleus surrounded by a series of electrons kept together by attractive forces from the nucleus: the total negative charge of the electrons is equal to the positive charge of the nucleus." Rutherford also assumed the nucleus to be "the seat of the essential part of the mass of the atom" with "linear dimensions exceedingly small compared with linear dimensions of the whole atom."

The "Bohr atom" improved on the Rutherford model in significant ways. In its original form, Bohr's atomic model consisted of electrons orbiting in circular paths around a nucleus in the center. Bohr further theorized that electrons move in elliptical orbits of limited range. Each range produces a certain energy. Light is produced when electrons shift orbit.

Bohr's theory of atomic structure opened up entirely new approaches to traditional physics research. For example, his ideas, so elegantly expressed in articles such as the Trilogy, were applied to define the precise measurements of colors or spectra radiated by the hydrogen atom. His conceptual model demonstrated how atomic particles are shaped and why they are a certain size.

Bohr used the establishment of his Institute for Theoretical Physics in 1920 as a forum for distinguished young physicists to probe deeper into the theories he first conceived. The Institute fostered the so-called Copenhagen School of physicists. Eminent (some future Nobel Prize winners) young physicists such as Werner Heisenberg and Wolfgang Pauli worked with Bohr at the Institute. Although some would surpass him in certain areas and others would further elucidate theories Bohr could not, for whatever reason, complete, he was their ethical master, a source of inspiration for decades and the person who synthesized their findings often into something greater than they may have intended. Bohr's many dialogues with Einstein, such as those at the

famous conferences at the Solvay Institute, stimulated a generation of young scientists with their profundity and what C.P. Snow
called "noble feeling."

Bohr resisted the Nazi occupation of Denmark until he was
forced to flee to Sweden or be made to work on the German
bomb effort. He was directly responsible for influencing the
Swedish king to accept five thousand Danish Jews (almost the
entire Jewish population of Denmark) who facing sure death in
1943 at the hands of the Nazis fled into safe and neutral Sweden.
At great personal risk, Bohr later flew to Britain in the bay of a
British bomber. His work on the Manhattan Project in America
followed.

With the war won, he returned to Denmark. His remaining
years were spent fruitlessly trying to make the world powers face
up to the responsibility of harnessing and controlling nuclear
energy.

Bohr's perhaps most permanent theory has been his principle of complementarity. He posited that a physical system may
possess differing and opposing conditions that nevertheless are
all necessary to formulate its description. The complementarity
principle has been used to explain seemingly unrelated ways of
life, from Eastern religious philosophy to Marxist-Leninist
dogma.

Bohr's personal legacy also extended to his talented son,
Aage, who also won the Nobel Prize in 1975 for physics.

18

Moses Mendelssohn

(1729–1786)

For over 1,500 years from the destruction of ancient Judea by the Romans and the dispersion of Jews throughout the empire, world Jewry lived and prayed in medieval seclusion. Small communities were organized around powerful rabbinic councils. Always careful to preserve spiritual values, the rabbis guided their people through the tribulations of an often hostile gentile culture.

Moses, the son of Mendel the Torah scribe, was born in 1729 at Dessau, Germany. Jews in the Germany of that time did not have last names. Instead, they followed the biblical tradition of listing their first name followed by their father's. Only later would German authorities demand that Jews become more secular and take last names (often chosen for each Jew by an unsympathetic German civil servant).

Moses suffered from curvature of the spine, was soft-spoken and rather diffident. Growing up in medieval surroundings, he studied traditional Jewish law and bookkeeping, learned to trade silk.

In 1749 the German playwright and poet Gotthold Lessing introduced a one-act play, *Die Juden (The Jews),* that depicted Jewish people not as horrid bloodsucking stereotypes, but as rational, kind human beings. Unlike their French counterparts (such as Voltaire, who was virulently anti-Semitic), many German Enlightenment figures sought to "rescue" the Jewish population from medieval confines. These moderate German thinkers sought to understand the religious spirit of man and to bring about a reconciliation of Christian and Jewish cultures.

Mendelssohn met Lessing, who introduced him to literary society. To prove his philosophical worth, Moses entered a writing contest, competing against (and beating!) the great philosopher Immanuel Kant. Lessing encouraged Mendelssohn to continue writing philosophy, and helped the mild-mannered trader to get his works published.

Mendelssohn's early text *Phaedon,* written in German, explored Platonic philosophy and the immortality of the soul, using classical (not Hebraic) imagery to illuminate his argument. Following Lessing's revolutionary example in not writing in more fashionable French or Latin, Mendelssohn chose everyday German as his language of discourse. He desired a national German audience for his writings.

This contemporary of the Baal Shem Tov and the Vilna Gaon (see later chapters) sought through his philosophy to bring Jewish society out of the ghetto and into the modern secular world (as his friend Lessing had made the son of Mendel into a "Mendelssohn"). The Jewish Enlightenment or Haskalah was the outgrowth of the attachment of many Jews of the era to German culture. "Germans first, Jews second," became the motto of those who mistakenly viewed the relaxing of medieval restrictions on movement and dress as the softening of Teutonic hatreds. This fatal delusion continued during 150 years of artistic and economic triumph, ending in the fires of the Third Reich.

Mendelssohn's great goal was to reconcile exposure to secular life with religious thought. Attendance at synagogue was voluntary, not mandatory, said Moses. The political dominance of the rabbis was over. Their power of excommunication was no longer legal. But the state, as in Jefferson's America, should allow its citizens to choose their house of worship freely. Reason would overwhelm hatred and persecution.

Jews must remain Jews at home and in their temples, but be loyal citizens of the state, active in public life. When God revealed His law to Moses on Sinai, it was to impose only on His people a system of internal rules personal to the Jews and no one else. Yet Jews did not have a mission to improve humanity.

Mendelssohn urged the study of Hebrew and the silencing of Yiddish, which he considered vulgar ghetto slang. He translated the Old Testament into German. Millions of copies were sold although their purchase was banned by the traditional rabbis.

He met many important rulers and thinkers. In a famous encounter with Frederick the Great, Mendelssohn criticized the monarch for writing in French (a bold move at a time of government-sanctioned Jew baiting). A Protestant theologian, Johann Lavater, questioned in public why, if Mendelssohn thought Jews and Christians should come together, he did not convert to Christianity? Moses retreated into a rationalist defense of Judaism.

At the time of the American Revolution, he became concerned with the civil rights of Jews. Returning to visit his birthplace, Dessau, Mendelssohn was required, before entering the city, to pay the head tax reserved for cattle—and Jews. A lifetime of struggle, culminating in the conflict with Lavater and the head-tax incident, convinced Mendelssohn of the superiority of the American model separating church and state.

Mendelssohn's secular view was always tempered by deep respect for customary religious practice. In the tradition of Maimonides, he sought out reason in all human endeavors. For Moses Mendelssohn, the Christianity of the Immaculate Conception and Resurrection was far more irrational than rule-guided Judaism. The leap of faith must always be accompanied by reasoned thought.

Mendelssohn's influence on the development of Jewish life remains vital. His philosophy permanently severed Eastern European Jews from a village culture that had kept them together during the long years of Diaspora. He hoped for a merging of Jews and Christians into a reasoning, emancipated society. However, Mendelssohn rejected conversion, pleading for tolerance and mutual respect. Jews should be Jews and Christians Christian. There was so much in common. The great lights of German literature, Goethe and Schiller, later acknowledged their debt to Mendelssohn for his liberation of the German language and rationalist universal philosophy.

His efforts led positively to the creation of schools to teach young German Jews with modern curricula. The Jewish Free School, founded in Berlin in 1781, was a model of its kind. Joseph II of Austria rejected the hatred of his mother, Maria Theresa, and issued edicts calling for the civil emancipation of his Jewish subjects.

Moses could not foresee the results of his liberating philosophy. On a personal level, all of his children (including his composer grandson, Felix) except one would become Protestants. Almost ten percent of German Jews in the late 1700s converted to Christianity (some of their descendants became Nazis). Secularism led in many cases to total assimilation (an issue that still troubles Jews in Europe and America).

The followers of the Vilna Gaon and the Baal Shem Tov reacted to Mendelssohn's Haskalah with virulence. Out of the turmoil of the period, the Orthodox, Conservative, and Reform movements developed, dividing Jewish sacred observance for generations.

Mendelssohn's life and work raise disturbing questions, but also provide paths of resolution. Jews are still faced with reconciling modern existence and religious tradition. Since the Holocaust, ecumenical gestures by Christians are met with warmth by Jews, but hesitantly, with some suspicion. On the other side, Jewish concern for civil rights started with Mendelssohn. For him, Judaism guides mankind's behavior with reasonable rules of living, a beacon of hope and challenge to the world.

19

Paul Ehrlich

(1854–1915)

Paul Ehrlich was the most renowned, successful, and influential medical scientist of his generation. Ehrlich's research led to the development of important medical disciplines—immunology, chemotherapy, and hematology (the study of blood and blood-forming organs). Although he received the Nobel Prize in 1908 for work in immunity, Ehrlich's most famous contribution was his creation of the cure for syphilis, the synthetic drug Salvarsan, commonly known as the "magic bullet."

Central Europe in the late nineteenth century was fertile
ground for creative thinkers. The number of influential scientists
and musicians born during this era in the German-speaking
countries was disproportionately higher than in other areas of the
world. The effects of migration, culture, industrialization, improved education, political movements, religious emancipation,
and nationalism gave rise to seminal minds whose work still
marks our lives today. Ehrlich's early years were indeed similar in
many respects to those of Mahler and Freud.

Raised in a small town in the Silesian countryside (now part
of Poland), Ehrlich was the only son of an eccentric innkeeper
and distiller and a likable mother of considerable intellect.
Ehrlich inherited many of his parents' good qualities. He was well
liked as an adult, known for his crotchety good spirits and
liveliness, sprinkling his speech with Latin sayings to make a
point, the archetype of the German professor.

His early education in German school or gymnasium was
typical of the age. He enjoyed mathematics and classical training
in Latin, but was burdened by rote training in German composition. Ehrlich's intellectual curiosity was not completely triggered
until his exposure at eighteen to natural sciences and chemistry.

During subsequent medical studies he became fascinated
with the use of dyes in researching cells and tissues. It was during
his early twenties at leading universities that Ehrlich gained the
knowledge and skills required for the remarkable chemical experiments of his maturity.

After graduation in 1878, Ehrlich went to Berlin to practice
medicine at a prominent hospital. His research there soon
produced breakthroughs in the methods of recognizing leuke-
mias and anemias. His medical training combined with a unique
gift for chemistry led quickly to the discovery that chemical
relationships control biological functions. This simple axiom
underlies much of the unbelievably broad research Ehrlich would
develop.

Some of Ehrlich's most unusual discoveries over the next
fifteen years until 1900 included the categorization of bodily
organs into classes according to their reaction to oxygen, the use
of dye to relieve pain and diagnose acute infections, the building
up of immunity in mice and their offspring (the so-called "wet
nurse" experiments) by injection of mother mice with small doses

of antigens and the consequent suckling and immunizing of their babies, the investigation of poisons in bacteria, and the use of serum to counteract potent infections such as diphtheria and tetanus.

Ehrlich's discoveries through the turn of the century would have been sufficient to mark his treasured place in medical history. However, in his final years he displayed an even greater scientific mastery. Although many of these last years were spent in fruitless cancer research, Ehrlich's international fame was established by his prophecy of chemicals which seek and destroy parasitic targets within bodily organisms. In 1910 he announced to the scientific world the creation of a synthetic drug called Salvarsan, a magic bullet which rid the body of the spirochete causing syphilis.

Before Ehrlich's discovery of Salvarsan, he had been a respected doctor, winner of the Nobel Prize for his work on immunity, and director of prestigious research institutes. The controversy over his cure for syphilis raged, however, until his death five years later during the second year of the First World War. Demand for Salvarsan could not be satisfied. Ehrlich personally checked the testing and production techniques of the new drug. His notoriety led to vicious accusations of fraud, risky experimentation, and profiteering. Although he was exonerated by the German Reichstag, these falsehoods and the onset of the war troubled him greatly, leading to illness, stroke, and death at sixty-one.

20

Rashi

(1040–1105)

As for the wise, their body alone perishes in this
world.   —Rashi on Psalm 49

The commentaries on the Babylonian Talmud and the Bible of
Rabbi Shlomo Itzhaki, commonly know by the acronym Rashi,
place him at the core of Jewish rabbinical thought. Very little is
known about Rashi's life. There are many fables about him,
wondrous tales invented to accentuate his importance, but they
are really unnecessary (except for enjoyment). Rashi is primarily
remembered for his magnificent and massive writings. What we
know about him is gleaned from his lively thought and clear

guidance. It was Rashi whose commentaries opened the window for countless readers to the often obscure and mostly difficult words of the Talmud, written largely in ancient Aramaic. Rashi's guide, expressed in transparent, easy-to-understand prose, made even the lowliest woodchopper in the smallest forgotten village a master of the Word, of God's law.

He was born and died in the Champagne region of northeast France, living most of his life in a town called Troyes. His maternal uncle was a well-respected rabbi who had studied with Rabbenu Gershom of Mainz (dubbed the "Light of the Diaspora"), the leading Talmudist of the tenth century and a forerunner of Rashi. He studied for a time in Worms and at Mainz under Isaac ben Judah, a rabbi dubbed the "Frenchman," whom Rashi always considered his master. Rashi's study at various Talmud schools reflected his aim first to absorb the disciplines of several traditions and then to incorporate them into a new vision.

Rashi stressed that the truly learned man must support himself with work "of the hands," and to prove his point he labored in his family's vineyard. Failing to till and irrigate the soil would surely leave it barren—and so the mind. To be a rabbi was an honor.

When he was about thirty, Rashi founded a school in Troyes. It became the center of Talmudic studies for the region and served as a catalyst in reviving Jewish learning and scholarship (especially after the devastation and massacres brought about by the Crusaders during 1096 in Central Europe). Rashi's brilliant teaching and extraordinary example contributed greatly toward the reinvigoration of Jewish culture and morale during a time of extreme religious persecution. His *Responsa* or answers to questions on the law served as models for generations of students. The revival of scholarship inspired by Rashi was also in many ways comparable to the rise of Christian literary movements led nearby by Peter Abelard and Bernard of Clairvaux.

Rashi's commentaries on the Talmud and the Bible are glosses, usually short discussions on individual words or small phrases from the holy text. Rashi was the perfect commentator, never a gigantic, universal thinker like Philo or Maimonides, never seeking to compose a grand compendium of all philosophy and logic or reconcile his conclusions with natural science. Rashi's goals were simple. He wished to explain the law in clear, comprehensible terms. "To write like Rashi" came to mean to write intelligibly, similar to the modern computer jargon term WY-SIWYG ("what you see is what you get").

Rashi was a master grammarian and lexicographer. He established the correct text of the Talmud, then a confusing jumble of conflicting scrolls. His biblical commentaries, while more subjective in presentation than those on the Talmud, were for hundreds of years devotional best-sellers, accessible to the general reader. The commentaries on the Talmud, on the other hand, were academic texts comprehensible to both the interested student and the learned rabbi. The more you knew, the more meaningful they were, Rashi's clear descriptions coming into sharper focus with expanding knowledge.

Rashi's work exerted lasting influence on almost nine centuries of rabbinical thought. How many other writers (perhaps other than the great Greek philosophers) have exerted such influence for so long? After Rashi's death, his sons-in-law and then his grandsons established a kind of Rashi dynasty, earning the honored acronyms of Rashbam, Rabbenu Tam, and Ribam, contributing *tossafot*, additional glosses on his commentary and further enrichening the Talmud.

But the institutionalized prejudice of the Church kept this great thought out of view, away from the mainstream of the world's intellectual development. Copies of the Talmud were burned in bonfires of hate. However, until the Enlightenment and emancipation in the 1700s, in little Jewish villages all across the Diaspora, geniuses and simpletons toiled together, hidden from the fires of Inquisition, quietly and patiently studying Talmud, Rashi's wondrous commentaries always leading the way.

21

Benjamin Disraeli

(1804–1881)

Like the wealthy banker Sidonia in his novels *Coningsby* and *Tancred*, Benjamin Disraeli, Earl of Beaconsfield, first Jewish prime minister of England, was a potent mixture of idealism and impassioned reason. One of the greatest exponents of the parliamentary system, Disraeli possessed a biting wit and fluency of tongue unmatched in democratic history. More books have been written about this fascinating and infuriating man than about any other British politician before Winston Churchill. While his great Liberal opponent William Gladstone remains to us forever caught up in the mores of the Victorian era, Disraeli seems timeless, a modern and ancient man who would have been equally comfortable debating Pericles or Margaret Thatcher.

Gladstone ruled England on and off for over a dozen years, through four administrations. His archrival, Disraeli, served as the British leader for only a little over six years. However, Disraeli's contributions to British and world history were as or more important than Gladstone's. Surely Disraeli's influence has lasted longer.

Briefly filling out Lord Derby's last term, Disraeli became prime minister in 1868, making little effect in the short time available. However, his second term, from 1874 to 1880, proved to be decisive years for the British Empire. A bold, some would say reckless, adventurer, Disraeli expanded British dominion over the Suez Canal and India. He passed legislation that reformed England and developed the founding principles of the Conservative (Tory) Party. At the Congress of Berlin in 1878, Disraeli acted as peacemaker, thwarting Russia's colonial intentions in the Balkans while preserving his own. Through his popular novels, he made his political views widely known. Disraeli espoused strange racial ideas, stressing his own "pure" origins in the sands of the Middle East as somehow superior to those of "barbarian" Anglo-Saxons. He tried to reconcile a Jewish background with his Christian conversion. Disraeli asserted that Christianity was completed Judaism, a declaration that satisfied no one, angering most, but was for him, more than a rationalization. Familiar as a dandy when young, dubbed "Dizzy" by his friends (and worse by many enemies, including the malicious "Jew *d'esprit*"), Benjamin Disraeli was the most controversial politician in British history (again before Churchill) and an essential, civilizing force.

The son of Isaac D'Israeli, an historian, essayist, and admirer of Moses Mendelssohn, Benjamin was of Italian Jewish descent. Reacting to a silly dispute with his Sephardic synagogue, Isaac had his children baptized into the Anglican faith when son Benjamin was thirteen, and brought up as Christians. But for this conversion, Disraeli would never have become in 1837 a member of Parliament and later prime minister. Indeed, Lionel de Rothschild (some say Disraeli's true model for his fictional character, Sidonia), elected to Parliament in 1847, was denied entry to the House until 1858, for his refusal to utter the required oath "on the true faith of a Christian."

Disraeli's early business undertakings were all failures (wild investments in South American mining shares and a daily newspaper). However, in 1826 he began to write under an anonymous name a series of novels, satirical in tone, on the contemporary political scene. The books were widely read but savagely criticized when the identity of their author was uncovered. He then suffered something of a nervous breakdown.

With his sister's fiancé, William Meredith, Disraeli left Britain in 1830 for a "Grand Tour" of the Mediterranean. The sixteen-month trip made a permanent impression on him. Disraeli was particularly taken with Jerusalem. He began to understand the relationship between his Jewish heritage and Christian assimilation. Indeed, this Middle Eastern journey inspired creation of the protagonist of his novel *Alroy* (1833). Set in an exotic twelfth-century milieu, the character, David Alroy, fails in his attempt to restore the Holy Land to Jewish dominion. Later, in his novel *Tancred,* Disraeli's early Zionism would result in the often quoted line that "a race that persists in celebrating their vintage although they have no fruits to gather, will regain their vineyards."

When Meredith died of smallpox in Cairo, Disraeli cut short his extended vacation and returned to England. Due to his burgeoning literary fame and stylish reputation as a fop with a lively wit, he soon gained entry into fashionable society and the bedrooms of extravagant ladies of high birth. In 1831 he decided to enter politics and become in real life a hero of the same epic proportions as his fictional ones. Associated initially as a radical of questionable background (in other words, a Jew) and of immoral sexual habits, Disraeli was trounced repeatedly.

Learning from his failures, he allied himself with the Conservative party and was returned to Parliament in 1837. Disraeli consolidated his position in 1839 by marrying the respectable and rich widow (twelve years his senior) of a fellow former member. The brief support of the Tory leader, Sir Robert Peel, gave Disraeli added prominence as well as his developing talents as a master orator skilled at ripping his political enemies apart in cascades of brilliant argument. When Peel failed to name him to his cabinet, Disraeli countered by founding a group of young Tories bent on reforming the government. The "Young England" movement sought to change the party from a stuffy bunch of aristocrats concerned only with preserving the status quo to an organization more representative of the British people. Despite the escapist and rather romantic notions of his group, Disraeli tried to rally the common people about the crown led by aristocratic leaders enlightened by religious feeling. Even with all this nostalgic nonsense, Disraeli expanded his party's political base and in effect brought the Tories into modern times.

When Lord Derby became prime minister in 1852, Disraeli became the leader of the House of Commons and chancellor of the exchequer. He returned to power in the second (1858) and third (1866) Derby administrations, succeeding the party leader as PM in 1868. During Disraeli's short first stay as prime minister in 1868, he expanded an already close friendship with Queen Victoria. The queen grew to despise the taciturn Gladstone, but almost fell in love with the charming Mr. Disraeli, whose every audience brought her pleasure and stimulus.

Ironically, Disraeli's defeat in 1868 was largely due to the electoral reform bill extending the right to vote to the working classes which he had vigorously supported and helped to carry. In 1874, however, the Conservatives won a clear mandate. Prime Minister Disraeli then embarked on a historic series of governmental innovations. With the able initiative of his home secretary R. A. Cross, Disraeli passed laws to clear the slums, improve public health and factory conditions, and regulate the sale of food and drugs. Much of this legislation was fifty years ahead of its time, establishing England as the most progressive government of the era and a model for other democracies.

Disraeli's greatest concern as prime minister was his overwhelming desire to maintain Britain's power in Europe. He viewed foreign policy as his most important duty and criticized Gladstone's reaction to continental crises as unnecessarily pacifist. The Rothschilds, on Disraeli's urging, provided the capital in 1875 for England to purchase shares in the Suez Canal from the khedive of Egypt. The shares became known as the "Key of India," confirming British occupation of Egypt and control over a vital route to South Asia.

To commemorate expanding British dominion, Disraeli's government declared Queen Victoria Empress of India. Her thanks to Disraeli was the granting of a peerage, making this Sephardic Jew the first earl of Beaconsfield.

Benjamin Disraeli from a painting by Sir Francis Grant.

From 1876 to 1878 his administration was preoccupied with international power politics. England and Russia had become rivals, playing with developing countries in the Mediterranean like pawns in a global chess game. Disraeli forced his upper hand when Russia, exhausted by its war effort against Turkey, was made to submit the terms of the peace to international mediation. At the Congress of Berlin in 1878, Disraeli met with Chancellor Bismarck, whose words *"Der alte Jude, das ist der Mann!"* ("The old Jew, that is some man!") remain the most memorable from the conference. By the clear threat of British military power, the Ottoman Empire was preserved (to become forty years later an enemy of England) and the route to India secured from Russian hegemony.

Thereafter, petty wars in Afghanistan and South Africa dominated Tory foreign policy concerns. Viewed today, this colonial involvement in "Third World" countries was both civilizing and oppressive, subjugating unique cultures to the grave sameness of the British Commonwealth. After these foreign mishaps and troubles at home and the return to power of Gladstone in 1880, Disraeli moved houses, dominating Lords in his last year of life (and wrote the splendid semiautobiographical *Endymion,* his last completed novel).

22

Franz Kafka

(1883–1924)

The British poet W.H. Auden noted that Kafka was "the author who comes nearest to bearing the same kind of relation to our age as Dante, Shakespeare and Goethe bore to theirs." Born and raised in Prague, a Jew who spent most of his life working in what was to become Czechoslovakia, Kafka spoke and wrote only in German, the language of his oppressors. He felt perhaps more sensitively than any other writer in history that special separateness now known as alienation.

Kafka's carefully crafted literary works have the clarity and ambiguity of dreams. His fiction is always easy to read, yet difficult to comprehend. In this "Kafkaesque" world, stories are told only from the protagonist's point of view. Readers never have the comfort of a writer's detachment. We see what happens in a story not safely from the outside, but from the inside out. This perspective makes Kafka's tales terrifying real. This great author does not throw us into a stream of consciousness, not knowing where we are, but sure that what rushes about us is there, is true. Rather, Kafka insists we know where we are, in sharp, bright light, then blinds us from the truth in language that implies, makes us guess, traps us, imprisons us without hope of release.

Like his fellow German-speaking Bohemian the composer Gustav Mahler, Kafka was a prophet of the horrible events of the twentieth century. *The Penal Colony* and *The Trial*, written before the First World War, are remarkable predictions of Hitler and Stalin, show trials, totalitarianism (whether Nazi or Communist), brainwashing, the Final Solution. Indeed, Kafka's beloved sister Ottla died in a concentration camp.

To hold back the most deeply felt truths, Kafka often engaged in masochistic fantasies. The prisoner in the penal colony is punished by the law he violated literally being imprinted in his flesh. Metaphor becomes metamorphosis when Gregor Samsa awakes one morning from "uneasy dreams" transformed into a massive insect. Gregor has become his own worst nightmare.

Kafka's dream stories seem to recreate thought before its expression in words. A human bug unable to flip over in bed, faceless judges condemning the damned at trial, murky castles looming overhead, metaphors represented in powerful visions difficult to understand, but simple to feel—and fear.

Franz was the eldest of three girls and three boys. His two brothers died in infancy. Kafka's father, Herman, supported the family with a dry goods business that flourished through the support of his wife Julie's wealthy family of Prague brewers.

Herman was a rough, physically imposing man. Julie largely ignored Franz when he was young, consumed with helping Herman in his business. Her family, although successful businesspeople, were descendants of rabbis and scholars, wise men and religious cranks. Franz Kafka was their natural progeny. Always accompanying his sensitive artistic nature were deep-seated feelings of inferiority and inadequacy. He felt that his slight physique and failure to achieve any meaningful commercial success could not live up to his father's imposing presence. When Franz grew up, his mother compensated for her earlier abandonment of him with smothering, overwhelming attention—too late for Franz. He did not have the strength to leave his parents until he was thirty-one or part from his "little mother Prague" until just before his death ten years later (only to return home to die).

He dutifully attended law school, never to practice law. Instead, Kafka was content to work as an administrator in a workmen's compensation firm. This menial job left his afternoons and evenings free for what he called his night work—writing. This dual existence, the bureaucrat-artist, produced enormous tensions within him, leading to suicidal thoughts and the darkest visions.

Leading Kafka away from death were wonderful friendships with talented young men and women, including Max Brod (who was to become his literary executor and most admired biographer), and a series of fiancées and liaisons. He kept a diary, wrote countless letters to his friends and lovers, reveled in performances by visiting Yiddish theater troupes, and studied Hebrew and Jewish history with insatiable curiosity. Three engagements were ended either by fright at his own perceived inability to share his life or by his father's disapproving glare. In 1917 tuberculosis began its relentless attack on his health, ending in death at forty-one years of age.

While on his deathbed, Kafka instructed Brod to destroy all his works, correspondence, and diaries. Few of Kafka's books had been published during his lifetime. He was unknown. He may likely have felt that it was better for the world that he remain so. But for Brod's unwillingness to destroy Kafka's writings, the modern world would not have been revealed through his special lens.

Hitler's rise to power in the 1930s slowed German literary attention to Kafka's masterpieces. After the war, largely through Brod's prodding, most of Kafka's books and letters were published, translated into several languages, and popularly read. The French existentialists Jean-Paul Sartre and Albert Camus discovered in Kafka a rich source of inspiration. Isaac Bashevis Singer, the great Yiddish writer and Nobel Prize winner, thought Kafka an immense influence of revelation and terror.

Franz Kafka's cold night world of isolation and enigma is both the recounting of modern history and his autobiography. In Kafka the cosmos is found in the most minute, the insect, a symbol of humanity laid bare to its most horrid self.

23

David Ben-Gurion

(1886–1973)

Born in Plonsk, Poland as David Green, he chose as his own the name of one of the last defenders of ancient Jerusalem against the Roman army. Ben-Gurion or "Son of the Lion Cub" was the man most responsible for the creation of the Jewish state of Israel in 1948 after almost two thousand years of dispersion. Ben-Gurion, or "B-G" as he was known to many, transformed Theodor Herzl's vision of a revived Jewish Zion into reality.

The world remembers him as the symbol of his people's will to fight to survive, to water the desert sand until it bloomed into a land of rich bounty, quoting biblical text to prove a point, and always talking with overwhelming authority. His plain-speaking wife, Paula, said that he should be called Ben-Gurion, not prime minister, because anyone could be prime minister, but only he could be Ben-Gurion.

The son of an unlicensed lawyer, at age ten David lost his mother during her eleventh childbirth. His schooling was primitive; he was largely self-taught, reading constantly and teaching himself over a half dozen languages. His interest in languages remained a lifelong obsession. Consumed during his later years in reading the Septuagint, the hellenic version of the Old Testament, and the lessons of Buddha, Ben-Gurion taught himself ancient Greek and Sanskrit.

His intellectual pursuits and admiration for his father's legal interests led to socialist and Zionist activities. When he was twenty, pogroms were launched against Jewish settlements with tsarist support. Repulsed by the carnage and the futility of Jewish life in Eastern Europe and inspired by Herzl's example, David emigrated to Palestine. In 1906 only sixty thousand Jews lived there, under the rule of the Turks. Frustrated also by the apathy of the Palestinian Jews to self-determination, the activist Ben-Gurion joined the Zionist movement in Palestine to make the Jewish Zion a reality.

Writing articles for the Zionist press under a nom de plume, "Ben-Gurion" urged (as early as 1907) the creation of an independent Jewish country. For the next forty-one years his constant goal was its creation. He journeyed to Turkey in the attempt to convince the rulers of the Ottoman Empire to cooperate in the institution of a loyal Jewish state. The Turks expelled him as a subversive. He fled to New York (where he met and married his Paula, a young nursing student from Brooklyn). Recognizing that England would control Palestine after the fall of the Turks in the First World War, he helped create two Jewish battalions to fight in the British army. There would be many other examples of his joining in with the powers that were to get what he wanted on *his* timetable.

Chaim Weizmann, the brilliant leader of the World Zionist Organization, had been the prime architect behind the Balfour Declaration of 1917 which called for the creation of the Jewish state. But the intellectual Weizmann did not possess the personal drive and charisma to mold a fractured Jewish populace into a cohesive force for change. Returning after the war to a Palestine controlled by the British, Ben-Gurion became Zionism's voice of the working people. He formed a labor party called Histadrut and as its secretary general established his party and himself as a powerful force in the union movement. Later, in the 1930s, he founded a political party called Mapai and became chairman of the Jewish Agency for Palestine.

Just before the outbreak of the Second World War and the almost complete annihilation of European Jewry by the Nazis, the British issued their official instrument of Palestinian policy. The infamous and shameful White Paper was an apologia to the Arabs, seeking their support in the coming conflict against Germany. Just as Hitler's demons began the systematic murder of over six million Jews, British policy sought to ensure a Jewish minority in Palestine by severely limiting Jewish immigration and land ownership.

Ben-Gurion urged opposition to Hitler and the White Paper concurrently. His movement also faced the challenge of civil war from the violent Jabotinsky movement led by the young, secretive Polish-born immigrant Menachem Begin. After the war Ben-Gurion sought to bring the survivors of the Holocaust to the Middle East. He pronounced that Eretz Yisrael, the Land of Israel, was the only refuge for the European Jew. Ben-Gurion transformed the illegal Jewish defense force, the Haganah, into what would become the Israeli Defense Forces, led by young generals named Dayan, Yadin, and Allon, and recruited Jewish American and European veterans of the Allied armies to man war surplus equipment purchased with donated funds.

When Begin's terrorist Irgun faction sought during a United Nations truce to deliver a secret cache of arms to Palestine aboard the ship *Altalena*, Ben-Gurion dispatched the Haganah in opposition. Jew battled Jew in what became for Ben-Gurion a test of wills, the imposition of his authority, and a demonstration to the British and the world of the Israeli rule of law.

When independence was declared on May 14, 1948, Ben-Gurion became the de facto premier and minister of defense of his beleaguered nation. Arab armies attacked Israel from all sides, seeking to eradicate the Jewish state. Supported by his able young officers and volunteers, Begin organized a rout of the inefficient Arab forces. For the first time since Judas Maccabeus had defeated the Syrians over more than two thousand years before, a Jewish army had defended its homeland.

Except for a brief retirement to his beloved kibbutz in the Negev in the early 1950s, Ben-Gurion would lead his country as prime minister through 1963. In those years he never failed to inspire, cajole, and stir controversy.

Ben-Gurion recognized that the borders of partitioned Israel could hold as many of the world's Jews as wished to come (always asserting however that a unified Jerusalem and control of the Golan Heights were essential). He flatly stated that a Jew was not a true Zionist unless settled in Israel. This stand caused great upset in America, alienating many of his former supporters. He also envisioned opening Israel's borders to millions of oppressed Soviet Jews who could start afresh in a democratic state where socialism was made to work. Judaism, to Ben-Gurion, was viewed not just as a religion but as a clarion call to nationalism.

Although the Soviet Union had been among the first countries to support Israeli independence at the United Nations, Ben-Gurion in 1951 took steps to align his country with the United States. He rejoiced in the shared values of the two nations. The U.S.-Israel partnership has had its troubles over the decades, yet remains an essential link in the brotherhood of democratic nations.

To Arab attacks on Israeli settlements, Ben-Gurion responded with swift retaliation, a practice that has been official Israeli policy ever since. When Egypt's president Nasser took control of the Suez Canal, Ben-Gurion ordered the Israeli army (with the aid of the French and British) to invade the Sinai peninsula. The Sinai crisis in 1956 was halted when President Eisenhower, wishing to assert American moral capital in light of the Soviet invasion of Hungary, threatened U.S. intervention. The war led to U.N. control of the Gaza strip and the opening of the Gulf of Aqaba to Israel allowing international navigation without Egyptian interference.

When the Mossad, Israel's CIA, was ordered by Ben-Gurion to kidnap the former Nazi officer Adolf Eichmann from his hiding place in Argentina for trial in Israel for war crimes, a great outcry of protest was heard throughout the world. When it became obvious that Eichmann was receiving a fair trial and when the enormity of his involvement in the Holocaust was made clear, the protests subsided. Ben-Gurion made it clear that Jews would never again be slaughtered without retribution.

His final years were spent on the kibbutz and at official gatherings, his large head framed in wild white hair, an icon of his country's birth and proud future.

24

Hillel

(ca. 70 B.C.E.–10 C.E.)

Love your fellow as yourself:
I am the LORD.
                    —Leviticus 19:18

A pagan asked the sage Hillel to explain Judaism while standing on one foot. If Hillel succeeded, the non-Jew would convert and become a true believer. Hillel replied, "What is hateful to you, do not do to your neighbor. This is the entire Torah. All the rest is commentary—now go and study it."

Mark relates that the teacher Joshua, known to his followers through the centuries as Jesus, preached around 29 C.E.: "And the second *is* like, namely *this,* Thou shalt love thy neighbor as thyself. There is none other commandment greater than these."

Some believe Hillel was Jesus' teacher.

Hillel the Elder, or the Babylonian, is regarded by many rabbis as the most perfect Jew, comparable in character to Confucius or Lincoln. Like them, he brought himself up out of overwhelming poverty. He spoke in proverbs. Speaking simply great truths, Hillel condensed centuries of Jewish learning in aphorisms which people could easily grasp. Many of his short sayings are remarkably similar to those of Jesus.

Little is known of Hillel's life. He is known more for his words and his presence as an influential teacher. Hillel is credited with the founding of a classical Judaism based less on temple ritual and more on biblical teachings and ethical precepts. His concentration on learning, the search to comprehend the essence of Jewish law, the creation of a portable religion (thought can be taken anywhere), enabled his people to remain together in the Diaspora to come, and for that great storehouse of Jewish law, the Talmud, to be written. His ethical yet loving embrace of *tikkun olam* (the improvement of the world through moral values) formed the basis of postbiblical Judaism and the beginnings of Christianity.

Hillel was zealous in his pursuit of knowledge. He left his home in Babylon to venture to study in Judea. It is related in a popular tale that one snowy Sabbath, he was too poor to pay a fee to enter the study house in Jerusalem. Not wanting to miss even one day of learning, he climbed to the roof and listened through a skylight. The teachers soon noticed that the study room was unusually dark. Looking up, they saw a snow-covered figure blocking the sun. Violating Sabbath restrictions against work, the students climbed the roof to rescue the frozen Hillel. The teachers and students then bathed, dried, and clothed him. Anyone so interested in learning, they remarked, must be taken care of, even to the extent of disobeying the law. A precedent was set.

Hillel would return to his home in Babylon for a time, only to come back to Jerusalem to assume the leadership of the Sanhedrin, the high court of ancient Judea, presided over by rabbis. Hillel found the members of the Sanhedrin of his day inadequately trained in Jewish law. The oral tradition had weakened under the Roman occupation and the vicious tyranny of King Herod.

Hillel appointed the severe, tough, arrogant, and legalistic Shammai as second in command of the Sanhedrin. For hundreds of years their followers would be known as the School of Hillel and the School of Shammai. They were the optimist and the pessimist, one content with just being, the other sure not being would have been much better. Hillel never got angry; Shammai always seemed mad. Hillel would compromise any point; Shammai never quit from a position taken. Although it is also said that God when asked preferred Hillel's life view, the visions of both formed the basis of Talmudic thought and debate, thus molding the mind of the Jewish people.

Both Hillel and Shammai were Pharisees, the precursors of modern Jewry. Many Christians view the Pharisees of Jesus' day as rigid and crippled by blind obedience to the law. Yet Jesus practiced Pharasaic Judaism and made it clear that he did not come to abolish the law. His admonition that many obey every dot and every stroke of Jewish law paralleled the teachings of Hillel and Shammai.

25

John Von Neumann

(1903–1957)

John Von Neumann, a Hungarian Jew, was perhaps the last example of what is now a vanishing breed, the mathematician comfortable in both pure and applied mathematics (as well as other branches of science and the arts). Of an extraordinary generation of Hungarian scientists, mathematicians, and artists including Leo Szilard, Fritz Reiner, Dennis Gabor, Eugene Ormandy, Edward Teller, George Szell, and Eugene Wigner, Von Neumann was perhaps the most brilliant and facile. He is credited with enriching, or even creating, whole areas of mathematical research, including logic and set theory, lie groups,

measure theory, rings of operators (now known as "Von Neumann algebras"), the theory of games (most particularly his
famous minimax theorem), and concepts of automata. While
serving as the inspiration for Abraham Wald's statistical theories
of the 1940s, game theory was also applied in the 1950s most
prominently in American economic, military, and political decision making. Von Neumann's most lasting influence, however,
lies in his development of new procedures of programing and the
development of mechanical devices which form the basis of
computing machines. After Charles Babbage, Von Neumann is
rightly dubbed the "father of the computer."

Von Neumann's father was a prosperous banker who purchased the royal "Von" from the Hungarian government. The
oldest of three boys, John, born Johann, at a very early age
displayed a remarkable talent for math. He was so proficient at
the subject that his grade school teachers brought in university
professors to tutor him. John showed an almost Mozartean ability
to synthesize widely disparate concepts with uncanny accuracy
and lightning speed. By the age of nineteen, he was teaching
advanced mathematics in Berlin (where he attended Albert
Einstein's lectures). John also took the time to visit in Göttingen
the great mathematician David Hilbert, whose personality and
work became perhaps Von Neumann's greatest inspiration.

After engineering studies in Zurich and teaching posts in
Berlin and Hamburg, at thirty Von Neumann joined the Institute
for Advanced Study in Princeton, New Jersey as its youngest
member. During the Second World War he worked in Los
Alamos on the secret construction of the atomic bomb. After the
war, he served on the Atomic Energy Commission. He died in
1957 from cancer.

Enormously influential and brilliant in their own right,
many of Von Neumann's illustrious contemporaries were as-
tounded by his ability to process with extraordinary rapidity
complex data into axiomatic language. Almost every branch of
mathematics and physics during the era was touched by his
original thought and wit.

Frustrated by the computers available during the bomb-
making years of the Manhattan Project at Los Alamos, Von
Neumann studied how the machines worked and then developed
new methods of computing. He specially designed codes that

triggered a wiring system to provide answers to a multitude of questions. This apparatus and the programing he invented in its service are the models upon which modern computer devices are based.

Unlike Szilard and Bohr, who sought to control the spread of nuclear weapons, Von Neumann, an ardent anti-Communist, supplied much of the intellectual justification for the American military's arms buildup during the Eisenhower administration. Although he opposed Senator Joseph McCarthy's attacks on J. Robert Oppenheimer and other scientists (which reminded him of Fascist persecution), Von Neumann in his last years vigorously assisted the defense establishment, adapting his theory of games and mathematical wizardry to more deadly schemes of warlike strategy.

Simon Bar Kokhba

(fl. 135 C.E.)

> I shall see him, but not now: I shall behold him, but
> not nigh: there shall come a Star out of Jacob, and a
> Scepter shall rise out to Israel, and shall smite the
> corners of Moab, and destroy all the children of Sheth.
> —Numbers 24:17

Simon Bar Kokhba, Simon "son of the Star," led the last Jewish
revolt against the Romans, an immeasurably bloody rebellion
which resulted in the final destruction of ancient Judean civiliza-

tion. Bar Kokhba is an enigma, still a person of great controversy. Opinions differ on whether he was a grand freedom fighter in the mold of Judas Maccabeus or an irresponsible tyrant as brutal to his own people as he was to their oppressors. The Roman historian Dio Cassius is the main source for our knowledge of the period. According to Dio, 580,000 Jews perished in the war. With the Great Revolt of 70 C.E., the Bar Kokhba rebellion ranks as the most catastrophic event in Jewish history before the seventeenth-century Chmielnicki massacres and the Holocaust.

After the fall of Jerusalem in 70 C.E. to Titus, son of the emperor Vespasian, the land of Judea was like an armed camp. The Romans had suffered heavy losses during the revolt. Whole legions had been wiped out by the rebels. The emperors who succeeded Vespasian did not want another uncontrollable conflict with the Jews. Martial law and persecution were preferred to rein in the populace under firm Roman control. During this period the officially approved writings of the important Roman historian Tacitus provided the beginnings of state-supported anti-Semitism.

Although initially a sympathizer with Jewish religious values, the Emperor Hadrian in 128–32 C.E., while stationed in the east, initiated policies aimed at unifying the disparate cultures of the empire. His most controversial idea was to build a Roman temple with a statue of Jupiter on the ruins of the destroyed Second Temple in Jerusalem. While Hadrian was still in the east with his two legions, the Jews were afraid to strike back, but began to rearm in secret under the single leadership of the man who would become known as Bar Kokhba. However, it is unclear whether the Romans were seeking to eradicate Judaism totally. Many Jews in the Galilee did not support the revolt, and after the war was over were allowed to practice and develop their religion.

The particular force of the Bar Kokhba rebellion came not only from its charismatic leader but from the support provided by the most prominent rabbi of the period, Akiba (ca. 60–135). Rabbi Akiba was perhaps the greatest scholar in the history of the Jewish religion. Unlike many of the other important scholars in Jewish history, Akiba grew up in poverty. It was said that he was the son or grandson of converts. He began as a shepherd and did not receive an education until the age of forty. By the time of the revolt in 132 C.E., he was the leading Torah scholar in Judea, with dozens of followers.

When Hadrian returned to Rome, Bar Kokhba's army struck at once. He seized Jerusalem, forcing the Roman legion encamped in the capital to retreat to Caesarea. It is said that Akiba joined in the rebellion and proclaimed Bar Kokhba the Messiah. Plans were made to rebuild the Temple. Sacrifices were reinstituted there in the ancient tradition. Coins were struck (they can still be seen today), and a new calendar dedicated. Bar Kokhba ruled by edict (many of his original edicts were found centuries later in the desert near Qumran). Out of Egypt a Roman legion advanced into the center of Judea. Bar Kokhba's men eliminated the Roman forces to a man.

The emperor pulled twelve legions from as far away as Britain to crush the revolt. However, no forces were rushed into the center of the country. In a brutal war of attrition each fortification was taken separately. Conventional strategies were adapted to guerilla warfare. The Romans were forced to hunt each rebel down. At their last stronghold in Betar, Bar Kokhba's army was defeated, and he was slain. Rabbi Akiba was captured, tortured to death, his skin ripped from his body by iron combs. Tradition relates that he died smiling in the realization that he was loving God with all his might. The religious center of Yavneh was destroyed, most of its students dead in the fight. In all, Dio relates, fifty forts and 985 towns or settlements were laid waste. The entire land of Judea was scorched clean.

For 1,800 years the Jews would have no home of their own. For those eighteen centuries, they would be a minority wherever they went, with no army to protect them, and only their thought and religious culture to guide the way.

The destruction of ancient Judea would also spur the early Jewish Christians to action. Before the revolt, they had coexisted quietly with other Jews as just another sect. Many Jewish Christians however saw the failure of the Bar Kokhba rebellion as a sign of the failure of orthodox Judaism and a confirmation of the righteousness of their own beliefs. Thereafter, they became more aggressive in their proselytizing.

The Galilean Jews were allowed to continue practicing their faith—though not without some persecution. Less than a century after the fall of Betar, the Mishnah, the systematic codification of the oral law, was composed in the Galilee under the guidance of Rabbi Judah the Prince. Over the next four hundred years scholars would comment on the Mishnah. Their commentaries became known as the Talmud, which would serve after the Bar Kokhba revolt as the rule of law for a people dispersed into the centuries.

27

Marcel Proust

(1871–1922)

Marcel Proust, the son of a Jewish mother and Catholic father, was, with James Joyce and Franz Kafka, one of the three most influential novelists during the first half of the twentieth century. His masterwork, *A la recherche du temps perdu (Remembrance of Things Past),* is a set of seven novels without conventional plot or traditional structure. Proust was a peculiar, reclusive man who spent his early years dawdling in fashionable drawing rooms in an almost ritual observance of upper-class gossip and pitter-patter. For the final thirteen years of his life, sequestered in a cork-lined room, he wrote and continually revised in strange, narrow notebooks an immense seven-part opus, incorporating his experiences of high society into a fictional universe of extraordinary power and beauty.

Although he wrote other novels before *Remembrance,* Proust is primarily remembered for the unique slant of his masterpiece. It is related to the reader by a Narrator, not by an all-powerful and all-seeing author. The events and characters of the novels are viewed through the sight and emotions of a fictional person, who is not necessarily Proust, the author. The Narrator appears to be motivated to tell what he remembers for reasons of his own, his judgment entirely his, seemingly divorced from the usually omnipresent opinions of a writer creating a book.

Before Proust, the great novels of Balzac, Dickens, Tolstoy, Flaubert, Dostoyevsky, and Zola were narrated by the author as chronicler (even when the story was told by a character such as Pip in *Great Expectations*). One always feels the presence of the creator, the author, guiding and observing the story. Not so in Proust. Although derived from his experiences in upper-crust salons, *Remembrance* is a work of fiction, not autobiography, and fiction, Proust seems to proclaim, demands, a radically new perspective.

He also changed how novels can be structured. Prior to *Remembrance,* novels had clear plots, usually culminating in the protagonist's death. Proust wrote novels without plots, without climaxes, without abrupt melodramatic shifts or coincidental happenings. In sometimes impossible to follow, seemingly endless sentences, reality is presented the way reality is. Events inexorably follow each other. People and places flow past. Time passes and is lost.

The story of his life is simply told. His mother, Jeanne Weil, was the daughter of a wealthy stockbroker. Marcel's father, Adrien, was born into modest circumstances, the son of Catholic shopkeepers, but rose to become a respected physician and expert in municipal hygiene. Adrien Proust is largely responsible for creating modern sanitation methods that helped to control in European cities the spread of cholera and infectious diseases. Dr. Proust however could not prevent his son's developing a severe asthma.

Despite attempts at a normal life (Marcel volunteered for cadet duty and attended law and political science classes), the future novelist preferred to experience the joys of *la belle époque*, the so-called banquet years during the gay 1890s. Supported by his mother's inheritance and his father's social standing, Marcel lounged away his early manhood in the private rooms of great hostesses (usually royalty). He established lasting friendships with creative artists such as composer Reynaldo Hahn, poet Anna de Noailles, author Anatole France, and the sarcastic writer Baron de Montesquieu. All of these friends (and some of his countesses) were immortalized as characters in *Remembrance*. His parents vehemently objected to Marcel's rich, idle life, citing his brother Robert's acceptable career as a doctor (it was Robert Proust who cared for Marcel in his final difficult years and made sure his works were published posthumously).

By his early thirties he could only show for his life's work countless hours wasted in salons and two unsatisfactory, derivative, and incomplete novels. The relatively premature deaths of his parents apparently galvanized Proust out of inaction into a life with purpose. Realizing his life might also not last long, Proust cloistered himself in his apartment and began writing his account of what he knew best—fashionable society around the turn of the century. To aid his concentration and ensure the perfect quiet he required, Proust had the walls of his bedroom work room soundproofed with cork. After writing uninterrupted for thirteen years, he died in 1922 while editing the seventh book of *Remembrance*.

Proust tended to writing much as a vintner cultivates vines. In his literary horticulture, conventional plot and character development are irrigated by the great streams of life. How and why men and women love, remember over time, remain happy, or lose themselves in jealousy or hate, are intertwined in flowery, almost verdant prose. The example of the madeleine dipped in mint tea unleashing the odors of the narrator's youth is the most famous image in Proust's luxuriant, symbolic garden.

He overthrew nineteenth-century conceptions of reality and time. Earlier writers had conceived of time by observing the progress of recognizable events. In Proust, "real" time was replaced by an examination of the reality playing out within his characters. Proust carefully dissected the development of people's inner selves over time, not simply their outward appearances revealing themselves in melodrama.

With magnificent sweep, in a tidal movement of impressions and gestures, *Remembrance* ends as the Narrator decides to write a novel telling everything he can remember. The end is as it was at the beginning. The circle closes in on itself.

28 *Mayer Rothschild*

(1744–1812)

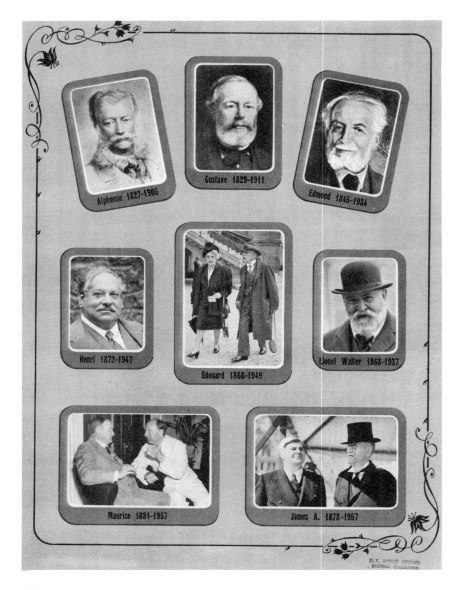

On Judengasse (Jew Street) in the ghetto of the German city Frankfurt am Main, colorful house signs predated numbered addresses, serving as pictorial markers of business and family names. "Rothschild" or "red shield" was derived from such a sign.

Although there is no known portrait of him, Mayer Amschel Rothschild, as few men in history, influenced the progress of world history over a century after his death. With the development of his family as a cohesive unit of economic and political might, he shaped the future not only of the Rothschilds but of their many countrymen.

Mayer placed his five sons, Amschel, Solomon, Nathan, Kalmann (later Carl), and Jacob (later James), just out of their teens, in five European capitals, establishing the first international banking and clearinghouse system—essentially the first privately owned multinational company. Although the sons lacked their father's ghetto-trained diplomatic abilities and subservient manner, they possessed instead raw cunning, technical expertise, and a ferocious drive for hard work. Their creation of banking houses in the German confederation, Austrian Empire, Great Britain, Italy, and France led to enormous political influence and a concerted desire by the family to keep Europe at peace. War hindered economic development and upset their carefully planned spheres of control. Although their political power would wane after the First World War as more banking houses rose to prominence and competition set in, the Rothschilds helped shape the political fortunes of many of the great figures of the age, including, but certainly not limited to, Napoleon, the Duke of Wellington, Talleyrand, Metternich, Queen Victoria, Disraeli, and Bismarck (and the futures of their countries).

Mayer's ancestors had been ordinary peddlers for generations in the Frankfurt town ghetto. Although Jews could journey outside the ghetto walls during the day, they were required to wear traditional hats and garb identifying their religion. A Jew wandering outside would invariably subject himself to anti-Semitic toughs. A religious slur was preferred to the beating and robbing a Jew could not safely defend himself against and from which no one would grant any protection.

With his parents' support, Mayer studied to become a rabbi

in the ancient city of Nuremberg. These studies were cut short, however, by their premature deaths. With the help of relatives, Mayer then secured a clerk's position at the banking house of Oppenheimer in Hanover. Mayer prospered and seemed set on a successful career, but was unsatisfied and quit to seek his fortune back in the ghetto where he was born. Returning to Frankfurt, he was stopped at the river crossing and required to pay the Jew toll. Behind the ghetto gates manacled with heavy chains every night by German soldiers, Mayer planned his future.

He started out as a dealer in old coins and heirlooms. His buyers turned out to be the highest royalty (the only ones interested in so esoteric a hobby). Noticing that the rival German kingdoms had different currencies and no readily available trading method, Mayer established a *Wechselstube* or simple bank in which these monies could be traded at varying rates of exchange. Mayer used the profits from this exchange business to develop his numismatic line, investing in coins of greater value and antiquity and developing a richer clientele.

In 1770 he married seventeen-year-old Gutele Schnapper. She would give birth to five sons and five daughters and live to the age of ninety-six, rarely leaving her ghetto house. In her old age Gutele was a revered figure visited by nobility and people of influence.

Mayer, supported by a growing family, began to sell coins to the richest noble in Europe, Prince William of Hesse. Students of the American Revolution may remember the Hessian soldiers who fought with the British in their losing attempt at subjugating the colonies. These Hessian mercenaries were subjects of Prince William and were sold, like chattel, to the British at immense profits. Prince William and his treasurer (who became a silent partner in the Rothschild businesses) increasingly relied on the respectful and talented Mayer. When William succeeded in 1785 to his father's throne, Mayer had a reliable sinecure at William's court at Kassel to develop his international contacts.

Over the next two decades, Mayer would use his connections at William's court, his noble clients, low prices on his coins (in return for friendship and IOU's), and his young sons, to build the financial foundation and political network of the Rothschild family. An example of Mayer's resourcefulness occurred at the time of Prince William's lending of Hessian mercenaries to the

British. Mayer observed that William received British bank drafts in return for the soldiers. At the same time Mayer was engaged in paying for cotton cloth from the textile manufacturers in Manchester. Why not somehow combine both enterprises and make bigger profits? Mayer arranged for the Manchester manufacturers to be paid directly with William's British bank drafts—and for the discount fees saved to be pocketed by both William and himself. The revolt in the American colonies would be the first of many wars during which the Rothschilds would earn enormous sums.

Mayer inserted Solomon at William's court as the monarch's newest financial adviser. Amschel began to serve as William's mortgage broker, arranging enormous loans throughout the continent with royal borrowers. Nathan went to Manchester to perfect the textile trade—and managed somehow during the French Revolution to send cheap cloth to Mayer's store in Frankfurt just as prices were sent soaring by rebellious unrest.

An international network of family was formed that would survive revolutions, Napoleonic wars, counterrevolutions, and the industrial age. Even when Napoleon swept away William, sending him into exile, Mayer continued to guide the finances of his prince. Mayer's sons were spread throughout Europe and were always a step ahead of Napoleon's secret agents, collecting interest on loans, selling contraband and food in markets stripped bare by the ravages of European war. The Rothschilds communicated through a highly developed system of couriers, letters, and even carrier pigeons, using a bizarre lingo of German, Yiddish, and Hebrew sprinkled with amusing pseudonyms.

The Rothschild sons developed quickly from cotton traders and smugglers into international bankers. From 1810 on they would sell money only. They would use many of the techniques and networks developed by their father in their conquest of Europe's financial markets. Nathan, for example, knew of Napoleon's defeat at Waterloo before anyone else at the London Exchange and used the information to sell English bonds high and then repurchase very low (just as the news arrived of the great victory and prices soared!).

By Mayer's death in 1812 his sons were firmly in place in their respective European capitals. They would help finance the restoration of the continent after the wars, the development of modern governments during the rapidly developing industrial era, and the building of railroads across Europe. Nathan's son Lionel after many attempts would become the first unassimilated Jew elected to Parliament, his way paved by Benjamin Disraeli and others. Lionel would not join the Parliament unless he could take his oath of office wearing a traditional Jewish hat and swearing over the Old Testament. In 1858, with his head covered in accordance with Jewish practice, Lionel was sworn in as a member of Parliament.

Despite all their accomplishments, since the late 1800s anti-Semitic perceptions of Jewish financial power and prowess centered on the Rothschilds. The Rothschilds have been viewed by many bigots as the archetype of an "international Jewish bankers' conspiracy."

Yet, out of Jew Street, in anti-Semitic Frankfurt, arose a family that would engage the greatest figures of modern European history, change the course of human events—and survive to this day.

29

Solomon

(ca. 990–ca. 933 B.C.E.)

Solomon "in all his glory" ruled for over forty years the greatest and most powerful kingdom in the history of Israel. A master at achieving peace through artful negotiation, Solomon often married to forge alliances and to avoid war. Aided by heavy taxation and vigorous trade policies, the royal treasury swelled under his rule. His wise guidance was sought by other leaders who respected his proverbs and feared his chariot army. Not innately religious and pious like his father, David, Solomon was a man of the world consumed with temporal power and earthly pleasures.

On the backs of his people, he built a great Temple to house the Ark of the Covenant, at the same time constructing shrines to display the idols of his foreign queens. He is credited with inspiring the composition of the biblical *Song of Songs*, the *Proverbs*, and *Ecclesiastes*, expressions of a literary renaissance sheltered by his wealthy and powerful regime.

Of all the major figures of Jewish religious history, Solomon (in the traditional sense) was the least God-filled. His methods of statecraft and poetic impulse were closer to Middle Eastern or Oriental values than Hebraic. Not able or willing to follow his father's more obedient example, Solomon used his seemingly infinite wisdom to rule absolutely. Throughout the Middle Ages, European nobility pointed to Solomon as an exemplar of the purest king, absolute monarchy at its peak, intentionally forgetting the negative results of his governance.

He was the most polygamous Jew in history. The royal harem was said to number in the thousands. Marriage to foreign princesses bought peace. Through nuptials with Pharaoh's daughter, a close alliance was forged with Egypt. His affair with the Queen of Sheba benefited the Hebrew spice trade.

Whether or not Solomon wrote the *Song of Songs* is unclear, yet its author surely knew a great deal about erotic love. The *Song of Songs* served as the model for medieval French and Spanish love poetry, a biblical source poets could safely emulate, free from official repression (although there were Christian attempts to suppress it).

Ecclesiastes is the words of an old man, experienced and exhausted with the trials of life. It is the first literary statement of world weariness, thousands of years before the *Weltschmerz* of German Romantic poetry. Ironically, *Ecclesiastes* would later find perhaps its most perfect expression in the monologue "Wahn! Wahn!" of Hans Sachs in *Die Meistersinger*, the folk opera by the anti-Semitic composer Richard Wagner. A very different sort, contemporary minstrel Pete Seeger, found inspiration in *Ecclesiastes* for his moving antiwar song, "For every season, turn, turn, turn..."

Although Solomon ruled in peace for so many years, his legacy was one of division and chaos. Immediately after his death, his son so antagonized the tribes in the north that they split away,

Solomon and the Queen of Sheba from a painting
by the Swiss artist, Konrad Witz.

forming the separate kingdom of Israel centered in Samaria. This schism would last for almost four hundred years.

Jews and Christians today remember the wise Solomon, his gift of judgment most colorfully displayed in the famous incident of the two prostitutes and a baby. A mother distraught at the death of her baby steals a neighbor's infant. Both mothers ask the king for custody of the living child. When Solomon threatens to split the live baby with a sword and give one half to each woman, the real mother rushes forward, pleading with her sovereign to spare the child. The other whore insists that the baby is neither of theirs, but should be cut in two. Solomon awards the child to its real mother. This Judeo-Christian image of Solomon the judge exercising divine wisdom over two anguished women has had a lasting influence on the development of civilization and its jurisprudence.

30

Heinrich Heine

(1797–1856)

Born Chaim, in his early adulthood called Harry, finally assimilated as Heinrich, he was the greatest lyrical poet of the Romantic period and the first literary modernist in the German language. To German readers, Heinrich Heine is acclaimed as their most beloved poetic voice, a close, intimate friend, never distant like the Olympian Goethe, almost as if Keats, Byron, and Shelley had been rolled into one.

120

Heine is known to English-speaking audiences today mostly through the musical settings of his poems by the great composers such as Schubert, Mendelssohn, Schumann (especially), Liszt, and even Wagner. A kind of literary Chopin, Heine, the German poet exiled to France, influenced generations of writers and composers. Wagner's operas *The Flying Dutchman* and *Tannhäuser,* as well as the novels, poetry, and prose of Matthew Arnold, George Eliot, Longfellow, Tennyson, Shaw, and Nietzsche, were directly inspired by Heine's masterpieces.

Heine's life is also tragicaly representative of the problem of the Jewish artist creating in a largely Christian society. Like many of the German Jews of his time, Heine was influenced by the example of Moses Mendelssohn and the German Enlightenment. Napoleon's conquest of Europe led to the emancipation of Jews out of the feudal restrictions of ghetto life. After more than a thousand years of degradation, Jews had their first opportunity to improve their well-being in the open. When Heine changed his first name (his grandfather's name was Chaim Bückeburg; Chaim was made Heymann, Heinemann, and then finally Heine), it was more than just a recognition of a German equivalent. The young Heine thought of Judaism as a "calamity." He viewed its ritual as an unenlightened sickness. Heine believed that conversion to Protestantism would serve as his "admission ticket" to the greater world (later in the century, the Bohemian Jewish composer and conductor Gustav Mahler converted to Catholicism to win a post as head of the Court Opera in Vienna). Rather, conversion brought Heine, in his own words, "misfortune."

Despite his conversion, Heine remained for the rest of his days obsessed with his Jewishness. He was bitterly sarcastic of those German Jews who had become holier than their most Christian thou. Heine made vicious fun not only of bearded talmudists but also of the newly Reform worshipers, whose services in the vernacular required the flavoring of organ music to be socially acceptable. Yet, in his final years, when a venereal spinal disease confined him to what he sarcastically called a "mattress grave," Heine dubbed himself a "mortaly ill Jew" and wrote the most Judaic poetry. His Jewish self-hatred was emblematic of many other Jewish artists and thinkers of the period, including, most prominently, his acquaintance Karl Marx.

Heine's poetic works include dream pictures, songs, romances, sonnets, lyrical intermezzos, paeans to the North Sea, romantic histories, lamentations, epics, and Hebrew melodies (inspired by the example of the medieval Jewish poet Halevy). He is credited with creating a new literary form, the *feuilleton* or short essay, which he regularly contributed to French and German newspapers and reviews. While his early poems represent a culmination of German romanticism (and he effectively supplanted Byron in the 1820s as the public's favorite Romantic), his last works predict the experiments later in the century of Verlaine and the Symbolists (many of whom acknowledged his influence).

Although in many ways a conservative, Heine became a symbol of freedom. Supported most of his life by his rich uncle Solomon Heine, a banker and philanthropist (and later, somewhat notoriously, by the reactionary French government), Heine was something of a professional schnorrer, living most of the time far beyond each handout. Unable to secure a teaching post in Germany (despite his conversion), his publications suspended by a repressive local government, he fled his homeland in 1831 for Paris and the liberal atmosphere of the "citizen king" Louis Philippe. Dubbed the "German Apollo," Heine became a staple of an incredibly rich Parisian culture of Hugo, Sand, Delacroix, Balzac, Berlioz, and Meyerbeer. For a time he allied himself with a group of German expatriates nicknamed *"Jungdeutschland"* ("Young Germany"). Later, Heine also found in the quasi-socialist teachings of Saint-Simon a welcome respite from the petty bourgeois. The French were the first to recognize Heine's special genius. German adulation only followed France's infatuation. The public perception of Heine was that he was a radical, his life perpetually viewed as a symbol of liberation.

In brief quatrains Heine was capable of instantly conjuring his own uniquely poetic worlds. He has been compared to Chopin for a parallel ability to evoke in just a few sounds any desired lyrical imagery. For all their economy of expression, Heine's poems elicit unbounded expression.

Many of his poetic works are so widely known in Germany and Austria that they have become a part of the vernacular. Even the Nazis could not deny his importance to German culture. Heine's popular poem *Lorelei* was included in Nazi poetry collections, identified as a "folk song." Yet, Fascism had much to fear from Heine's deeply emotional, personal, and Hebraic legacy.

Hitler even ordered Heine's grave in Montmartre destroyed.

Initially attracted to Napoleon's revolution, Heine, like Beethoven, saw the tyranny behind the "liberator." Although romantic in his choice of pastoral themes, Heine was a brutal realist. Not content to sigh, like so many of his contemporaries, with nostalgia for a greater pan-German past, Heine, "citizen of the world," warned the French to remain vigilant against a future Teutonic threat. No less worried by the violent dreams of Karl Marx, Heine foresaw the rise of a communism more interested in brutal control than in helping people. Shocked by the Damascus blood libel of 1841, he retreated in his last years to a personalized Judaism. Only when the Christians were fully liberated by their Messiah, he argued, that is, stayed true to his message of peace, would all humanity, and not only the Jews, forever end its suffering.

31

Selman Waksman

(1888–1973)

Winner of the 1952 Nobel Prize in physiology and medicine, Selman Abraham Waksman is generally credited with the development of antibiotics as the most effective means (along with penicillin and sulfur drugs) of eliminating bacterial infections (and the first efficient method of curing tuberculosis). Waksman's lifelong obsession with the study of microorganisms led to the isolation of the "mycin" drugs (streptomycin, actinomycin, and neomycin), antibiotics that have been clinically applied with great success.

124

Waksman's remarkable discovery of these antibiotics (and several others) was an outgrowth of his studies of soil organisms. He identified minute organisms active in the earth which produced soluble substances containing antimicrobial properties. Indeed, before he became widely known for his work on antibiotics, Waksman had achieved an international scientific reputation for his work as a soil microbiologist.

Often people with major influence on the world can trace the reasons for their work to experiences in their youth. Waksman spent his early years near Kiev in a small Jewish town or shtetl. Under the watchful eye of the aristocracy, the rich black soil of the Ukrainian steppe yielded bountiful harvests of grains. Yet the Jews of this area in Poland and Russia, referred to as the Pale of Settlement, lived a simple but difficult and poor existence. Threatened by pogroms and sickness, Jewish culture turned inward into Bible and Talmud studies. At a time when antitoxins were readily available in more developed areas, Waksman's little sister died of diphtheria, an unnecessary death not to be forgotten.

Schooled in traditional Jewish education, Waksman as a young man showed his dedication to public causes. In his early teens he organized with friends a school for poor children, cared for the ill, and formed a youth group to defend his little town against threats of persecution.

Like so many of his generation, Waksman sought opportunity in America, settling at age twenty-two in New Jersey. His undergraduate and graduate studies at Rutgers University exposed him to agricultural and bacteriological disciplines. His first paper at twenty-seven was on soil bacteria and fungi. After a short stay in California, Waksman with his young wife put down roots in New Brunswick, near Rutgers, where in the 1920s and 1930s he became a full professor and examined with associates and students the world of microorganisms in the soil. During this period he also began consultations with industry, aiding in the production of nutritional substances and enzymes derived from bacteria and fungi. During the summers, Waksman worked at a laboratory involved in the study of marine microbiology he founded at Woods Hole on Cape Cod.

Faced with the oncoming surge of the Second World War and armed with his immense knowledge of many kinds of soil microbes, especially the actinomycetes, Waksman attempted with his colleagues in 1939 to isolate products that would destroy bacteria and thus control infection. With meager resources, Waksman developed during the 1940s simple techniques which served to identify many antibiotics. Later, with the support of the pharmaceutical giant Merck and Company and the collaboration of the Mayo Clinic, Waksman's laboratory established the efficacy of these wonder products. Waksman was touched in particular by their application to childhood disease, his memory of his sister always with him.

Some scientists who make great discoveries do not live to see the benefits of their research. Waksman fortunately enjoyed the accolades of the political and religious leaders of his time, culminating in the award of the Nobel Prize in 1952. The Merck royalties from the sale of antibiotics led to the development of the Waksman Institute of Microbiology, a world center of research in microbiology.

His influence has been worldwide. Waksman research institutes operate in Asia and Europe. Antibiotics have saved countless millions of lives. To organize international efforts to bring these crucial substances into remote regions and poor cultures continues to be a world priority. Waksman carefully noted the helpful application of microorganisms in producing foodstuffs such as cheese, wine, and vinegar; but, most important, in the chemical warfare of antibiotics he made real his apocryphal statement that "out of the earth shall come thy salvation."

32

Giacomo Meyerbeer

(1791–1864)

Born Jakob Liebmann Beer near Berlin into a family of wealthy bankers and traders, Giacomo Meyerbeer is largely credited with creating grand opera. His influence, first felt strongly in the operas of Verdi, Wagner, and Bizet, reached into the twentieth century. The lavish productions of Florenz Ziegfeld and Andrew Lloyd Webber owe their sense of opulence and splendor to Meyerbeer. Meyerbeer's musical style was the antithesis of that of his younger colleague the gentle Mendelssohn, choosing rather than reflection, grandiose gestures, spectacular effects, overripe melodrama, unending sentimentality, and great length. No composer until Richard Strauss was as popular and made as much money.

Exposed (like Mendelssohn) at an early age to a rich cultural milieu, Meyerbeer studied piano with the great Muzio Clementi and composition and theory with Carl Friedrich Zelter (teacher also to Mendelssohn) and with the famed theoretician Abbé Vogler in Darmstadt. Meyerbeer's fellow student in Darmstadt was Carl Maria von Weber, composer of *Der Freischütz,* later recognized as the first great German Romantic opera. Vogler secured a position for Meyerbeer as a court composer. He also began to be known in his mid-twenties as a virtuoso pianist.

Antonio Salieri, the famed rival (and alleged assassin) of Mozart, encouraged Meyerbeer to study Italian melody. He traveled to Italy, which became his home until 1825 when he was thirty-four. Meyerbeer wrote operas in Italian that were marvelously successful, rivaling even the great Rossini. Yet it was not until his move to Paris and the production of *Robert le Diable* and *Les Huguenots* that Meyerbeer's international fame and lasting influence was secured. These works (and the massive *Le Prophète* and *L'Africaine* which followed) established the style commonly known as grand opera, employing enormous spectacle and heroic imagery.

Grand opera was as much Meyerbeer's invention as that of his extraordinary librettist, Eugène Scribe. It was a form which appealed to the vulgar tastes of a new ruling class of bourgeoisie rising out of the trades and industries of developing Europe. Great operas before Meyerbeer are not numerous. The Renaissance masterpieces of Monteverdi were followed by the baroque dramas of Handel, then the classical theater of Mozart and Beethoven and the wonderfully witty works of Rossini. Meyerbeer's invention of grand opera transformed the way composers viewed the stage. The ten great operas of Wagner and the over twenty important operas of Verdi were directly influenced by Meyerbeer in subject matter as well as form. Meyerbeer experimented with orchestral color, and each of his compositions was serviced by an increasingly larger orchestra. The listener is often hard-pressed to identify the composer he is listening to when first exposed to a Meyerbeer opera—is it early Wagner or early Verdi?

Meyerbeer's borrowing of French, German, and Italian musical models is reflected in his name. Jakob became Giacomo, Beer was merged with his maternal grandfather's last name, Meyer, and the Italian first name was combined with a new German last name, both worn by a composer who wrote his operas mostly in French.

Meyerbeer the internationalist also incorporated historical elements from many countries into his works. His choice of subject matter would influence the historically correct works of Verdi (*Joan of Arc* and *Aida*) and Wagner (*Rienzi* and *Die Meistersinger*). Meyerbeer was also the inventor of the modern-day press conference, bringing groups of journalist into his splendid home for extended interviews.

Although he was not a prolific composer, Meyerbeer's operas were the most popular of his day, eclipsing Rossini and the other bel canto composers, particularly in France and Germany. Yet his work does not, after all, contain much great music; rather it is a pastiche of French, German, and Italian styles patched together in a bright, flashy quilt. After their very strong initial commercial success, and amazing influence on younger composers, Meyerbeer's operas slipped away, forgotten by the public (except for infrequent revival).

His influence also had an unintended but historically tragic effect. The young Richard Wagner sought Meyerbeer's help. Meyerbeer aided the younger composer with money and letters of recommendations which helped Wagner secure important positions and early productions of his Meyerbeer-influenced operas. Then when Wagner criticized Meyerbeer to mutual acquaintances and in the press, the older man cut off all support. Wagner followed with a lengthy diatribe called *Judaism in Music*, which attacked what he termed the pernicious and degrading effect of Jews on German music. Wagner's pamphlet, which espoused racial theories masked by hollow reasoning, would have enormous influence on the fascist anti-Semites who followed and served as one model for Adolf Hitler's *Mein Kampf*.

33

Isaac Luria

(1534–1572)

$\mathbf{W}$e owe much of what we know of the sixteenth-century kabbalist Isaac ben Solomon Luria to the writings of Gershom (Gerhard) Scholem, childhood friend of the philosopher Walter Benjamin and later professor of Jewish mysticism at the Hebrew University in Jerusalem. In a series of books and lectures revealing the mysteries of the kabbalah, Scholem examined the remarkable lives and works of Jewish mystics and magicians, heretics and saints. Of all the kabbalists, Scholem rated Luria the most influential in Jewish history. For Scholem, Lurianic kabbalah was the last great rabbinical movement to affect Jews everywhere.

130

Luria was known to his followers by the acronym Ha-Ari ("sacred lion") from the initials in Hebrew for "the divine Rabbi Isaac." Out of a European, rather than Middle Eastern or Spanish, background, he was known to his followers in the Galilee as Rabbi Isaac Ashkenazi.

Unlike many great figures in Jewish religious history, Luria left few written works of importance. Similar in curious ways to Jesus of Nazareth, Luria is remembered largely from the remembrances of his disciples. Like Jesus, Luria was a visionary, professing to confer with the souls of dead holy men, pointing out their forgotten graves to his students during their walks through and about the city of Safed.

Very little is known about his early life. His father emigrated to Jerusalem from Poland or Germany, married into a Sephardic family, and died when Isaac was young. Isaac was raised by his widowed mother in Cairo at the home of her brother, a farmer. In Egypt, Luria studied Jewish law with prominent masters, became highly proficient in its intricacies, and sold pepper and grain.

Sometime in his twenties he retreated from trade and his young wife (his uncle's daughter) to an island on the Nile for seven years of seclusion and study. Luria pored over the sacred book of the kabbalah, the Zohar, as well as the mystical writings of his contemporaries, including the highly influential Moses Cordovero. During this period Luria wrote his only important work, a commentary on a section of the Zohar. Little of the work, Scholem related, reveals the mystical universe of Luria's maturity.

After a short period of study with Cordovero, Luria attracted a group of disciples to his new home in Safed. In Luria's time, the Galilee was once more a center of revelation. Luria preached and his followers recorded what he preached. Hayyim Vital became his most famous student, preserving for future generations the treasures of Luria's mind in a book called *The Tree of Life*. Lurianic thought could only be understood by passing through "gates" of knowledge.

Luria's mysticism was based on a principle he called "Tsimtsum" ("withdrawal"). For Luria, our universe came into being when God shrank Himself—the "big bang" theory explained centuries before twentieth-century scientists in kabbalistic terms.

When God created the cosmos, divine light shone about,

caught by God for his special purposes in the creation of orbs, things, and beings in magical bowls or vessels. When the vessels were broken, the turmoil of life was unleashed.

Scholem noted that Luria's mystical philosophy was "permeated with messianic tension." Unlike Cordovero, who viewed life as riddled with confusion, Luria taught that we live in a "world of restitution" or "Tikkun." Only by restoring the inward and outward worlds of our universe through prayer and moral behavior (making our existence ideal and perfect) will we be redeemed, made ready for the inevitable coming of the Messiah. Every Jew's redemption is necessary for the redemption of all.

When Luria died at age thirty-eight in an epidemic, his followers, most notably Vital, spread his contemplations in what Scholem dubbed "saint's biographies." Lurianic kabbalah invigorated Sephardic worship in particular, but also lent visionary fervor to the messianic claims of the false messiahs Sabbatai Zevi and Jacob Frank. Luria's most lasting influence however has been the resonant philosophical framework he gave Judaism. For underneath all the talmudic reasoning, legalisms, and rituals lie visions of light eternally seeking their return to the beginning of creation.

34

Gregory Pincus

(1903–1967)

His name is not widely known. Yet his influence on our reproductive lives is immeasurable. In Boston in the early 1950s Gregory Goodwin Pincus and his associates developed the birth-control pill.

The pill is a pharmaceutical marvel. It contains a chemical agent that is almost 100 percent effective. The pill has changed family planning worldwide. Governments concerned with too rapid population growth have legislated its use. Gregory Pincus is largely credited with its development.

Pincus devoted his life to the study of mammalian reproduction. From his early seminal work *The Eggs of Mammals* to the more than 350 papers he wrote with colleagues on hormones, aging, metabolism, and rodent genetics and infertility, Pincus was at the center of twentieth-century reproductive research.

Born in New Jersey, Pincus studied at Ivy League colleges followed by advance research with well-known specialists in genetics, animal physiology, and reproductive biology at Cambridge and Berlin. After work during the Second World War for the U.S. Army on the effects of stress, he founded the Worcester Foundation for Experimental Biology. The foundation became regarded as the international center for research on mammalian reproduction and steroid hormones. Pincus also initiated important annual conferences as well as editing valuable studies on hormones.

After the war, Margaret Sanger, the famed pioneer of planned parenthood, encouraged Pincus and his colleagues to reproduce in the laboratory synthetic compounds which, when administered orally, could prevent pregnancy. Although others were working at the same time in studying the effects of newly created hormones on reproduction, it was Pincus who coordinated and adapted these studies to human beings. The contraceptive pill, ingested orally, prevented pregnancy by inhibiting ovulation, leaving the female reproductive system intact yet dormant, until needed later for pregnancy.

Although its long-range effects have not yet been definitely settled, the pill when systematically used has been an extraordinarily effective family-planning device. Use of the birth-control pill has surged in the United States, for example. Many more women are taking it even later in their childbearing years, and fears of adverse effects have been subsiding. Contrasted with other methods of contraception which are much less effective, the pill (other than sterilization) has become the most desired method.

Some observers of birth control such as the Population Council have reported that the use of contraceptives such as the pill has been as revolutionary as changes in agricultural development in Third World countries. Contraception in these developing nations has led to a decrease in the average number of births per mother from six children in 1965 to just under four (3.9) today. If properly administered, this substantial decrease in births could lead to a stabilization of population growth in the next century, along with positive changes in food supply, education, and mortality.

The pill is also widely credited with being the most important reason for the sexual revolution of the late 1960s and 1970s. Until the threat of AIDS cooled the ardor of free sexual behavior, liberation from the fear of unwanted pregnancy through the use of the pill enabled countless women to engage in premarital and even marital sex without inhibition. This sexual liberation presented difficult challenges to traditional Jewish ethics and values.

The use of oral contraception to avoid pregnancy has also raised moral questions which challenge the basic tenets of organized religion. Orthodox Jews and observant Roman Catholics not only oppose abortion, but view the pill as morally repugnant. The official stance of the Vatican and Orthodox Jewry against contraception has had the unintended effect, however, of turning many away from religious practice.

The pill has also been noted by advocates of birth control as affording women the opportunity to have control of their own bodies. This freedom of choice will have as equally lasting a result as the sexual revolution on humanity, the relationships of women with men, and cultural development.

35

Leon Trotsky

(1879–1940)

Facilitator of the Russian Revolution, "genuine revolutionary leader," right hand of Lenin, hated enemy of Stalin, Leon Trotsky (born Lev Davidovich Bronstein) was one of the most influential—and hated—political figures in modern history.

Without Trotsky, Lenin would most likely not have been able to succeed in imposing Marxism on Russia. The history of the world since October 1917 would have been markedly different had comrades Lenin and Trotsky not prevailed. Founder of the first *Pravda* ("Truth") newspaper, Trotsky provided much of the intellectual basis for the rebellion, even though he came late to bolshevism. He showed Lenin how to use a confederation of soviets or elected councils to consolidate power. It was Trotsky, not Lenin, who led and organized the armed revolt that after the fall of the tsar overthrew Kerensky's provisional government and established communist rule. As commissar of war, Trotsky founded the Red Army and used it to brutally suppress the massive civil unrest plaguing Russia after the revolution.

So talented and necessary in the progress of violent revolution and civil war, Trotsky was incapable of being an "apparatchik" or bureaucrat in the monolithic Soviet state that followed. Overwhelmingly vain and arrogant, Trotsky lacked Lenin's political skills and Stalin's deviousness. In the waning days of Lenin's rule, Trotsky appeared bored with the proceedings of party meetings, openly reading novels while Stalin quietly consolidated his own power base. Trotsky's underestimation of Stalin and proud reluctance to enter the political fray ensured his fall and exile from Russia.

During the 1930s, Stalin purged the party of almost all its founding fathers in a series of show trials and executions. In 1940, Stalin's secret agents conspired to murder Trotsky in a frontal assault on his fortresslike home in Mexico City with machine guns and bombs—and failed. Later, a sole assassin ingratiated himself with a friend of Trotsky, secured a private audience with the great man, and drove an ice pick into his brain. Trotsky fought back, but died the next day.

More than any other leftist figure, including Karl Marx, "the Jew Trotsky" came to symbolize revolution and communism. During the Russian civil war just after the revolution, the "evil" person of Trotsky spurring them forward, antibolshevik troops massacred more than fifty thousand defenseless Jews in the Ukraine. Later, on the Eastern Front during the Second World War, Nazi soldiers were told that they were waging holy war culminating in the ultimate defeat of the bolshevik Jewish Christ killers. The horrors of implementing the Final Solution came easier to Nazi death squads believing they were ridding the world forever of Trotsky's image.

The great irony of the Trotsky symbol was that he was a self-hating Jew. Many of the important revolutionaries of the period were Jewish. Revolutionary leaders such as the German Rosa Luxemburg and Hungarian Béla Kun were non-Jewish Jews.

They either denied their heritage or went out of their way to humiliate their brethren. At an early congress of Russian Marxists, the Bund or General Jewish Workers Union was ferociously beaten down by Trotsky. He also largely ignored the pogroms that ravaged his people during the Russian civil war.

Again, other than Lenin, Trotsky was the prime force behind the Communists' success. He had spent most of his adult life fomenting revolution. The son of a prosperous farmer, Lev Davidovich Bronstein was sent to Siberia in his early twenties for subversive activities against the tsarist regime. In Siberia he married another revolutionary, fathered two daughters, escaped to England (with the blessing of his wife, but without his family), assumed the alias of his jailer, one "Leon Trotsky," and became the personal propagandist of Lenin. Lenin sent Trotsky back to Russia to work undercover. Trotsky organized workers' councils, and in the dress rehearsal for the 1917 revolt, led in 1905 an abortive attempt to overthrow the government. Tried, imprisoned, and again exiled to Siberia, he escaped once more, voyaging this time as far as America. In 1917, just after Lenin, Trotsky returned to Russia, leading the charge on the Winter Palace, the Communists seizing control over Russia that would last for over seventy years.

Trotsky's vision of a perpetual revolution played out on an international stage almost came to pass. Both Trotsky and Lenin assumed that their idea of a workers' revolution would spread to Germany, France, and England, painting Europe's flag a deepest red. Their Russian revolution did serve as a model for successfully brutal rebellions in China, Vietnam, Korea, and Cuba. Third World, more agrarian states seemed to adapt more readily to communism than highly industrialized nations. However, Stalinism, that twisted outgrowth of Leninism, overwhelmed the more utopian and intellectual niceties of the Trotskyites and became the favored example for developing leftist states.

In his dozen years in exile from Russia, Trotsky worked hard at exposing the terrors and hypocrisy of Stalin. Trotsky was of course no liberal democrat, believing in the total supremacy of the Communist party. The savagely uniform Soviet state he had helped found could not contain so independent a voice. When exile would not silence him, Stalin made sure an assassin's blow to the head did.

36

David Ricardo

(1772–1823)

Much of modern economic and political theory was first
formulated in the late eighteenth and early nineteenth centuries
by British thinkers such as Adam Smith, Thomas Malthus,
Jeremy Bentham, James Mill and his son John Stuart Mill, and
the Sephardic Jew David Ricardo. Along with Smith, Ricardo, the
author of *The Principles of Political Economy and Taxation* (first
published in 1817), is credited with founding the "classical school"
of economics.

Ricardo's family were Dutch Jews who emigrated to England
in 1760. Abraham Ricardo was a prominent member of the
London Stock Exchange and an Orthodox Jew, who sent his son,

David, to Holland to study Talmud. At age fourteen, David joined his father at the exchange, exhibiting an unusual talent for business. It is both fascinating and useful to note that David Ricardo was one of the few economists in history who was not just a theorist but a successful businessman.

Despite his traditional upbringing, at the age of twenty-one, David left Judaism to join the Unitarian Church and married a Quaker's daughter. Ricardo's family disowned him (the separation would last eight years), and he was left to fend for himself. He won the support of a prominent banking house and, soon thereafter, financial independence.

While still working at the exchange, Ricardo dabbled in several intellectual pursuits, settling on economic theory in 1799 after an almost random encounter with Adam Smith's *Wealth of Nations*. Ricardo's first pamphlet on economics (published in 1810) was called *The High Price of Bullion, a Proof of the Depreciation of Bank Notes*. This writing, esoteric as it may seem today, was highly controversial in its time, leading to the formation of a committee in the House of Commons to investigate the issue and corrective legislation. The article also prescribed the method of valuing currency and the power of a central bank to regulate the money supply (issues which plague the Federal Reserve to this day).

Ricardo began a series of correspondence with the leading economic thinkers of his era. Many of his most influential theoretical ideas were first expressed in letters to Malthus, Bentham, and Mill Senior. In 1815, Ricardo presented an *Essay on the Influence of a Low Price of Corn on the Profits of Stock*. The basic tenets of Ricardo's economics were first stated here. In rigorous theoretical language, he proposed the role of wages in price fluctuations (a rise in wages did not increase prices), how profits could be fattened (only by a drop in wages), and the importance of food production to the overall enrichment of society. A year later, Ricardo offered *Proposals for an Economical and Secure Currency*, another writing exhibiting his concern to stabilize money supply.

In 1817 his magnum opus, *The Principles of Political Economy and Taxation*, was issued. Continuing to develop his theories of an "economical and secure currency," Ricardo lay the basis of the monetary policy of capitalist nations for more than one hundred years. He expounded theories ("the laws which regulate") of production and income and of economic control, describing how and why people consume and invest, use and waste what they have. With an almost scientific thoroughness, Ricardo sought to explain the workings of international trade and its impact on domestic economies. He provided a conceptual methodology which remains influential, and was the first to identify economics as a set of principles concerned with material wealth.

Ricardo's interest in the economy led to a political awareness and involvement. In 1819, he became the second person of Jewish origin to be returned to Parliament, remaining until his death in 1823.

Many of Ricardo's theories were scrapped by later theorists. However, his influence on John Stuart Mill and Karl Marx is well documented. Ricardo's narrow, quasi-scientific approach, with little room for social philosophizing, continues to win adherents to this day.

37

Alfred Dreyfus

(1859–1935)

"Death to Dreyfus! Death to the Jews!"

On January 5, 1895, at the parade grounds of the military school in Paris, shrieks of hatred pierced the ice-cold air. An immaculately dressed Captain Alfred Dreyfus, standing proudly at attention in freezing rain, was publicly humiliated before hordes of soldiers and city people. A noncommissioned officer cut off Dreyfus's suit buttons, then his badges, and finally grabbed his sword and broke it across a knee. Dreyfus was marched about the square to vicious taunts and curses. Although he shouted, "I am innocent!", the crowd ridiculed him. Dreyfus was led away to a life's sentence in exile on dreaded Devil's Island.

142

The Dreyfus affair, known to the French as simply *"L'Affaire,"* was, before the pogroms in Russia and the unique tragedy of the Holocaust, the most publicized and perhaps the most influential event of anti-Semitism in modern European history. It spawned the pernicious growth of modern state-supported campaigns of persecution culminating in the tsarist and Nazi oppressions. The affair destroyed the myth that highly cultured societies were immune from irrational bitter hatred or could chill insane prejudice with developed civilization. The beautiful era of the 1890s in Paris, *la belle époque* of Renoir, Toulouse-Lautrec, Debussy, and Eiffel, was stained forever by the great lie of bigotry and fear. Only through the gallant and heroic efforts of writer Emile Zola, politician Georges Clemenceau, Lieutenant Colonel Georges Picquart, and other Dreyfusards, were the ideals of the French Revolution reaffirmed, and Dreyfus freed.

Dreyfus himself was not a remarkable man. He was from a wealthy Alsatian family, overbearing, ambitious, thought of as a bit of a prig. His supporters would say that he was not a committed individual. If the victim had not been himself, Dreyfus would surely not have supported the accused. He would not have been bothered by the affair. It is rather his story, not his person, that is so remarkable.

The origins of the Dreyfus case lay not in Jewish affairs, but in centuries-old antagonisms separating France and Germany and in petty anti-Semitism in the armed forces. In the early 1870s, France had lost the Franco-Prussian War. The industrially rich region of Alsace-Lorraine was taken by the Germans, not to be returned until the First World War. French authorities were suspicious of all things German and saw the need to spy incessantly on their adversary.

Disturbed by the sudden disappearance of military maps, a certain Major Henry of the Statistical Staff of the French General Staff enlisted the help of a maid at the German Embassy to deliver him paper discarded as trash by its diplomats. These papers noted a "Scoundrel D" as the source of French military secrets. The highest levels of the French government ordered the apprehension of the spy at once, at any cost.

When Henry was on leave, another, even more zealous officer on the Statistical Staff stole from the unattended lobby of the German Embassy a catalog of French military secrets. This list (French *"bordereau"*) with its references to artillery formations and the promised delivery of a firing manual would become infamous. The Statistical Staff reviewed the names of officers attached to the General Staff, hoping to match the handwriting of the *bordereau* with that of one of its officers. "Scoundrel D" was quickly assumed to be a somewhat pompous, Alsatian artillery officer, and the only Jew on the General Staff, Alfred Dreyfus. Examples of Dreyfus's handwriting on file were compared to that of the *bordereau*. A handwriting expert concluded that the *bordereau* was *not* written by Dreyfus; there were no similarities. So to justify their belief that only a Jew could commit such vile treachery, similarities were manufactured. A Police Department statistician, one Alphone Bertillon, was brought in and confirmed that the writing *was* by Dreyfus. The war minister, General Mercier, seeking to further his career, wanted a traitor, found desired confirmation in Bertillon, and ordered Dreyfus arrested.

Catholic newspapers, aligned with the anti-Semitic organ *La Libre Parole* (edited with virulent prejudice by the Jew-hating Edouard Drumont), launched a series of attacks on "spy" Dreyfus. Some in the official Catholic establishment saw in the affair an opportunity to regain religious authority lost since the Revolution and subsequent industrialization of the nation.

They were not alone. Major Henry with the help of his anti-Semitic superior, Colonel Sandherr, produced a file of supposed state secrets claimed to have been passed to the enemy. The military tribunal judging Dreyfus, assured by the War Ministry that the matter was one of essential state security, unanimously rendered a guilty verdict. Dreyfus was condemned to the most severe sentence permitted under law. Stripped of his military rank in the most degrading fashion, he was deported and imprisoned in a living hell.

As soon as Dreyfus was incarcerated on Devil's Island, the French public forgot about him. France was now safe from traitors. Dreyfus eked out a bare existence on the desolate isle with guards who were forbidden to speak with him, gradually losing all hope and slowly his health.

A year after Dreyfus's imprisonment, Lieutenant Colonel Georges Picquart was appointed to replace Sandherr, who had resigned due to a terminal illness. Picquart, a thorough officer,

A caricature of Dreyfus as a traitor.

began to research Dreyfus's unclear motives in committing the great crime. Picquart examined the dossier given to the military tribunal by the War Ministry that had led so quickly to the conviction. He was amazed to discover how skimpy and unconvincing the allegedly conclusive evidence was. Picquart also received at the time a small card that had been lifted in a cafe by a French surveillance agent from the pocket of the German military attaché. The card had as its addressee Major Ferdinand Walsin Esterhazy, a French officer of noble heritage but dubious reputation.

At about the same time, Esterhazy applied for a position on the General Staff. Esterhazy's application was reviewed by Picquart and compared with the *bordereau*. The handwriting was identical. Esterhazy was the spy! Picquart's superiors, however, would have nothing of it. High officials of the French government had sanctioned the case, even the war minister. The case was closed.

Dreyfus's family began spreading rumors in the press about

his escape. They sought to get some interest, any interest in the case. Perhaps it could be reopened. Instead, the anti-Semites in the press and the military went to work. Newspapers printed inflammatory stories about international Jewish syndicates organizing to release Dreyfus and overwhelm France. Dreyfus was put into iron shackles. When his guard protested at the treatment, he was relieved and replaced with a sadist. Disturbed by Picquart's assertions about Esterhazy, Major Henry enlisted the help of a forger and fattened the Dreyfus file with "new" evidence. Picquart was ordered to Africa and replaced by Henry. The cover-up continued.

The Dreyfus family would not give up. After a photograph of the *bordereau* was published in a popular newspaper, Dreyfus's brother Mathieu distributed pamphlets throughout Paris with copies of the *bordereau*. The handwriting was recognized as Esterhazy's. With the help of a prominent French senator, Auguste Scheurer-Kestner, the government commenced an inquiry into Esterhazy's possible involvement. The state investigation decided Mathieu's proof was inadequate. Esterhazy, however, would have none of this. He demanded a full trial, a court-martial, to clear his name.

The court-martial was a farce. Despite the testimony of Scheurer-Kestner and Picquart and the production of damaging evidence, the military tribunal (possessed as it was of Major Henry's expanded file) exonerated Esterhazy, who was carried to his carriage to the hero's welcome of "Long live Esterhazy and the army! Death to the Jews!"

The Esterhazy case, however, did have the effect of mobilizing the forces of progress in France. To the assistance of the estimable Scheurer-Kestner came the journalist and later premier of France Georges Clemenceau and the popular novelist Emile Zola. Zola responded to the Esterhazy fiasco immediately with his brilliant article *"J'Accuse...!"*, which endures as a testament to blunt truth in the service of justice. Zola accused Mercier and the other generals of being accomplices in one of the worst crimes in history. The anti-Semites reacted with pogroms in most of the French cities, the worst occurring in colonial Algiers. The government charged Zola with libel. He fled to England to escape imprisonment. Picquart was also arrested, and on trumped-up charges, imprisoned.

But in the end, miraculously, truth won out. In 1898, a new minister of war, General Godefroy Cavaignac, interviewed Major Henry, questioning carefully the supposed proofs that had led to Dreyfus's conviction and Esterhazy's vindication. Henry broke down and confessed everything. Cavaignac had Henry arrested. That night in his prison cell, Henry committed suicide, slicing his throat with a razor. Esterhazy, shorn of his well-known mustache, slipped into Belgium.

Despite all this, the French government and many Frenchmen would still believe that the army could do no wrong. Dreyfus was returned to France, his hair all white, racked with malaria, his naturally high voice reedy and hollow. Retried, he was again convicted. Offered a pardon, he accepted. Clemenceau and the others were outraged by his cowardice. But Dreyfus seemed to know better. He was later made a general, helped defend Paris during the First World War with an artillery battery, and died in 1935, five years before the fall of France to Hitler. Although Clemenceau and other leftist politicians took over the government in an overwhelming victory in 1906, anti-Semitism became part of the official French body politic, which led directly to complicity in the Holocaust. The vicious anti-Dreyfusards would have their murderous way with French and refugee Jewry during the Vichy years of the Second World War. The Gestapo found ready accomplices in the sons and daughters of Esterhazy, Drumont, Henry, Sandherr, and too many others.

In the courtyard of those military parade grounds that bone-cold January day in 1895, witnessing the degradation of a proud but stuffy Alsatian officer who happened to be Jewish, was a reporter from Vienna. Theodor Herzl's short life would never be the same. To escape this kind of persecution, this infamy, the Jews must have their own homeland. Out of the Dreyfus affair, Zionism was born.

38

Leo Szilard

(1898–1964)

Although not as commonly known as Albert Einstein or Niels Bohr, Leo Szilard was one of the most original and creative scientists of the twentieth century. With Enrico Fermi, Szilard is largely credited with creating the first nuclear fission reactor and for fundamental work in modern cybernetic or information theory. It was also Szilard who convinced Einstein to write the famous letter to President Franklin Roosevelt in 1940 resulting in the establishment of the top-secret Manhattan Project and the atomic destruction of 170,000 Japanese at Hiroshima and Nagasaki ending the Second World War. Szilard was active as well in biological research, was concerned, especially in his last years, with the role of science in keeping the peace, and developed the idea of the "think tank" where distinguished thinkers could combine social and scientific ideas into something new (first realized at the Salk Institute in La Jolla, California).

He was born in Budapest. Szilard's father was a successful engineer and architect who raised his three children in affluence. Szilard, however, was not well as a child and in his early youth was tutored at home by his mother. Later, he trained in electrical engineering, only to be interrupted during the First World War by military service in the Austro-Hungarian Army. continuing his studies after the war in Berlin, Szilard found himself drawn to physics, seeking out the best teachers and gradually taking his place in prestigious research laboratories.

During these early years in Berlin, Szilard became a regular visitor to Einstein's home. Szilard displayed to Einstein an inventive and practical side marked by remarkable theoretical intuition. They soon secured a series of patents in Great Britain, Germany, and the United States for a heat pump which later would be used to control the temperature of nuclear reactors.

With the rise of Hitler in 1933, Szilard fled Germany for England. On March 12, 1934, Szilard applied to the Admiralty for a secret patent. He sought it in secret out of the fear that its use could lead to the most violent explosion. The patent was for a nuclear fission chain reactor.

Szilard's concept of a chain reaction came to him in a flash. He had been reading a newspaper story of a scientist's hopes for freeing atomic energy. Szilard observed that if one could find an element which when split by neutrons would absorb one neutron while releasing two neutrons, such an element if put together in a large mass might sustain a nuclear chain reaction.

The English, however, did not provide Szilard with the support he needed for his research. When he reached the United States in 1938, Szilard learned for the first time that the German Otto Hahn had split the uranium atom, thereby uncovering nuclear fission. Confirming his later nickname as the "gray eminence of physics," Szilard carefully noted that the German discovery of fission would most likely lead to the release of nuclear energy through an explosive device.

Under the auspices of Columbia University, Szilard began experiments to show the number of neutrons released during

fission and how they were released. His research with Fermi led
to the first controlled chain reaction on December 2, 1942. This
experiment as well as Szilard's pressure on Einstein to write to
Roosevelt led the U.S. government to establish the top-secret
Manhattan Project which produced the bomb that ended the war.

Niels Bohr had predicted that the manmade creation of
nuclear energy would not be practicable. Through a superhuman
effort, Szilard and other immigrant physicists proved Bohr
wrong. Indeed, the German effort was hampered by the loss of
Jewish emigrés like Szilard to America. In 1945 the U.S. military,
rather than invading Japan and exposing its forces to countless
casualties, chose to explode the bomb over civilian populations.
Szilard, again with Einstein's help, had sought to influence
President Harry Truman to display the first atomic bomb to the
Japanese in a nonlethal way. Truman's choice to ignore their pleas
ended the war, but left a scar on human history that will not heal.
Despite the bitter experience of the firebombing by conventional
methods of Tokyo and Dresden (far more destructive than the
first atomic weapons), mankind now knew full well the wider
implications of nuclear holocaust.

The incredibly destructive force of the bomb was however
only one use of the nuclear chain reactor. Szilard's discoveries led
to the establishment of nuclear fission as an alternative (yet still
controversial) energy source. His scientific impulses tied to political action before the war enabled America to be on guard against
Germany's nuclear threat and to halt the Pacific war. After the
war, Szilard's lobbying for the peaceful development of nuclear
energy successfully influenced postwar congressional legislation
to establish civilian controls.

Not surprisingly, Szilard's research after the war turned to
life. After important studies of viruses and bacteria, Szilard
published a paper on the aging process which today remains
influential. It was as if the horrors of the atomic forces he had
helped release (guided by the theories and presence of his
mentor, Einstein) made him seek comfort in the life-giving
secrets of biology.

39

Mark Rothko

(1903–1970)

Fourteen years after Jackson Pollock's tragic death in a wild car accident in East Hampton on the South Fork of Long Island, his great rival, Mark Rothko, committed suicide in a New York City studio by slitting his wrists and draining his red blood slowly in the sink. Rothko had told his friends that while it could not be definitely proven that Pollock's death was a suicide, everyone would know when Mark Rothko ended his life.

When Pollock died, his wife, the painter Lee Krasner, had him buried beneath a great rock in the local town cemetery, not far from the scene of his fatal accident. Due to Pollock's notoriety and the sensationalism that surrounded his death (one young woman died in the accident and the only survivor, his mistress, was thrown safely into the brush), Pollock's final resting place, Green River Cemetery, became a sort of gathering spot for art world figures dead and alive. In the macabre words of a local, everyone was dying to get in. The remains of the poet Frank O'Hara and the painters Ad Reinhardt (a suicide by hanging) and Stuart Davis joined Pollock in a final who's who of postwar artists.

Rothko, however, was buried by his friend the painter Theodoros Stamos in a small church graveyard in East Marion on the North Fork of Long Island. Stamos had built a dramatic house on stilts near the bluffs facing Long Island Sound and chose in a dramatic gesture (some people felt aimed at Pollock) the less trendy, quiet North Fork town for Rothko's last resting place. His gravestone was more modest than Pollock's big boulder. Rothko's last resting place was to be with strangers, far away from the art world.

Although Jackson Pollock is viewed by many as the leading advocate of the school of painters known as the New York School of Abstract Expressionism, Mark Rothko remains its most humane and expressive proponent. Rothko in life as in death was separate and apart from the other abstract painters. As Pollock freed line from the constraints of known shapes, instilling his paintings with a newfound energy and spirit, Rothko's equivalent achievement was the liberation of color from realistic confines. In the 1950s and 1960s he displayed in a trailblazing series of paintings the power of pure color to evoke deeply felt emotion, solemnity, and majesty. His release of color from recognizable designs forever influenced how art is viewed and created.

A painter's work is best viewed rather than written about. Imagine, then, large canvases with blocks of color floating against each other in horizontal duos, trios, and quartets. It all seems so simple, yet simply right, as if one had never seen colors interact like this before.

The Abstract Expressionists (Rothko hated the label) were reacting against the almost socialist realism of the Depression years with revolutionary approaches to painting. Pollock led the fight with his remarkably energetic paintings of dancing lines. Rothko turned away from his early socially concerned realistic style and used the primacy of color in amorphous shapes to express tragedy, ecstasy, or doom. Using compelling coloristic images, Rothko was able to evoke a religiosity, mystery, and timelessness unique to his generation. None of the other painters of the period, including Barnett Newman, Reinhardt, Willem de Kooning, Adolph Gottlieb, or Franz Kline, achieved as consistently as Rothko the immediacy of feeling and thought brought about by his friction of colors, glowing and shifting, vibrant or restrained, always alive (that is, until the dark last years).

Rothko was born Marcus Rothkovich in an area of Latvia from which Aaron Copland could also trace his roots. His father was a prosperous pharmacist who enrolled his youngest son, Marcus, in religious school or heder. Like many Jews of that time, faced with the conscription of his two eldest sons into the Russian army, Rothko's father brought the family to America in 1913. Upon arrival their name was changed to Rothkowitz, and they made their way west, settling in Portland, Oregon. Raised in Portland by his widowed mother (his father had suddenly died shortly after they came to Oregon), Rothko's teens were spent in poverty. Nevertheless, in the early 1920s he went to Yale, did not finish his schooling, acted for a while (Clark Gable was once his understudy), and then journeyed to New York to study painting at the Art Students League, eventually under the influential Max Weber. Soon he married, seemingly just to get married, was then bitterly unhappy, and worked in a series of menial jobs to support his new family. These odd jobs were finally interrupted by that great artists' collective supported by President Franklin Roosevelt's New Deal, the Works Progress Administration (WPA). While working for the WPA during these Depression years, he first met de Kooning, Gottlieb, and Pollock, and as the war approached, many of the great contemporary European painters threatened by the Nazi peril arrived in New York. The combination of European influence, the Depression, and American patriotism seemed to have a catalytic effect, for in the early 1940s the styles of many of the young Americans began to change, marking the beginning of a golden age of modern art. Toward the end of the war, Rothkowitz changed his name to Rothko, divorced his first wife, remarried (this time happily), and suppressed his earlier socially realistic paintings, displaying with gradual success a more abstract style.

After the war, New York became the world capital of art
(although most people did not yet realize it). The great European
refugees had returned home, leaving the younger men and a few
women to develop their unique ways. The works of these mostly
New York artists hang now in our most prestigious galleries, but
in the late 1940s, they could not sell a painting. The WPA had
brought many of them together, and they continually influenced
each other, frequently visiting one another's studios, meeting
socially to discuss literature and politics and to drink, standing
apart from the conventional mores of society, often identifying
with the downtrodden and the poor. They began to show their
works, often together, in the handful of galleries which would
recognize their emerging talents. They experimented with new
concepts of form, line, color, and shape. The message was often
in the materials used, not in the use of materials.

Although very much a part of the New York School, Rothko
never forgot to instill in his paintings strong emotive messages.

Artist Mark Rothko and his three-year-old son Christopher.

He desired to elicit not only intellectual responses or excitement from his viewers, but preferably their deepest feelings and wants. As his art gained wider recognition, Rothko, like most of his generation, did not know how to react. The incredible surges of emotion required for his art taxed him severely. He made bad business connections which would later lead to the great scandal surrounding his estate and the theft of many of his paintings. His bright colors gradually deepened in shade, reflecting a darkening mood. Rothko's increasing fame brought important commissions, including the request by the wealthy de Menil family of Houston to create a chapel with huge murals. These dark, brooding works, in shifting browns and black, are more gloomy than tragic, large screams of pain rather than majestic symbols. After the de Menil chapel, his final paintings continued to display the darkest hues available; in their smaller scale they were more expressive, but still cold and tired.

As Pollock led by converting active lines into pure abstractions, Rothko instilled colors with emotion, foregoing the necessity of shapes drawn from real things. The tension in his paintings was often derived from the elemental force of the colors themselves. For example, he was concerned with the effect of how a certain kind of yellow might react with a certain kind of red or purple and how their relationship might inject an emotion into the viewer. Rothko did not name his paintings, but assigned numbered dates to them. The viewer then had to react to what was on the canvas without any help from everyday images or literary or historical references. Pure art for art's sake, colors melting into colors, were to take us away from the pain of the real world into visions of infinity.

40

Ferdinand Cohn

(1828–1898)

The magic of science reveals itself when research, first intended to produce one result, surprises with the unexpected. Ferdinand Julius Cohn, son of the German Jewish ghetto in Breslau, studied to become a botanist. His studies of microscopic plant organisms, such as fungi and algae, were innovative and influential. Yet these studies led Cohn to unimagined discoveries in an entirely different field—bacteriology.

Cohn shifted his focus away from plants to different but remarkably similar living things called Vibronia (a form of bacteria). He identified these bacteria as a form of plant life, not the animals scientists then assumed they were. This identification and his related discovery of spores built the foundation of modern bacteriology.

The son of a merchant, Cohn was a child prodigy who was first thought to be slow and difficult. Overcoming a hearing defect, he attended the University of Breslau, studying his beloved botany. Cohn was refused a degree, however, because he was Jewish. Despite emancipation from the ghetto, for most of the nineteenth century, Jews could not enjoy equal rights in most of Europe. He ventured to Berlin, where he received his doctorate at the age of nineteen. While studying microorganisms, he became interested in the politics of revolution. During the 1848 rebellion Cohn made clear his radical support, and during the ensuing suppression was barred from a teaching position in the Prussian capital. At age twenty-two Cohn returned to Breslau where he would remain for most of his life. Securing a teaching post at the university, Cohn began to research the cell lives of the tiniest creatures.

Scientists during the 1850s were looking within cellular structure for the very substance of life. Cohn was sure he had located the driving force of life in a single material called protoplasm. Although his research on protoplasm would prove very influential during the nineteenth century, it was a way station along a path of much more important exploration.

In a major text on fungi and algae published in 1854, Cohn identified a bacterium called Vibronia, asserting that it was a form of plant, not animal, life. Vibronia had been thought to be an animal due to the way it moved, propelled quickly by cilia or long tendrils. Cohn, the master botanist, recognized how Vibronia was similar to, yet different from, fungi and algae. He noted, in addition, the particular ways this bacterium developed, remarkably close to the growth of algae.

After establishing a prestigious institute on plant physiology, Cohn began the second phase of his career, primarily studying bacteria. He began an academic journal to record and publicize his findings. The journal would contain articles which would serve as the basis of contemporary bacteriology. Cohn's major work of this period included the classification of bacteria into groups according to their shapes, the discovery that fungi and bacteria had no genetic relationship, but that bacteria ate much like plants, ingesting their nitrogen from the same source but carbon differently (bacteria loved carbohydrates), and the notation of the temperatures at which bacteria could survive (they can be frozen, only to thrive again when thawed) or be boiled to death (eighty degrees Celsius). Cohn also greatly influenced the pioneering work of Robert Koch, whose discovery of the cure for anthrax revolutionized farming.

As the father of modern bacteriology, Cohn merits inclusion on the list of the Jewish 100. His analysis and cataloging of bacteria enabled other scientists not only to identify bacterial hazards to good health and hygiene, but also to develop effective means of defense in humanity's continuing war against microbes.

41

Samuel Gompers

(1850–1924)

Samuel Gompers was an organizer of the cigar makers' union, founder and first president of the American Federation of Labor (AFL), and leader in what was truly a class struggle for equitable wages, reasonable work hours, child labor laws, industrial regulations, workers' compensation, the right to bargain collectively, and the use of strikes and boycotts to force economic concessions. Most of the power of organized labor over the past one hundred years, not only in America but across Europe, arose from the work of this tireless man.

The ability of labor to organize seems today almost an inalienable right. Before Gompers, this was not so. In the early days of the sweatshops, laborers had no rights. Men, women, and children worked all day and night, six or seven days a week, in substandard conditions for inadequate pay. Many of these workers were Jewish, most refugees from tsarist and Polish persecution, all seeking a better life in America only to find unending hardship, drudgery, and degradation.

Gompers was born in London in 1850 to Solomon Gompers and the former Sara Rood. In 1863 the family emigrated to America, where Solomon became an expert laborer making cigars. Samuel followed his father's example, apprenticing for small cigar-making companies. Although Samuel married another London-born Jew, Sophia Julian, he never practiced Judaism (except for wearing a cantor's skullcap as an older man to hide his thinning hair). First, Ethical Culture, then trade unionism, would supplant his origins.

After the Civil War, mechanized means of mass production overcame the skilled art of expertly rolling cigars by hand. Cheap labor was supplied by slum workers, mostly newly arrived from Bohemia. Faced with the threat of the loss of their livelihood and a nationwide economic depression in the 1880s, the skilled cigar makers organized. Gompers worked as a local union organizer, becoming known for his talented oration. He was soon named president of his local union. Because of his union activities, Gompers lost his job and was out of work for several months, his family subsisting on flour soup and handouts from relatives. The life of a union man was not easily chosen.

Gompers rose quickly to national prominence. He acknowledged that the union could not resist either improved industrial methods or the entry of legions of unskilled workers. Gompers' "new unionism" recognized the need for central management of work stoppages (not the random, ineffective strikes cigar makers were unfortunately so fond of), securing benefits for the unemployed, coordinating local activities with national labor groups, and publicizing union issues in newspapers and magazines.

Largely resulting from the failure of the most prominent of national groups of the time, the Knights of Labor, to protect workers adequately, Gompers formed the AFL in 1887. Gompers, thirty-seven years of age, was elected its first president, serving, except for one year off, for thirty-eight years until his death. In the early days of the AFL, Gompers was its only full-time officer. He developed its own journal, built up a strike fund, and brought many disparate, sometimes conflicting trade movements under one umbrella. The AFL consisted for many years primarily of skilled workers who were employed by small owners. Gompers refused to admit migrant laborers or workers without skills. He publicly opposed an open-door immigration policy (a position the major labor unions continued to endorse in their opposition during the 1990s to NAFTA), showing particular resentment of Chinese immigration. He who had been an immigrant himself as a young boy chose to ignore his own tale.

Gompers remains a controversial figure in labor history. He founded the first great labor federation committed to many of the guiding principles of the movement. However, he considered the goals of trade unionism to be paramount. The period between the Civil War and the First World War was a time of bitter hostility toward the labor movement. Anything that stood in its way had to be overcome, whatever the cost. Gomper sought to make labor unions respectable, not an easy task in an age of extremely violent anarchism, vibrant socialism, and abundant radicalism. As head of the War Committee on Labor during the First World War and in his aggressive stance against the "Red Scare" that followed the Russian revolution, Gomper did much to gain respectability for his federation. He was also active in early legislative efforts to protect children in the workplace, establish the eight-hour day, and provide for compensation to injured workers. His lack of foresight in welcoming semiskilled and unskilled laborers into the AFL was rectified by its merger in 1955 with the Congress of Industrial Organizations (CIO), which represented many of those workers.

A tireless traveler while the head of the AFL, Gompers logged tens of thousands of miles per year in journeys across the country extolling the virtues of trade unionism. On one such trip to San Antonio in 1924, a weary, now blinded Gompers succumbed, leaving the future of the labor movement to mostly lesser men.

42

Gertrude Stein

(1874–1946)

Finding the right way to express oneself is the challenge of everyday speech. Do we say what we think, do we think what we say, do we repeat what we should not have said, do we fail to say again what we should have repeated? Do our words mean what we think they mean, or can they mean something different, something not burdened by custom, expectation, convenience?

Gertrude Stein was a Jewish American woman born in the 1800s who showed twentieth-century writers how to write. From a

162

prosperous background, she provided psychological and edible sustenance in her Paris salon to a generation of great artists. Painters such as Picasso, Matisse, Rousseau, and Braque, as well as a later group of American expatriates—authors Hemingway, Fitzgerald and Anderson and composer Thomson—feasted on her sage counsel.

Stein believed that for the United States, the twentieth century began just after its Civil War. Since Europe entered the modern era only after the First World War, America was therefore the oldest country in the world, and by its innovative spirit, the newest. For Stein, the American century was not about people living on top of each other in antique European cities, reflected in a continental literature obsessed with itself. Rather, modern art was about wide, open American spaces, large shapes and angles, broad vistas, the thing being what it is and isn't it fine as it is!

Ernest Hemingway owed his mostly nonrepresentational work largely to her direct influence. The familiar Hemingway style with its taut, plain sentences, letting in no extraneous emotion, is what it is because of Gertrude Stein. She helped him clean up his plodding early prose into powerfully expressive poetry.

Before Hemingway, Pablo Picasso had found spiritual and intellectual support in the Stein living room at 27, rue de Fleuris (as well as in the delicious cuisine and warm hospitality of her lover, Alice B. Toklas). Surrounded by walls crowded with his paintings and those of his contemporaries or just predecessors, Picasso sought Stein's guidance at a crucial period. While he was leaving the Italianate lyricism of his rose, blue, and harlequin paintings for abstract cubism, she was separating words from conventional usage, making them live the life "they have to live," in what became an almost exact science of literature without subject, a word being what it is it is. As Picasso painted his *Portrait of Gertrude Stein* (filling in her face well after the weighty body was painted) and the *Demoiselles d'Avignon* with their African heads and multiangled features, in such early works as *Three Lives* (years before James Joyce's comparable experiments with language) Stein was tearing sentences apart, reducing words to their essential meanings, separating substance from form, making form substance, "composition as explanation."

Composer Virgil Thomson also found in Stein's wordplay a

parallel universe to his "white note" music (plain Jane melodies set in hymnlike chords). These two Americans in Paris created profoundly Yankee songs and operas together. It was a strange irony that somehow being physically separated from the United States inspired them to part from traditional European operatic and song forms. *Four Saints in Three Acts* (1929) premiered in New Haven, Connecticut with an all-black cast (Toscanini attended and liked it). More about the visions of saints than about any plot or story, the piece was fresh and lively. Word patterns like "pigeons on the grass alas" were meaningful primarily as a ballet of consonants and vowels, precise improvisations. Their last work, *The Mother of Us All,* about Susan B. Anthony and assorted friends, presented historical characters in amusing juxtapositions with alarming vibrancy.

Her life with Alice B. Toklas, another Jewish woman from the United States, is best remembered in the *Autobiography* Stein wrote for her (which is actually more Gertrude's story). Their rich love for each other survived the Nazi occupation (amazingly they sat the war out in a Vichy French village) and Stein's death (Alice died twenty-one years after Gertrude, cherishing her memory more with each passing day). The image of Gertrude Stein, shorthaired, strong, plump, and dominant, accompanied always by her soft, kind Alice B., set a proud example for now three generations of lesbian women.

43

Albert Michelson

(1852–1931)

Albert Abraham Michelson was the first American scientist to win a Nobel Prize (the first American to win any Nobel was President Theodore Roosevelt, awarded for his role during 1905 in settling the war then raging between Russia and Japan). Honored by the Nobel Prize committee in 1907 "for his precision optical instruments and the spectroscopic and metrological investigations conducted therewith," Michelson is widely recognized as the father of modern theoretical physics. Although there is some controversy over his direct role, many have claimed that Michelson's collaboration with chemist Edward Morley (in the famous Michelson-Morley experiments) provided the basis upon which Albert Einstein formulated his special theory of relativity.

The focus of largely all of Michelson's life's work was his desire to measure with precision instruments the physical properties of light. He is credited with proving that light travels at a constant speed no matter the direction it is heading, in any and all conditions. Michelson's development of the spectroscope afforded proof of the movement of molecules. He was the first to measure the diameter of a star. His determination of the speed of light was the most accurate of the era.

Michelson was born in western Poland. In 1856 his family emigrated to America, settling in San Francisco. During the waning days of the gold rush in California and Nevada, his father labored as a merchant to miners. Albert was sent to San Francisco to attend public school. At Boys' High School the principal, noticing Michelson's aptitude for science, encouraged the young student. After being rejected initially for admission to Annapolis (and despite an unsuccessful petition to President Grant), Michelson convinced the commandant of his merit and was accepted to the U.S. Naval Academy in 1869.

Two years after graduation he returned to Annapolis to teach physics and chemistry classes. While there, using simple devices, Michelson measured the speed of light closer to what became the accepted figure of 186,508 miles per second than any scientist before him.

After studies in Europe in the 1880s, he was appointed professor of physics at the Case School of Applied Science in Cleveland, Ohio. In 1885 Michelson began his now celebrated association with Morley of Western Reserve, who as senior researcher had at his disposal a large laboratory with up-to-date equipment.

The Michelson-Morley experiments of 1887 proved a negative. Their so-called null result profoundly affected the way physicists viewed the world. Physicists in the 1880s assumed that light was created by unequal changes in an amorphous substance that filled up all space. They called that substance "ether." The widely accepted theory was that ether was stationary. Light moved through ether at different speeds, depending on the direction from which it came. In their experiments, Michelson and Morley shot out two beams of light, reflecting them off each other at a ninety-degree angle. Their instruments were able to show that both beams had traveled at the same speed. The experiment rendered the theory of ether unacceptable and obsolete.

The ramifications of their experiments were overwhelming to many scientists. Was it possible that the earth stood still, and Copernicus had been mistaken? Physicists had already proven that ether was not brought along by the earth in its travel through the cosmos. Most of Michelson's contemporaries (and to a certain extent Michelson himself) could not bring themselves to believe that ether itself did not exist. Many scientists reacted to the Michelson-Morley experiments, attempting to work out its implications. Finally, Einstein's special theory of relativity solved the questions first posed by Michelson's experiments.

Despite the immense influence of his work on subsequent generations of physicists, Michelson was never totally comfortable with their mathematically derived science. He considered the true mission of physics to be the development of new instruments to measure physical properties with total accuracy.

In 1892 Michelson became professor of physics at the University of Chicago, where he remained until 1929. In 1920 at a dinner held in Pasadena, California honoring Einstein and himself, his esteemed German colleague recognized that Michelson had "uncovered an insidious defect in the ether theory of light, as it then existed, and stimulated the ideas of H.A. Lorentz and Fitzgerald, out of which the special theory of relativity developed."

44

Philo Judaeus

(ca. 20 B.C.E.–40 C.E.)

We know little about his life, other than that in his last year he traveled to Rome at the behest of the Jewish community of Alexandria to seek the aid of the emperor Caligula in protecting Egypt's Jews from religious persecution.

A contemporary of Jesus of Nazareth and his early followers, Philo had ideas of God, creation, history, nature, soul, knowledge, virtue, and government which served as the basis for the philosophical thought of Judaism, Christianity, and Islam for seventeen centuries until Spinoza's great revolution of thought in the 1600s.

168

Philo was the first philosopher of major influence to attempt to understand biblical teachings in light of Greek metaphysics. His work also aimed to rewrite hellenistic philosophy in scriptural terms. To justify his conclusions, Philo often quoted various Greek philosophers backed up by Jewish law. He rejected Greek philosophy opposite to biblical teaching, accepting hellenism only when it could be bent to his metaphysical will.

Influenced by the Bible, Philo was also the first philosopher to refer to God as unknowable, incomprehensible to humanity. Plato and Aristotle had asserted that man was capable of knowing and describing God. Philo rejected their view, making the distinction that God is unique, is the most generic of beings, and being *sui generis,* cannot be described.

For Philo, all human knowledge and activity was directed by God. Prophecy, a special kind of knowledge, may only be achieved by divine intervention or what the Christians would later call revelation. He also organized man's ideas of life, the earth, and the cosmos into what the intellect could comprehend. Philo named this intelligible sphere "Logos," a word derived from Scripture and new to philosophy.

Plato had alleged that the soul is immortal, incapable of being destroyed by God and natural causes. Philo disagreed. God grants immortality as a gift, only if the soul, empowered by God's will, has been worthy of its heavenly birth.

Contrary to most of the Greek philosophers before him, Philo believed in free will. God can do whatever God chooses, and so could mankind. Man could work with and oppose nature absolutely.

One of Philo's greatest influences is his attention to democracy. He is one of the first major philosophers to urge that all people are equal before the law. This is a concept of justice which did not enter American life, we must remember, until after the Civil War and in practice, has not completely yet.

Attempting to pull together all of his philosophic ideas, Philo believed, in his *Allegories,* that the tides of historical change are controlled by a divine Logos; God has intended that the world is to become a perfect democracy.

With the decline of the vibrant Jewish community, in Alexandra, Philo's influence on Judaism waned. The influence of Greek philosophy on Jewish thought would only arise again in the work 1,200 years later of Moses Maimonides. Talmudic teachings would venture into a wholly new direction, urging a more Hebraic notion of law and philosophy. However, Philo's philosophy exerted important and crucial influence on the early Christian fathers (Saint John) and Muslim scholars who viewed his thoughts as the intellectual basis and justification for their preaching.

45 *Golda Meir*

(1898–1978)

Her earliest memories were of her father nailing wooden boards across the front door of their house in Russia. A pogrom was rumored, a state- and church-endorsed massacre of Jews. Golda later remarked that it was typical of her father not to think of hiding his family.

Golda Meir, prime minister of Israel for five years, was among the most beloved leaders and admired women of the twentieth century. Although criticized by Israelis for her late response to Egypt's sneak attack that commenced the 1973 war, she is remembered by the world as the mother of her nation and its symbol of peace.

Golda's early life is crucial to an understanding of her actions and to the difficulties this extraordinarily humane woman faced. Born Golda Mabovitz on May 3, 1898 in Kiev, at eight years of age she emigrated with her family to Milwaukee. The father had preceded the family to America by three years, seeking to bring a fortune back to Russia. Her parents had had eight children, four boys and four girls. Golda and her two sisters were the only to survive past infancy, and one of the other five lived to two years of age, two small ones having died in the same week. Life in Russia was severe, poverty overwhelming, *"essen teg und trinken trehen"* ("to eat days and swallow tears"). In Pinsk (the family's hometown to which they had returned after a short stay in Kiev), her elder sister, Sheyna, engaged in illegal political activities as a Zionist socialist. Surrounded by cold, lack of food, marauding Cossacks, police persecution, and lack of opportunity, the women of the family fled to their father in free America.

In Milwaukee the family eked out a living. Father found carpentry jobs, mother operated a grocery, and Sheyna labored during the day as a seamstress and at night as a Zionist, then ran away to Denver. Golda helped her mother in the grocery, opening the store early each morning and arriving late at school, her eyes full of tears. She still managed to get good grades, but as her teenage years approached, resentment of her parents grew for their opposition to her desires to become a teacher and marry a man of her own choice. At fourteen Golda ran away to her sister in Colorado where she met her future husband, Morris Meyerson, a refugee from Russia, a kind intellectual who painted signs for a living.

Molded by her sister and the freedom of living on her own, she returned home at eighteen to teach school and preach Zionism. Her father initially opposed her speaking in public on the grounds that such activity was not ladylike—that is, until he heard her powerfully orate on a street corner. After meeting David Ben-Gurion, who had visited Milwaukee seeking followers, she left for Palestine, followed reluctantly by her new husband, Morris.

Morris and Golda were invited to live in a small kibbutz called Merhavia (meaning "God's wide spaces") largely due to Morris's phonograph and record collection. Golda adapted herself quickly to pioneer kibbutz life, caring for the livestock, working in the fields, washing clothes, baking bread. Recognized by her comrades as a hard and innovative worker, Golda was chosen to represent the kibbutz at the General Federation of Labor, the Histadrut. Even in these harsh rural circumstances her leadership qualities stood out.

Morris, however, could not stand the pioneering life. They moved to the cities, finally settling in a dusty quarter of Jerusalem. Golda soon gave birth to her two children, Menachem and Sarah. Their life in these years was to Golda "poverty, drudgery and worry."

Her parents, however, had settled in Herzliya on the seacoast, and Golda grew to adore her father's local involvement in security and Histadrut affairs. Golda rose quickly in the labor federation, first in 1928 becoming secretary of its council, then in 1934 a member of its executive committee. Her political activities, however, kept her away from her family, and her marriage deteriorated. She separated from Morris and moved with the children to a small apartment in Tel Aviv. Golda later often described what women's liberation meant in 1930s Palestine. She felt recurring pain over the looks of reproach from her little ones when she had to go away to work and leave them with strangers. Working mothers had to suffer for their chosen activities.

Attending a French conference on Jewish refugees in 1938, she witnessed firsthand the disinterest of European governmental officials in granting asylum to victims of Nazi persecution. During the war that soon followed, Golda organized opposition to oppressive British colonial rule. In 1939 the British had halted Jewish immigration into Palestine for fear that the influx of refugees would cause the Arabs to support Hitler (some did, including the Mufti of Jerusalem). Zionist leaders managed to smuggle in a small number of refugees. However, the British restrictions led to countless unnecessary deaths at the hands of the Nazi butchers at a time when Zionists like Golda could have saved many lives.

The indifference of British rule hardened the Zionists, preparing them for their great postwar endeavors. In 1946 many of the Zionist leaders were arrested for their secret political actions. The British authorities, however, left "that woman," Golda, alone. She quickly started running the affairs of the opposition, networking with underground military units and attempting to negotiate with the British.

When the United Nations recommended the partitioning of
Palestine and the creation of a Jewish state, Golda was on hand to
attempt difficult negotiations with the king of Transjordan and to
sign the Israeli declaration of independence. When Israel was
threatened by Arab attack, it was Golda who traveled to the
United States to raise money for weapons. Her extraordinary
speech to a Jewish group in Chicago led to an equally extraordinary fund-raising effort by American Jewry in support of the
fledgling state. Golda returned home with fifty million dollars.
Ben-Gurion later remarked that "someday when history will be
written, it will be said that there was a Jewish woman who got the
money which made the State possible."

After a brief stint in Moscow as Israel's first minister to the
Soviet Union (the Russian refugee had returned "home" representing the Jewish homeland), she was elected to the Knesset, the
Israeli parliament, where she served from 1949 to 1974. In
addition, between 1949 and 1956, as minister of labor, Golda drew
on her wealth of experience in the Histadrut to lead her country
in what were times of rationing and enormous economic hardship. She helped develop housing for immigrants then living in
tents, worked against sexual harassment of women in a male-
driven Mediterranean society, and introduced social programs
for the elderly, needy, infirm, and unemployed.

In the mid-1950s, on Ben-Gurion's urging, she changed her
name to the more Hebrew-sounding Meir. She did not look back
much to Russia (other than with bitterness) or to America (always
in gratitude). Israel was home right from the first days on the
kibbutz.

During the 1956 Suez war she was appointed foreign minister. Her defense of Israel at the United Nations during the crisis
received worldwide press coverage. During the same period she
developed technical and economic assistance programs for
emerging African nations.

In 1966 she retired from the cabinet to be a full-time
grandmother. She was almost seventy years old and tired of
public service and politics. During Prime Minister Eshkol's tenure in the late 1960s, she remained in public view, however
lobbying American Jewish groups for support and making clear
that Israel wanted peace, not war. Nasser, Egypt's leader, however,
failed to hear her and others' calls for peace, and the Six Day War

of 1967 soon erupted. Under Moshe Dayan's dynamic leadership the Arab forces were routed, Jerusalem unified under Israeli rule, and the Sinai, Gaza, and Golan Heights secured.

When the wise Eshkol died suddenly in 1969, the ruling Labor party turned to its secretary-general, Golda. Although tired of government life and already burdened by the leukemia that would end her life nine years later, Golda became Israel's first female prime minister.

The years until the Yom Kippur War in 1973 were spent in building up the armed forces with more sophisticated weaponry but also with continuing attempts to find avenues for a more lasting peace. During the summer of 1973, intelligence reports indicated a buildup of Arab troops and the withdrawal of Soviet advisers from Syria. Golda thought to put the troops on alert, but held back on her cabinet's advice. She was to regret following her instincts, as shortly thereafter, on the holiest day of the Jewish calendar, Yom Kippur, Anwar Sadat's forces broke through the supposedly impregnable Bar-Lev line at the Suez and threatened Israel with extinction. Only with massive American supplies and the loss of 2,500 Israeli lives was the country saved.

Golda was castigated by her countrymen for reacting too late to the Arab threat, and for ending the war too soon before conclusive victory. She would retire one year after the war, exhausted from the fray. But her instincts to save lives and seek peace would bear fruit three years later when the emboldened Sadat came to Israel in search of peace.

When cancer ended her life in 1978, Golda Meir was remembered by the world as the lioness of her people and an example for women and men everywhere. Her country had demanded that she lead it through difficult times. First as a pioneer in its early years, then in her dedicated efforts for social justice, she personified the best qualities of Jewish life. Like the biblical Prophetess Deborah, Golda showed all women how to lead an army of fierce fighters in defense of a country's life, never forgetting her humanity and always pointing the way to lasting tranquility.

46

רבנו אליהו מווילנא (הגר"א)

The Vilna Gaon

(1720–1797)

Elijah ben Solomon Zalman, known as the Vilna Gaon, or genius scholar of Vilna, Lithuania, was without question the greatest mind in the long intellectual history of Jewish sages. Contemporary rabbinical scholars liken his power of thought to the RAM (Random-Access Memory) of modern computers.

His influence on the development of Jewish intellectual and religious thought is undeniable, but his effect on the non-Jewish world is negligible. Why then include a cloistered ghetto cleric in the list of the most influential Jews in world history? The Vilna Gaon is the last of the great rabbis of what has been called the heroic age. With his contemporaries Moses Mendelssohn, the secular philosopher of the German Enlightenment, and Israel Baal Shem Tov, the founder of the ecstatic Hasidic movement, the Vilna Gaon represents the third course of Jewish religious development of the era, the pinnacle of rabbinical study of the Torah and its teachings. These three great eternal thinkers shaped modern Judaism at the dawn of the industrial age and made the religion what it is now.

The Gaon was one of the most remarkable prodigies in Jewish history. It is said that he began dedicated study of the Talmud, the commentaries on Jewish law, at age six, and was lecturing on its tractates (legal and moral expositions) at Vilna's main synagogue a year later. At eighteen he married a wealthy woman. They produced sons, and she provided him with comfort, no necessity to work to make a living, only to study Talmud eighteen hours a day, every day, year after year, until his death at seventy-eight. He never accepted any official positions. He did not have to; he only studied, wrote, declared. He became the undisputed leader of the traditional Eastern European Jews or Mitnagdim.

This ascetic genius, like Maimonides, appreciated the value of scientific learning to amplify one's understanding of Jewish law. He urged students to study Hebrew translations of science and mathematics texts. This was revolutionary and brought Talmudic study into touch with the mainstream of society. However, he insisted that such study must always be at the service, never defiant, of the law.

He revised the Jewish prayerbook, discarding thousands of years of poetry and introduced singing into religious services. Much of the Ashkenazic music pious Jews know today dates from the time of the Vilna Gaon.

Why did this genius demand of himself such rigorous and lengthy daily study? It was said that if the Gaon did not study eighteen hours a day, then other rabbis in the rest of Europe would study less—and forget what would happen to the assimilated Jew!

His piety was matched by a brutal, cold logic and an unparalleled memory of Scripture and commentary. He was never afraid to point out inconsistencies in the Talmud and suggest his own rational solutions. His analytic method anticipated by two centuries today's academic approach to the under-standing of Jewish law.

He barely ever slept. His sons said he needed only two hours a day. The Gaon often put his feet in cold water to stay awake while he studied and wrote.

When faced with the almost fanatic enthusiasm of the Hasidic movement and its tradition of wandering teachers, wild in their ecstasy of prayer, he urged persecution. The Gaon thought the Hasidic stress on praying to God with fervor, an almost mad passion, menaced traditional study of religious law. The Hasidic movement, however, brought the common man into the fold in a way that the reclusive Vilna Gaon could not and would not accept. He issued documents of excommunication, insisting that it was not proper to have anything to do with the Hasidim.

This schism in religious thought would only be healed after his death (there is a well-known tale that the Hasidim danced on his grave) when the threat of the Haskalah or Jewish Enlighten-ment threatened orthodoxy.

47

Henri Bergson

(1859–1941)

Born in Paris of a Polish musician father and an Irish-English mother, Henri Bergson was one of the most influential philosophers of his era. The Bergsonian worldviews of time, evolution, memory, freedom, perception, mind and body, intuition, intellect, mysticism, and society deeply affected the thought and writings of 20th century European politicians and authors. The Jewish novelist Marcel Proust, the Irish playwright and critic George Bernard Shaw, the American philosopher William James, and the English philosopher Alfred North Whitehead all acknowledged Bergson's profound influence. Along with Jean-Paul

179

Sartre, Bergson is revered as one of the leading French philosophers of contemporary times.

Bergson's philosophy was so attractive and popular due to his marvelous style as a writer and his ability to construct analogies which could be readily understood. Yet despite his 1927 Nobel Prize for literature, his flair for writing was criticized by some as too rhapsodic, his philosophy lacking precise justification or scientific proof.

Bergson could not have minded such criticism for he believed that the expression of his ideas demanded a new approach. No mechanical or material outlook would do. Time, for example, was not only a scientific concept that could be measured like the sand in an hourglass. Theories of natural science could not explain the way people directly experience time. The standard units of time measured by a clock were fine to express seconds, minutes, hours, and years. Much of what we do is marked by what time it is, what time has passed, and what time it will be.

For Bergson, however, time was not simply a unit measured by a machine, but a flow of life, what he called "pure" time or *durée reele* (real duration). Time is experienced not in spaces but as a continuing whirl, flowing inevitably. Trying to represent time in an abstract or spatial manner lessens our understanding of what we are. Unlike the great Descartes who stated "I think, therefore, I am," Bergson urged that "I am something which continues."

Bergson's concept of duration was revolutionary. Many philosophers since the ancient Greek Plato had assumed that time was an illusion, finite now and eternity all the same. Spinoza, for example, had represented reality as an aspect of the everlasting. Bergson viewed time in its durational aspect. When one contemplates time in its real duration, knowing that one is acting freely and not as an automaton, then personal freedom is achieved. Man's acts are never free until they are spontaneous, arising out of one's personality at that moment.

Bergson did not develop like many other great philosophers, uttering forth at a young age a grand philosophical system. Rather, he patiently addressed in a series of books single subjects, submitting all to his concept of time.

To understand the connection between the spiritual and the material, how our minds and bodies operate together, Bergson

sought to fathom the workings of memory. The brain, he asserted, is not a great storehouse of information, but rather a filter
that retains only what we practically need to go on. Indeed, the
brain works more to forget than to remember. Only man possesses consciousness or pure memory—the ability to remember
only what is needed. Man's pure memory unites with a quality
common to all living things, instinct or "habit memory," in a
uniquely human synthesis of remembrance.

Bergson also investigated how the intellect works. Likening
the intellect to his concept of time, he noted the "cinematic
method" of the intellect, a living and continuous motion picture,
consisting of individual static frames, understood one by one, but
also in a great kaleidoscopic wave. Although the intellect carves
up everything into easily recognizable pieces and remains outside
of what it knows, intuition allows the mind to wade into a sea of
consciousness, flowing without end, of never-ending duration,
becoming *part of* what it knows, producing knowledge absolutely.
Bergson recognized that intuition arises not necessarily from
flashes of inspiration, but rather from a heightened form of
thinking.

Expanding his concepts of time, mind and matter, intuition
and intellect, Bergson analyzed evolution. He felt that philosophy
must be added to biological history. Bergson believed that an
original impetus of life, the "vital impetus," gave force to all
living things. Such impetus was derived from human creativity.

Bergson's professional life was largely spent teaching metaphysics in French schools of higher education, culminating in a
position at the Académie Française. He served also as a diplomat
during the First World War and as an official at the League of
Nations.

Toward the end of his life, Bergson was drawn to the
teachings of the Roman Catholic Church. To be one with God was
only possible through a special intuition, akin to what is known as
mysticism. However, people are blocked by their everyday routine, strife, struggle to make a living, to stay alive, to reach very
often this special state of blissful consciousness. Although drawn
to Christian mystical thought, Bergson as a figure of international prominence during the Nazi era could not bring himself to
convert, remaining Jewish publicly for the rest of his life.

48

The Baal Shem Tov

(1700–1760)

Sometimes when religious or political movements become unresponsive to human needs, a great yearning for simplicity, a rebellious spirit, infects the common people, and they seek change. In the early eighteenth century, most Jews in Eastern Europe lived in small villages with little hope for any material comfort. Jewish society then favored the learned, the most highly skilled. Villages were run by families of wealthy merchants, rabbis, and lawyers. The poor were powerless before the might of the grand village councils.

Into this community of half of the world's Jews, led by oligarchy and oppression, was born the Baal Shem Tov, or the Master of the Divine Name. Israel ben Eliezer was a poor man, a wanderer, an orphan, a teacher's assistant, a Podolian lime digger, an innkeeper, a jack-of-all-trades, a maker of amulets, a faith healer. Most of the stories of his life were retold by his followers, simple tales woven into miraculous legends. He left no writings. We know of his wondrous deeds only through the recollections of disciples. Yet his influence on the development of modern Judaism is enormous. Along with the development of orthodox rabbinic Jewish thought culminating in the Vilna Gaon and the liberalization led by the Enlightenment philosopher Moses Mendelssohn, the Besht (the acronym for Baal Shem Tov), supplied the heart, brought ecstasy to prayer, passion to dry words of devotion.

To some contemporaries, the Besht was a leader of heretics, similar to the followers of the false messiah Sabbatai Zevi, or the mad Jacob Frank, who preached free love and later converted his group en masse to Catholicism. But the common people adored the Besht. He preached that anyone could commune with God. Scholarship was not as important as piety. Only through total abandonment of the self via spiritual exaltation would the righteous gain heavenly grace. Anyone could pray, even if he was not the most learned. The whistle of a simpleton reached straight to Heaven, carrying with it the prayers of a community.

To the Besht, since God was everywhere, from the lowly slug to the most magnificent forest, all was joy, happiness surrounded every living thing. God commanded us to be joyful, to sing and dance, to feel with each ounce of our beings his wondrous bounty. Hasidic prayer meetings were therefore very noisy affairs. He taught that Heaven lay behind the sacred words available to anyone who trusted the rapture of prayer to lead the way.

One of his most fundamental creations, the *tzaddik,* was used by his followers to create great dynasties of rabbis, some of which have continued to the present day (for example, the Lubavitcher Hasidic movement traces its origins back to the late eighteenth century and the disciples of the Besht). A *tzaddik* was a superior person whose unique righteousness brought him specially close to God. The *tzaddik* could even intercede with the divine will. The Baal Shem Tov's successors, Dov Baer and Rabbi Nachman of

Bratislava, contributed mightly to the expansion of the political importance of the *tzaddik,* also called the rebbe, whose spiritual values were the exemplar of his community, and the bearer of sacred gifts.

After the death of the Baal Shem Tov, Eastern European Jewry was for many years divided between his ecstatic ideals and his more traditional opponents led by the Vilna Gaon. The Hasidim dubbed his followers Mitnagdim, "opponents" of their greater joy. The Jewish Middle Ages ended in the conflict between the Hasidim and the Mitnagdim, later becoming relatively meaningless before the specter of the secular Jewish Enlightenment or Haskalah. Hasids concentrated more on Talmudic study. This brought them closer to mainstream custom and away from the raptures of the Besht. For without his pipe-smoking presence, apart from his physical example, some structure was required.

Yet his lessons remain the loving essence of Judaism. There is no greater joy than performing the commandments of God.

49

Felix Mendelssohn

(1809–1847)

Jacob Ludwig Felix Mendelssohn, grandson of the sage of the German Enlightenment, Moses Mendelssohn, was one of the most gifted and influential musicians of the 1800s. Child prodigy, virtuoso pianist, innovative conductor and pioneering administrator, composer of Romantic music of great classical beauty and restraint, Mendelssohn in a short period of time changed the way music is composed, played, and listened to. Mendelssohn's life is also symbolic of the rise of the nineteenth-century Jew out of centuries of oppression and degradation to the most enlightened level of expression, embodied in a personality of gentility and compassion.

Like his grandfather, Felix always strove to illuminate, to

express with the greatest clarity. Although his music often has literary or geographic reference (in keeping with the Romantic movement), it is tempered by a close attention to classical form. His *Violin Concerto*, beloved as the finest work of its kind, is the most perfect example of the fusion of the classical with the Romantic. Mendelssohn has been rightly compared to the great German poet Goethe for a unique combination of classical and Romantic influences. Although we hear echoes of Bach, Handel, Mozart, and Beethoven in his music, Mendelssohn also served as a model for many of the composers who followed him, including Wagner, Brahms, Dvořák, and Mahler.

Felix was born into a home of considerable wealth and influence. His father, Abraham, was a northern German banker who provided his family with a luxurious home made richer by the musical activities of his children. Felix's two sisters and brother were talented musicians who participated in the frequent family musicales organized around their prodigy sibling. In particular, his sister Fanny was an extraordinary pianist and composer as well as her famous brother's lifelong confidante.

Felix Mendelssohn was probably the greatest child prodigy in the history of music, including Mozart. Like Mozart, he had a keyboard-playing sister who aided his development and served as a sounding board for his ideas. Like Mozart, he was exposed early to the most important literary, artistic, and musical figures of his youth, in Mendelssohn's case, Goethe, the philosopher Hegel, and the composer-pianists Muzio Clementi, Ignaz Moscheles, and John Field. From the supreme German poet, Goethe, Felix was influenced to combine classical formal design with pure aristocratic expression.

By hiring large groups of professional musicians to come to their home and audition the teenager's works, Mendelssohn's father enabled Felix to mature much earlier than normal (even for great composers). A series of string symphonies composed in his early teens was followed at ages sixteen and seventeen respectively with the great chamber work *Octet* and the overture to Shakespeare's *A Midsummer Night's Dream*. The *Octet* and overture are so advanced harmonically and melodically that it is almost impossible to believe they were written by someone so young. It is also amazing to realize that when these works were written, Beethoven was still alive in Vienna writing his tortured final works. From his materially more comfortable perch, Mendelssohn, even before Berlioz and Schumann, Wagner and Liszt, set the musical stage for the rise of Romantic music. Although influenced by Beethoven in the use of the orchestra and formal patterns, Mendelssohn restored color and lightness to the musical palette. The Sturm und Drang of Haydn and Beethoven was relieved by a more pastoral outlook. Mendelssohn's music is so much more soothing and comforting for its relaxed line and easy grace.

At the Berlin Singing Academy the boy Felix had been exposed not only to Beethoven but remarkably to older music, most notably that of Johann Sebastian Bach. Bach was not then widely known except to the most learned musicians. Exposure to Bach's richly multilayered compositions enriched the free use of counterpoint in Mendelssohn's rapidly developing style.

An important result was Mendelssohn's revival of Bach's great masterpiece the *Saint Matthew Passion* in 1829. This first performance of the work since Bach's death seventy-nine years before permanently established the reputation of the great baroque composer and was the true beginning of an awareness and attention to music written earlier than the contemporary.

In Mendelssohn's time, concerts usually consisted of variety programs consisting of short, light pieces, individual movements from larger works, and always new music written by the performer, rarely an interpretation of an older master's work. When Mendelssohn took over the Gewandhaus concerts in Leipzig at the age of twenty-six, he changed forever how concerts are presented. Complete works were offered, famed soloists (such as Liszt and the Russian Anton Rubinstein) were featured, and the great masters revered.

Mendelssohn the conductor also shaped the Gewandhaus orchestra into a precision unit which played together and in tune, directed by him alone; one interpretative body, not several. He was the first modern conductor. Before Mendelssohn, conducting was largely limited to cues from the first violin. Mendelssohn used arm movements to mark beats, prodded dynamic reactions from his players, and supplied a continuing pulse and direction to the music.

He also organized the Leipzig Conservatory, the first great music academy. The faculty included the finest teachers including the immortal composer Robert Schumann and his great pianist wife, Clara Schumann. Mendelssohn traveled widely, celebrating his trips in Romantic works depicting his favorite places. The *Fingal's Cave* or *Hebrides Overture, Scotch* and *Italian* symphonies, evoked colorful European geography and culture. These works are early examples of a kind of nationalistic music which would dominate many of the emerging nations on the continent.

In addition, Mendelssohn championed the music of his contemporaries such as Chopin, Liszt, and always his dear friend Schumann. Mendelssohn also wrote extensive music for plays, elevating the incidental to the essential. With Bach and Handel as his guides, he composed oratorios on biblical subjects. His *Elijah* and *Saint Paul* generated such enthusiasm, in England particularly, that dozens of oratorio societies sprang up almost overnight, local communities competing with each other in quasi-religious celebrations of his music. The nineteenth-century oratorio, which definitely has its roots in Mendelssohn via Bach and Handel, dominated Victorian music making.

Mendelssohn's religious life is emblematic of the nineteenth-century German Jew. Grandson of the most influential Jewish philosopher after Maimonides and Spinoza, Felix converted at age seven to the Lutheran Church. His father later urged him to add the Christian surname Bartholdy after Mendelssohn as a kind of badge of assimilation. Although many of his compositions bear the name Mendelssohn-Bartholdy, and he considered himself a Protestant, his Jewish heritage was never forgotten. Mendelssohn considered Christianity a logical extension of his Judaism. Furthermore, virulent anti-Semitism was encountered in Berlin, and despite Prussian laws granting Jews political freedoms, greater equality and acceptance lay through conversion. Assimilation and wealth opened many doors for Mendelssohn. However, not satisfied with an easy bourgeois life, he worked feverishly in many fields with astonishing success and influence. Despite a happy marriage to the daughter of a Calvinist pastor and being father to five children, Mendelssohn was shattered by the death of his beloved sister Fanny. He suffered a series of strokes, dying at age thirty-eight, the most acclaimed musician in Europe.

50

Louis B. Mayer

(1885–1957)

Zukor, Laemmle, Goldwyn, Cohn, Thalberg, Loew, Fox, Lasky, Schenck, Mayer—these are some of the names of the Jewish men who created the American motion-picture business. Of all of them, the most influential on U.S. and world culture was surely Louis B. Mayer, head of the Tiffany of studios, Metro-Goldwyn-Mayer or M-G-M.

Intense in everything he did, fiercely patriotic, paternalistic, excessive in his passions, both love and hate, Mayer ran his studio like an extended family in which he was a doting, overbearing, omnipresent Big Daddy.

Born in Russia, unsure of his birthday (like so many Eastern European refugees), each year Mayer chose July Fourth as his special day of celebration. Supporter of Republican right-wing causes and figures from William Randolph Hearst to Senator Joseph McCarthy, Mayer set the political stage for the acceptability of blacklists of suspected Communist sympathizers by the Hollywood establishment in the 1950s. In an attempt in 1927 to form an organization to mediate labor disputes in the film industry, Mayer organized the Academy of Motion Pictures Arts & Sciences, whose annual awards defined Hollywood and its stars—at the same time influencing the public to view those movies that garnered the most Oscars.

Mayer's extreme rages led to a worldview in which men and women were either idealized or rarefied creatures like his megastar Greta Garbo or down-home, American-as-apple-pie townsfolk like the juvenile Mickey Rooney (in the *Andy Hardy* movies). "L.B.," as Mayer was affectionately known at M-G-M, lost his mother at an early age. It has been suggested that his fascination with having his films depict mothers as deeply feeling, caring matrons resulted from his loss of Sarah Mayer when he felt he needed her most. In Neil Gabler's words, the Jewish immigrants who headed the major film studios not only "invented Hollywood," but before the touting of "family values" by politicians of recent vintage, the movies of M-G-M helped create in the national psyche a utopian view of the home.

Mayer's origins were humble. His father, Jacob, was a peddler, seling scrap metal in a small town in New Brunswick, Canada. Leaving Canada in his late teens, L.B. sought his fortune in Boston. At the age of nineteen he married the daughter of a respected cantor and then worked at several odd jobs until purchasing and renovating a small burlesque house in Haverhill a village north of Boston. Mayer changed the name of the theater, introduced silent movies to the area, and with his profits, purchased other local theaters. Soon his chain of movie houses produced sufficient cash flow to enable him to become a distributor. When in 1915 he purchased the New England distribution rights to D.W. Griffith's *Birth of a Nation*, Mayer had reached the big time, earning a return ten times his initial investment. This first stupendous movie gave him a financial base first to go into theatrical production (a false start), then to travel out west to Los Angeles to make movies.

Arriving in Hollywood in 1918 at the age of thirty-three, Mayer found a society wide open to entrepreneurs. Most of the world's silent movies were made in the still rustic canyons of greater Los Angeles. Over seventy small film companies vied for the public's attention. Production costs were low, and the post-World War I economy supplied the necessary capital and audience to support a new industry.

Mayer's first great starlet, Anita Stewart, appeared in romantic features which brought Mayer's small film company, Metro Pictures, wide attention. In 1924 the powerful theater owner Marcus Loew purchased Metro, and Mayer became its executive vice-president. Metro then merged with Goldwyn Pictures (named after Samuel Goldwyn, its found and former owner—whose name, Goldwyn, was originally Goldfish). By 1926, the company became Metro-Goldwin-Mayer, with mayer its chief officer.

The studio chose as its motto *Ars Gartia Artis,* or art for art's sake. Quality filmmaking with such stars as Greta Garbo, Clark Gable, Joan Crawford, Robert Taylor, William Powell, Jean Harlow, Myrna Loy, Melvyn Douglas, and the actor's actor, Spencer Tracy (especially in the remarkable productions of Mayer's wunderkind Irving Thalberg—the model for F. Scott Fitzgerald's *The Last Tycoon*) earned the highest regard of the movegoing public. In the 1940s and 1950s the remarkable M-G-M musicals expanded Broadway theatrical forms into uniquely cinematic compositions of sound, dance,a nd color. even Mayer's personal life affected movie history. His daughter Edith married David O. Selznick, the son of L.B.'s former employer, Lewis Selznick and the creator of the most influential movie of all time, *Gone With the Wind.*

Mayer's Hollywood displayed to the world in simple and direct images the primacy of the home in the making of American culture and values. But it was a home idealized in a Mark Twain setting more Tom Sawyer than Huck Finn. His studio also recorded lush Art Deco escapism representing an urban, aggressive, yet stylized new America rushing into modernity. For millions all around the world, Mayer's M-G-M made the dynamic American ethic desirable, respected, and envied.

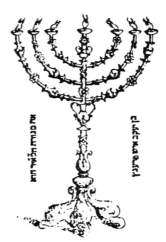

51 *Judah Halevy*

(ca. 1075–1141)

Judah Halevy, philosopher and poet, thought of himself as the harp for all the songs of Zion. Living during the turmoil of medieval Spain, Halevy was the greatest poet of what is now considered the golden age of Spanish Jewry. His *Songs of Zion* and his work of philosophy, *The Book of Argument and Proof in Defense of the Despised Faith,* known today as *The Book of the Kuzari* (or Khazars), continue to influence Jewish, and in particular, Israeli thought. After King Solomon and the Spanish religious poet and philosopher Solomon ibn Gabirol, and before Heinrich Heine and Marcel Proust, Halevy was probably the most important of all Jewish literary figures.

In the eleventh and twelfth centuries, Spain was mired in bloody religious wars. Christian armies slowly worked their way south as Muslim forces led by the fanatical Almohads out of Africa slashed northward, forcing Jews caught between to choose conversion, exile, or death. At the time of Halevy's birth, Toledo fell to the Christians. Throughout his life, Spain was disrupted by sudden shifts in power, cities observing the Prophet's precepts one day and the Gospel of Christ the next.

In the midst of all this turmoil, Halevy composed more than eight hundred poems. His subjects were those then most common in Spanish Jewish poetry: love, lament, lyricism, piety, and Zion. Possessing an extraordinary vitality, richness, and strength, they are unique treasures of European literature.

After a brief stay in Granada, Halevy wandered for twenty years (often accompanied by his friend the writer Abraham ibn Ezra). Halevy's travels as a stranger in a strange land are reflected in his poetic longings to return to Erez Israel. He did not believe Jews could be safe anywhere in the Diaspora, and preached an immediate return to the Holy Land. If Jews were not safe in glorious Spain, having prospered for hundreds of years despite their relatively small numbers (with a success comparable in many ways to the Jewish communities of nineteenth-century Germany and today's America), they were in danger everywhere but Israel. His call for a Return made him the first major Zionist. Poems of Zion, the so-called Zionides, reveal Halevy's intense pain and dreams. Spanish life made Jews slaves and betrayers of God. Inner freedom and redemption could be found only by emigrating to their homeland.

Dating from his early years in Córdoba, spent in a milieu of art and lovemaking, Halevy's paeans to love and drinking wine remain his most quoted works. Derived from forms prevalent in contemporary Arabic poetry, these erotic verses contain musically rich wordplays and imagery from nature.

He also composed just under two hundred eulogies to well-known people of his time, couched in elaborate language, grand and euphonious. Intellect and emotion were bundled together in powerfully poetic embraces of expression.

Halevy's 350 *piyyutim* or religious poems celebrated Jewish festivals, devotion to God, Judaism's special place in civilization, its superiority and loneliness, and the tragedy of separation from and a gnawing desire for redemption in the Holy Land.

The Book of the Kuzari, Halevy's only book of philosophy, rages against Aristotelian logic, Christianity, and Islam. Set in a question-and-answer format, the work presents the king of the Khazars in discussion with a Hellenic philosopher and Jewish, Christian, and Muslim representatives, seeking to determine for his people the one true and proper faith. After exposing the spiritual vacuum beneath Greek logic (all the time admiring it), Halevy acknowledges the debt of Christianity and Islam to Jewish sources while declaring their subsequent history as invalid. Halevy's views have been called racist by some. Yet the *Kuzari,* as it is commonly known, has exerted enormous influence on Jewish thinkers, from the kabbalists and Hasidic masters to twentieth-century philosophers such as Franz Rosenzweig and Abraham Isaac Kook.

Most historians believe that Halevy in his final years journeyed to Erez Israel only to die on route in Egypt. A tale persists however that Judah Halevy, the bard of the Diaspora, on the last day of life did finally make his way to Jerusalem, bent to kiss its sacred stones, only to be trampled to death by an Arab horseman.

52

Haym Salomon

(1740–1785)

He died penniless at the age of forty-five. Several years after Haym Salomon's death in 1785, his son Haym Moses claimed that the government owed his family restitution. Indeed, Haym Moses urged, his father had loaned General Washington, the Continental Army, and several Founding Fathers more than $354,000, had in fact financed the Revolution. The U.S. government has never recognized the Salomon claim.

Many in the Sephardic community, however, have long claimed Haym Salomon, Revolutionary War patriot, as one of their own, for Salomon had married into the Franks family of Philadelphia, Pennsylvania, a distinguished and prominent group of Sephardis. Yet Haym was Ashkenazic, born in Lissa, Poland.

Other legend has it that Salomon was a kind of American Rothschild, skilled in the financial complexities of European commerce. It was said that Salomon, the financier of American freedom, was as rich as Midas, with a bottomless well of fortune. In reality, Salomon, skilled in over a half dozen languages, worked first selling dry goods in New York, then at the request of Philip Schuyler, peddled supplies to the troops upstate at Lake George, and later worked as a broker selling war bonds, employed by the Philadelphia financier Robert Morris.

It has also been promoted that Salomon, as a personal lender to Washington, Jefferson, Madison, Monroe, Randolph, and the Polish patriots Kosciusko and Pulaski, had saved these Founding Fathers from penury. James Madison (who for most of his career had difficulty making ends meet) was truly one of Salomon's most famous debtors. Madison initially referred to Salomon as a "Jew broker." However, when his creditor did not call the loan, Madison softened, recognizing Salomon's kindness and unwillingness to be usurious.

Whether he was "just a broker," although an extraordinary one at that, there can be no dispute that Salomon was a patriot. Before he displayed patriotism through financial prowess, Salomon was arrested as a spy by the British for attempting to blow up the royal fleet in New York Harbor, then escaped for a better-paying job with Morris.

Many other Jews left their patriotic mark on the American Revolution (although there were also some Tories among them), despite the fact that during the eighteenth century their population in the British colonies in America was small. David Salisbury Frank, a relative of Salomon's wife, was implicated in the notorious Benedict Arnold matter (and later vindicated). Francis Salvador, a plantation owner from South Carolina, was the first person of Jewish origin to die during the rebellion (scalped by Indians after an ambush near Charleston). Barnard Gratz, an immigrant from Upper Silesia, frequently ran the British blockade, providing much-needed materials to the continental forces. Lastly, Benjamin Nones, a French Jew, came to America, volunteered for Washington's army, and was dubbed the "Jewish Lafayette" for his brave service in Pulaski's regiment.

Yet, when people think of Jewish patriots of the American Revolution, they most often speak of Haym Salomon and for good reason. Whether or not he "financed" the Revolution is beside the point. As Robert Morris's most able broker trading in government notes, Salomon raised fabulous sums for the cause while making himself huge profits. Some say he became (next to Morris) the richest man in the emerging nation. Salomon traded not only in securities but also in commodities. His trading network was so extensive that he became in his words "generally known to the mercantile part of North America."

The most persistent tale of his largesse took place on Kol Nidre, 1779, when a messenger from General Washington arrived with a plea for Salomon at the Mikveh Israel Congregation in Philadelphia. The troops, it was related, had not received their pay for many months, the army was about to disband, and the British were coming. Responding with mighty spirit and holy intention on this most sacred night of Jewish observance, Salomon organized a loan of $400,000 from his fellow congregants. Legend has it too that Haym put $240,000 of his own money into the kitty. Washington was then able to pay his soldiers their back wages and take the field.

Who knows if Washington would have won the war without Salomon's loan? However, it is clear that Haym Salomon, self-proclaimed Broker to the Office of Finance, was "useful to the public interest" in a time of desperate need in American history.

53

Roman victory
coin: "Judea
Captive."

Johanan ben Zakkai

(ca. 80 C. E.)

Legend has it that during the siege of Jerusalem by the Romans in 70 C.E. he was smuggled out in a coffin by students. The Jewish rebels, the Zealots, had sealed the city and were not letting anyone pass. The name of the students' master was the deputy head of the Sanherin, the Rabban, Johanan ben Zakkai.

Johanan ben Zakkai had opposed the rebellion. He did not believe in messianism, but in learning. He is justly credited with the preservation of Judaism, not grounded in sacrificial worship at the Temple in Jerusalem (destroyed by the Roman legions) but in the fortress of the Torah, of Jewish law.

This student of Hillel was considered by many Jews of his time to be a traitor. Upon his escape from Jerusalem, Johanan ben Zakkai ventured into the military camp of the Roman general

198

Vespasian. Pleased at the capture of so prominent a Jewish leader, Vespasian gave him an audience. The rabbi pleaded for asylum from the Zealots and predicted that Vespasian would become Caesar. "Give me Yavneh and its sages," said the rabbi. The Roman general (soon indeed to be declared emperor by his troops) granted the Rabban's request for the town near the coast west of Jerusalem called Yavneh (near modern-day Jaffa).

Under the auspices of the Roman authority, in a vineyard and on an upper story of a house, Johanan ben Zakkai established an academy in Yavneh for the study of Jewish law. Yavneh became for the first time in hundreds of years the center of Jewish thinking, one not located in Jerusalem. The initial codification of Jewish law and, most important in the history of western civilization, the putting of the Old Testament into final form, took place in Yavneh. The events of the Jewish calendar, including its wondrous festivals (Passover, Purim, and the like) and sacred holy days, were marked forever. The rabbinical court at Yavneh was for its people a house of judgment (*bet din*) and model for governance in the difficult dark ages that followed.

This retreat into the core of Judaism, away from futile battles with superior military powers, from the control of a central Temple in Jerusalem, and from the zealous yearning for a Messiah, gave the religion a new beginning. Johanan ben Zakkai, in the style of Hillel, urged simply that Jews not rush to tear down pagan altars. If you are planting a tree and someone rushes up to you and tells you the Messiah has arrived, continue planting, then go see. No more battles, no more sacrificial ritual, no more state, he urged—only study. Countless cultures would rise and be lost in the black centuries before the Renaissance. The Jews would survive, and it was because of this perspective, the example of Johanan ben Zakkai.

After the disastrous revolt of Simon Bar Kokhba in the next century, the academy ceased to exist at Yavneh, first transferred to the western Galilee, passed generation by generation through families of imposing patriarchs, then disappeared in the sandstorms of war and disruption. But its form of rabbinical government and its focus on study and the writing down and thus preservation of what had been a largely oral tradition, ensured the continuing development of Jewish life and influence on the world.

54

Arnold Schoenberg

(1874–1951)

The Austrian composer Arnold Schoenberg thought of himself as a kind of musical Moses. Schoenberg preached to his disciples musical laws achieved almost through divine inspiration. He brought forth out of the past only those musical techniques necessary for future creations. Schoenberg dictated that solely through strict obedience to his instruction would the faithful reach a promised land of perfectly ordered harmonies, melodies, and dissonances.

In the early 1920s, feeling he had exhausted traditional melodic and harmonic concepts, Schoenberg developed a method of musical composition later called twelve-tone, serial, or dodecaphonic music. His new system changed forever how composers think about composing.

Schoenberg's compositions and the works of many of his successors reflected his teachings. He believed that each tone possesses an expressive weight of its own, not reliant on traditional scales or melodic patterns. Rather, heightened expression was reachable only through a complex awareness of how musical lines interplay horizontally and vertically in the context always of a unified whole. Schoenberg sought an intellectual method of musical control, regulating with the utmost precision musical decision making—what form a piece would take. Only through this rigorous technique could the most intense expression be accomplished.

At the beginning of the twentieth century, Paris and Vienna were the two rival capitals of Europe. Vienna was a hotbed of new ideas, cultural clashes, and political unrest. Arnold Schoenberg was born there in 1874 and grew up in the city of Arthur Schnitzler's novellas, the great golden paintings of Gustav Klimt, the practical utility of the Secessionists (an artistic, architectural, and design movement that ignored Victorian sentimentality for rich pattern and color), Dr. Sigmund Freud's probing of the subconscious, and the titanic orchestrations of Gustav Mahler.

Vienna had been home to the composers Haydn, Mozart, Beethoven, Schubert, Brahms, and Johann Strauss, creators of many of the greatest works of classical tonality. Always interested in the study and teaching of their works, Schoenberg was intent on understanding and imparting just how their music worked. Like many of his generation, he was overwhelmed by the sorcery of the Richard Wagner of the operas *Tristan and Isolde* and *Parsifal*. Wagner's music in these works is highly chromatic, using chords that slip away from each other in a rich, harmonically liberated idiom. Wagnerian chromaticism provided a jumping-off place for Schoenberg's musical explorations. He sought a musical language that would impart extreme emotional states. Mahler's compositions also investigated similar feelings, but his sense of nature, love, death and resurrection were more lyrical than the younger Schoenberg's. However, although posterity has claimed Mahler as a greater composer, Schoenberg's tough brand of musical expressionism has had more lasting influence (at least in the short term).

The breakdown of classical tonality mirrored a corresponding breakdown of society. Listeners could find their way in works of the past. It was most often easy to understand, even on a superficial level, what the classic composers were saying. Beethoven's musical language was not far from common folk song; his expressions were a recognizable part of his culture. Schoenberg's music, on the other hand, seemed to most of his contemporaries separate and apart. Today's audience can recognize that he was putting into music the innermost feelings of his age; he was in essence recreating in sounds the tormented pulsing of a world about to go insane. Schoenberg's music to this day is disturbing and has not achieved popular success. It is as if he exposed in music a side of us we want to ignore. We hate him for writing with so much pain.

Born a Jew, raised a Catholic, Schoenberg converted to the Lutheran Church in his youth and back to Judaism in his old age. His search for religious identity paralleled his development as an artist. In his twenties he composed the ecstatic *Transfigured Night (Verklärte Nacht)* and the massive *Gurrelieder*. These works were touched by Wagner while remaining quite original. At the same time that Claude Debussy was composing his famous opera based on Maurice Maeterlinck's *Pelléas et Mélisande*, Schoenberg was composing an orchestral tone poem on the same subject. His *First String Quartet* and *Chamber Symphony* followed, displaying the same tendencies of stretching tonal resolutions over longer and longer time periods. The musical language of these works is overripe, excessive, and rich with symbolism. His *Three Piano Pieces* of 1909 are viewed today as the turning point in his artistic journey. For the first time in Western music every note and phrase had a separate purpose, liberated from conventional harmonic rules and expectations.

Schoenberg sought a technique or system that would organize all elements of musical composition. In the works that followed through the First World War he gradually amassed the creative materials to formulate the twelve-tone method. For the most part, these works contained ever more anguished emotions than his earlier ones. The short opera *Erwartung*, composed by Schoenberg in a delirious few days, and the fantastical *Pierrot Lunaire* for singer and chamber ensemble contain music of immeasurable density and weight. During this period Schoenberg also developed a way of speaking song called *Sprechstimme,* in which the singer declaims musical line in a limbo not quite song and not quite speech.

Schoenberg's reaction to the virulent anti-Semitism between the two great wars was to return to his Jewish roots in the oratorio *Jacob's Ladder,* the grand opera *Moses and Aron,* and the Holocaust memorial *A Survivor from Warsaw.* Schoenberg's later works made use of more tonal idioms, and is a kind of musical reconciliation expanded the expressive reach of his techniques.

Schoenberg's expressionism greatly influenced his students, most important of whom were Alban Berg, the composer of the seminal opera *Wozzeck,* and Anton von Webern, who wrote aphoristic pieces of immense postwar significance. Never part of the Viennese musical establishment, Schoenberg established the Society for the Private Performance of Music, which premiered many important works of the period, and established a segregated method of introducing new music away from the promotions of commercial concerts. The society was a forerunner of the many contemporary chamber music groups which dominated universities internationally for over forty years. With the rise of Nazism, Schoenberg fled to the United States, settling on the West Coast where as a destitute refugee he took private students to support his family, failed in an attempt to write film music, and then taught at the University of California at Los Angeles.

Schoenberg's influence spread to American composers, who viewed his compositional style as an ideal paragon of expression. The 1950s and 1960s were dominated by composers attempting to extend Schoenberg's revolution to all aspects of music. Many thought that the ability to organize every tone, pitch, color, and rhythm into a perfect unity could be reached only through logic and scientific analysis. Others seeking to write music that was more lyrical were abused by Schoenberg's academic followers as crass audience seekers chasing after applause with show-business tunes. A kind of cultural totalitarianism set in, separating audiences from new music and making the concert hall more museum than living theater.

Today, Schoenberg can almost be viewed as a musical Karl Marx and not as the Moses of his visions. His first true disciples, Berg and Webern, lived in the same era and composed music that truly expresses their time. Extreme states of feeling, psychotic episodes, and violence are the stuff their period's darkest night-mares were made of. The composition of neo-Expressionistic music after the Second World War during a long period of prosperity has seemed to most listeners just plain wrong and out of place. A wedge was created between Schoenberg's high culture and most concertgoers. Nevertheless, Arnold Schoenberg's true legacy still must be his freeing of tones from conventional expectations and his challenge to all music lovers not to remain complacent in the belief that what is beautiful is the expected.

55

Emile Durkheim

(1858–1917)

Emile Durkheim, the son of an Alsatian rabbi, was not only the founder of modern sociology, but with Freud, Marx, and Max Weber, one of the most profound thinkers of the nineteenth and early twentieth centuries. First at attempting to codify social science, Durkheim sought to explain rationally how societies develop and how people interact, divide their labor, become aware of values, learn restraint, resolve conflict, change together. His theories are mirrored and developed in the works of the French Jewish social scientist and philosopher Claude Lévi-Strauss.

205

Durkheim's theories of "collective representations" have been highly influential. He noted that ideas are often created by many and because of their common creation become forceful and binding. These group concepts are also referred to as the results of the "collective conscience" serving as the justification of laws and ethical behavior.

Many of Durkheim's studies reflect his obsession with morality. Highly influenced by Immanuel Kant's theories of moral obligations (and perhaps reacting to the bitter public events of his time), Durkheim sought to understand how societies could change in the service of justice. He urged that peoples living among one another must have a vision and understanding of humanity, not just for themselves but for other societies. This liberal humanism conflicts with Durkheim's often misunderstood persona as an agent of conservatism.

His life's work was centered in the ways in which society and individuals control their actions (or are controlled). Whether he studied suicide, Australian aborigines, educational methods, morality, law, or religion, Durkheim sought in each instance reconciliation and synthesis. How can man be free in the face of authority? Does tradition hamper choice? These were important questions first asked by Durkheim in a sociological context.

Durkheim viewed sociology as the result of history. Natural sciences had presented philosophers with a rational means to understand the world. The decline of monarchy and the rise of democratic regimes brought crisis and radical change to modern society. With scientific analysis, such change could be studied and analyzed. Durkheim studied the causes of breakdown in the old order and the reasons for the ascent of the new.

His philosophy of social change has been considered problematic by some. Durkheim's ideas were not readily identifiable or simply translated. He ignored the writings of Karl Marx, perhaps terrified at communist visions of brutal class conflict. Durkheim approximated answers, more willing to explain the gray than to draw in black outline.

The most appealing aspect of his work is a concern with healing. Often using medical symbols, Durkheim attempted to understand how societies interact or personalities develop for the just purpose of improving life.

His studies on the division of labor in primitive and developed societies and problems in personality development discussed in his work on suicide have also been highly influential, and show Durkheim's concern with curing. Primitive societies, he argued, have a kind of "mechanical solidarity" in which labor is barely divided, everyone helping each other in a ritual of interdependence. Personal decisions are rigidly sublimated to the will of the group. In more developed societies, labor is divided into many specialities and an "organic" solidarity takes hold, regulated by a much needed and complex judicial system to settle conflicts and impose direction. Similarly the act of suicide was viewed by Durkheim in its relationship to society and therapy. A suicide may be in the service of a cause (such as the altruistic death of a soldier on a suicide mission), or brought about by a belief that the society has totally disintegrated, been separated away, or justified by an ego shut off from the company and solace of other people.

Educated in law, philosophy, anthropology, and social science, Durkheim, despite being Jewish in a snobbishly anti-Semitic culture, had a very successful career in education. Like many of the important people of his day, he attended the Ecole Normale (one year behind the great French Jewish philosopher, Henri Bergson). After working from 1882 to 1887 in secondary schools (a prerequisite in France at the time for a position in higher education), Durkheim began teaching the first university course in social science at the University of Bordeaux. In 1896 the university created for him its first professorship and university chair in the new discipline of sociology. Durkheim went to Paris in 1902 to teach at the Sorbonne, where he spent the remainder of his life.

France's defeat by Germany in 1870, the Dreyfus affair, and the First World War defined Durkheim's philosophical outlook and the direction of his work. The fall of the Second Empire in 1870 and the establishment of the Third French Republic wrought immense social changes. The Dreyfus affair of the 1890s divided France's intellectuals into warring camps. Durkheim, a private and studious man, firmly and publicly came to Dreyfus's aid. For this, Durkheim's classes were disrupted and his life threatened. Later, the disintegration of the world as he had known it in the trenches of the First World War proved overwhelming, contributing to his death.

56

Betty Friedan

(b. 1921)

Born Betty Naomi Goldstein to Harry and Miriam (Horowitz) Goldstein in Peoria, Illinois, educated at Smith College, married in 1947 to Carl Friedan, the mother of three children, divorced in 1969, activist, best-selling author, professor, a founder of the National Organization for Women (NOW), the National Women's Political Caucus, and the First Women's Bank, researcher, journalist, Democrat, clinical psychologist, and grandmother, Betty Friedan was the most influential feminist of the postwar era. Deemed by Marilyn French and others as an "initiator of the 'second wave' of feminism," Friedan's writings and lectures, including the highly influential books *The Feminine Mystique* and *The Second Stage*, synthesized women's views on what equality meant and how women could achieve the right to choose, not only to have children but how to live and work. For over twenty-five years from the early 1960s, Friedan was a powerful spokesperson, always seeking rational, caring discussion and solutions, not just dogma.

The first push for equal rights for women ended in 1920 with the granting of the right to vote. Despite Emma Goldman's pleas that voting rights would not solve their problems, the American women's movement before the Second World War largely failed to carry on the fight (although the Equal Rights Amendment or ERA was first presented to Congress in 1923). The tremendous push to secure the ballot box had exhausted the suffragettes and given them a false sense of security.

When the war against fascism ended two decades later, four million women lost their jobs to returning GIs. Women were again told that their place was in the home. The freedom to work to build up and defend their nation was over. Men would earn the family's bread. What the boys needed was a warm place to come home to every night. Ironically, American soldiers had accepted some of the same values toward women (*Kinder, Küche, Kirche*— children, kitchen, church) as the Nazis they thought they had defeated.

The contemporary women's liberation movement began not in the 1960s as many believe, but gradually in those postwar years. Women in small groups started a process of consciousness raising and examining their history. The publication in 1963 of Betty Friedan's *The Feminine Mystique* crystalized the concerns raised by that process, igniting a worldwide movement not just for women, but for human rights.

The feminist historian Ginette Castro notes that *The Feminine Mystique* developed out of a desire to prove that it was possible to combine work with the home. Identifying "the problem that has no name," Friedan posited that American women were tired out and driven to boredom due to lives without any interests other than housekeeping and raising children. Friedan had lost a job as a newspaper reporter because she had requested maternity leave. In the magazines she then contributed to, Friedan noticed that stories about real women's lives were ignored, while fantasies about the "Happy Housewife Heroine" were eagerly sought. She dubbed the myth of the perfect domestic wife the "Feminine Mystique."

Castro remarks that Friedan's first goal in her book was to debunk the myth of this "new religion of femininity." Women were not special "Wife-Mother" goddesses, but victims of a system structured to subjugate them. Victims of a "Housewife's Syndrome," their only identity could be found in what objects (things and children) they possessed. "Imprisoned in a comfortable concentration camp," they had "forfeited" their self. Some women who found pride in their roles as housewives deeply resented Friedan's definitions, but the book struck a chord of outrage among many, and woke up a generation.

Her background in psychology also gave Friedan the tools to attack the sexual advice of certain followers of Freud. These post-Freudians, she asserted, overemphasized the importance of sexual fulfillment in a cult of the orgasm. Sex was not a substitute, Friedan urged, for self-realization as a person.

Neither were a woman's possessions the answer to her life's work. Housework had to be regarded for what it was—and finished "as quickly and efficiently as possible," said Friedan. Marriage and motherhood were not the culmination of all of a woman's goals, but part of a human being's life. More important was the knowledge that she can think for herself, work productively in her chosen field, mean something in her society beyond the home.

Friedan's first book energized the fledgling women's movement into a revolution in search of identity and place. It gave activist women a purpose and a direction, serving as a highly influential generator of future ideas.

The 1960s were busy years for Friedan. In 1966 she helped found NOW and acted as its president through 1970. One of the most visible feminists of her time, Friedan picketed, lectured, debated, stood up as one of the foremost "Women's Libbers," as they were somewhat disparagingly called then. Her liberal positions on issues were however often confused with those of radical feminists like Kate Millett or Ti-Grace Atkinson. As Friedan was to show in her three later books, *It Changed My Life,* and especially the wonderful *The Second Stage* and *The Fountain of Age,* she sought, in a consistent way, to free *all* people, young and old, from themselves.

Her later books posed difficult questions. Recognizing that in the increasingly difficult economy of the 1980s and beyond, men were doubting the purposes of having a career, whether "working hard" always translated into success. She related her fascinating experiences of working with the military at West Point, seeing in women's entry into our fighting force a symbol of the developing "personhood of women." Friedan rejected the "sexual politics" of many of the radical and lesbian feminists as deflecting the true purposes of their common rebellion. If love was improved between the sexes, then all of their relations would be equal. In caring and humane observations, Friedan the grandmother identified the family and men as partners in the journey toward equality. In Erica Jong's words, Betty Friedan wanted to bring women to their "senses," to recognize what was important so that they could do their important work and face their own truths. After all the rhetoric died down, people would be left to their own "evolving human condition."

No longer were the issues only about women caught in a mystique that robbed them of their humanity. The elderly too were trapped in a culture that idealizes youth, carelessly discarding the old. Friedan's message was that ultimately we must all free ourselves from the myths that limit us, face the pain, fight back restraints, learn from our own pasts, and forge ahead, caring for what we do and those we love.

57

David Sarnoff

(1891–1971)

Davis Sarnoff, born into poverty in Uzlian, Russia, a shtetl in the province of Minsk, was the greatest visionary in the history of broadcasting. His administrative genius developed RCA (the Radio Corporation of America) and its subsidiary, NBC (the National Broadcasting Company) into the first great manufacturing and mass-communication conglomerate, a model for other electronics companies and, with Ford Motor Company as the only other possible exception, the largest American corporation to grow mostly as the result of one man's efforts.

212

Sarnoff, skilled in the workings of telegraphy and nationally famous for his reception of distress calls from the sinking S.S. *Titanic,* foresaw in 1915 the utility of every house in America owning a "Radio Music Box." In the early 1920s he became popularly known as the "wonder boy of the radio." Seizing in 1926 the opportunity to control the then unfettered airwaves, Sarnoff created the first coast-to-coast radio network. A modern Medici, he developed alongside moneymaking commercial shows cultural programing such as a highly influential sponsorship of Arturo Toscanini's NBC Symphony Orchestra. Recognized in 1944 by the Television Broadcasters Association as the "Father of American Television," no person did more than Sarnoff to further the development of the medium. Against intense resistance from many at RCA, he later forced the growth of color television.

In each instance his vision became reality, largely due to incomparable administrative skills and a brutally direct manner. Sarnoff changed the way people get to learn about and entertain each other. He helped to create and then foster the growth of a communications industry limited only by the seemingly infinite ideas of its great inventors. Sarnoff would not be shocked at the growing obsolescence of the network system. Information highways, satellite and cable broadcasting, interactive movies and computers, video games, virtual reality, holographic images as real as Princess Leia in *Star Wars,* are all children of the revolution in communications led by Sarnoff. It is not enough now for the world to sit back and just laugh at Jack Benny's routines on their Westinghouse radios or watch *Bonanza* on RCA wood-cased TV consoles. The earth became a global village when entrepreneurs such as Sarnoff found a way for us all to communicate quickly in sound and later with sight.

Sarnoff's background in tsarist Russia could not have been further away from the powerful executive suites he later inhabited at New York's Radio City. His father, Abraham, an itinerant house painter, emigrated to America in 1896, bringing over his young family four years later. David grew up in the squalor of New York's Lower East Side. Except for his early years in Russia studying Talmud for long hours six days a week, he had little schooling. Sarnoff had no childhood. His father was incapable of supporting the family, and by the age of ten, David was earning the family's bread by peddling Yiddish newspapers. Noting that he could earn more if he hired others and by selling to small vendors in need of distribution, Sarnoff created his first profitable network.

In 1906 the fifteen-year-old joined the Marconi Wireless Telegraph Company of America as an office boy. Working as a gofer for the great inventor of the wireless telegraph, Guglielmo Marconi himself, Sarnoff learned how to speak English without much of an accent, to read from scraps of newspaper, and to manage the intricacies of running the office and working its equipment.

He was made the manager of the Marconi station in Sea Gate, Brooklyn, and then became the operator of the company's telegraph equipment at Wanamaker's Department Store in Manhattan. In 1912 he was one of the few telegraph operators to hear a distress call from the S.S. *Olympic* 1,400 miles out in the frigid waters of the north Atlantic radioing, "S.S. *Titanic* ran into iceberg. Sinking fast." The twenty-one-year-old became known throughout the country over the next seventy-two-hour period as he relayed to the nation periodic reports received from the rescue ships at sea with radios. President William Howard Taft ordered radio silence so Sarnoff could have no signal interference. Congress and the nation recognized from the disaster that radio was no longer just a scientific oddity. Transmitters were made a requirement by federal law on all large ships. The ability to transmit SOS calls was now viewed as a necessity. Sarnoff was later to recall that ironically the *Titanic* disaster made radio important—and incidentally himself.

RCA, the creature of General Electric, Westinghouse, AT&T, and the United Fruit Company, acquired Marconi Wireless in 1919. Sarnoff became RCA's commercial manager, in 1926 formed NBC, in 1930 was made the conglomerate's president. Unlike his archrival William Paley of CBS, Sarnoff did not have an innate sensitivity to popular programing. His public position was that he much preferred developing cultural programs, viewing his role as protective of the public good, not just to make money. Despite his refined taste, Sarnoff populated his radio shows with some of the greatest headliners, only to have many of them stolen by Paley just before the advent of television. Sarnoff also led Paley in the development of the necessary hardware to project the shows both would promote. CBS never successfully developed its own television sets. Sarnoff's RCA was for many years the Tiffany of electronics companies, a model for Sony and Mitsubishi.

The Toscanini concerts (first broadcast over radio, later over television also) not only exposed millions of Americans to classical music for the first time, but also saved the networks from governmental controls during the activist Franklin D. Roosevelt years. RCA also used the concerts to sell Toscanini records, one of the earliest and remarkably long-lasting examples of cross selling in the entertainment industry.

Like many titans of industry, Sarnoff was very active in government and philanthropic affairs. Appointed a brigadier general in the U.S. Army Reserve by FDR during the Second World War, Sarnoff was for the rest of his life known as "the General." Military rank fit him well. Unlike Paley, who tried to cover up his Jewish roots in an almost WASP genteelness, Sarnoff bristled at the slightest anti-Semitism, always making it clear what he was and from where he came (most notably face-to-face with Nikita Khrushchev).

58

Lorenzo Da Ponte

(1749–1838)

Madamina!
Il catalogo e questo,
delle belle, che amo il padron mio;
un catalogo eglie, che ho fatto io;
osservate, leggete con me!
osservate, leggete con me!...
—Leporello, in *Don Giovanni*

Mozart's librettist Lorenzo Da Ponte was born Emmanuele
Conegliano in the ghetto at Ceneda (now called Vittorio Veneto)
near Venice. It is not commonly known that Da Ponte was Jewish,

for he paraded around Europe most of his life as a priest, albeit a very sexually active one, and Mozart's life story still garners most of the attention. Friend of the infamous Casanova, the Abbate or Abbe Da Ponte wrote *The Marriage of Figaro, Don Giovanni*, and *Cosi fan tutte*, the three greatest libretti in opera history set to music by Mozart. Before the brilliant adaptations in the late 1800s of Shakespeare's *Othello (Otello)* and *The Merry Wives of Windsor (Falstaff)* for Verdi by composer-librettist Arrigo Boito, Da Ponte's *commedia per musica* represented the pinnacle of musical theater. Most important, without Da Ponte's collaboration, Mozart would not have been inspired to write music that lays bare human emotion in ways never before attempted and rarely approached since.

Nothing in Da Ponte's past foreshadows his miraculous life and literary achievement. Emmanuele's father, Geremia, was a leather merchant. When Emmanuele was five years old, his mother, Ghella (Rachel) Pincherle, died after giving birth to his younger brother. Geremia's second wife was a Christian. Whether to satisfy her religious needs or to find a way out of the ghetto, in 1763 Geremia took his three children by Ghella to be converted by the bishop of Ceneda (who was named Lorenzo Da Ponte!). As was the custom, the last name of Da Ponte was assumed by the Conegliano family, Emmanuele accepting the bishop's first name also. The bishop took in his new namesake and two brothers, enrolling young Lorenzo in the seminary.

By 1773, Emmanuele Conegliano, child of the ghetto, was the priest Lorenzo Da Ponte. Although an abbe, Da Ponte never practiced the priesthood. His temperament (as related in his lively and fanciful *Memoirs*) was hardly appropriate for celibacy and a chaste outlook. He was, however, a well-regarded teacher at the seminary in Treviso, fascinated with contemporary literature and ancient languages. An unfortunate series of love affairs culminated in his fathering a child with an aristocratic but married woman. The combination of his radical political views and libertine activities led to expulsion from Treviso. Da Ponte fled to Venice, it is said to the home of another lovely lady, then to Gorizia, and out of Italy on toward Dresden (where he picked up from another Italian the art of writing plays to be set to music as operas).

Finally, in 1782, armed with a letter to the court composer

Antonio Salieri (later falsely rumored to have poisoned Mozart), Da Ponte traveled to Vienna, hungry for work. The Austrian court was mad for Italian opera, and the fast-talking Da Ponte was engaged as a poet of the Imperial Theater. He wrote a libretto for Salieri and at the house of a Jewish aristocrat, Baron Wetzlar, met the twenty-seven-year-old Mozart.

Their first project together, loosely translated as *The Duped Husband*, never got off the ground. Mozart, only seven years away from his death, possessed at twenty-seven the full force of perfect inspiration and technique. He required something more than just another *opera buffa* with the typical clowning and sight gags of the day. Mozart and Da Ponte were instead drawn to the most revolutionary play of their time, Pierre Beaumarchais' *Le Mariage de Figaro*. It was about a philandering count (Da Ponte knew plenty of them) who wanted to cheat on his refined wife with her maid (engaged to marry his manservant!). All the elements of comic opera were there, with several exceptions. These were real people. They sang with real emotions. At times they were really frightened. They laughed and raged and sometimes sang arias with delectable words set to unforgettable melodies that cried.

Da Ponte's libretti for *Don Giovanni* (based on an old tale, *The Stoned Guest*) and the amoral yet original *Cosi* address other dramatic and poetic concerns. *Don Giovanni* is a wild tragicomedy, the story of a Don Juan or Casanovalike character not far from Da Ponte's own past. Like *Hamlet* or *Faust*, it is unique, resisting stereotypes or rigorous analysis. With a black heart at its core, *Don Giovanni* is majestic in an elemental, horrific way. *Cosi*, in contrast, bubbles like champagne but is somehow poignant. And what they say about the relationships between men and women— how they cheat each other, lie, are passionate, learn and forget about love—were entirely Da Ponte's invention.

Da Ponte's Italian positively glows with phonetic excitement. He was not only a great dramatist, but a dramatic poet of the first order. Characters and settings are defined instantly. Audiences are drawn not only into the action, but more important, into the thoughts and emotions of what seem to be living people. Despite the length of these works, there is no repetition, no wasted words, just golden expression. Recognize that before Mozart and Da Ponte, this depth of dramatic presentation existed only in Shakespeare and the ancient Greeks.

One year before Mozart's death in 1790, the Austrian emperor cut back support of artistic endeavors due to the rising cost of his war with Turkey. Da Ponte lost his position, journeyed to Trieste where he met a young Englishwoman named Nancy Grahl, then traveled with her to Paris, then London (where for thirteen years he worked with now-forgotten composers), and finally emigrated to America. Lorenzo and Nancy had four children. A struggling immigrant, advanced in years, he supported his family by tutoring the many European languages he knew. Da Ponte's work teaching Italian at Columbia College in New York City is still commemorated by alumni such as myself. He died at the age of eighty-nine and was buried in Brooklyn.

59

Julius Rosenwald

(1862–1932)

Charitable giving or "tsedakah" is a requirement of Jewish law. In ancient times, alms were given to the poor. During the industrial age, great philanthropic foundations were established by wealthy families to aid a myriad of causes. Often in partnership with government, private philanthropy was used to help the needy, educate the masses, defend the persecuted, and heal the sick. The whole concept of private philanthropy by businesspeople and not the nobility, on so large a scale, was a new phenomenon, one of the truly blessed results of the Industrial Revolution.

After the Civil War, immense fortunes were made in business by German Jewish immigrants whose names became synonymous with the development of America as a world power. Seligman, Guggenheim, Bache, Kuhn, Loeb, Warburg, Speyer, Schiff, Straus, Lehman, Wertheim, Goldman, Sachs, and Rosenwald were the founding families of many important financial institutions and retail establishments. Financial services firms such as Lehman Brothers; Goldman, Sachs; Wertheim Schroeder; foundations and museums created by the Guggenheims; and giant retailers like Macy's, Abraham & Straus, and Sears, Roebuck originated in and developed out of small family businesses which grew with the American colossus.

Julius Rosenwald often said that his financial success was ninety-five percent perspiration and five percent inspiration. He also claimed not to know the size of his fortune. Whether he was worth two hundred million dollars in the days before income taxes or $17,415,450 (net without deductions for taxes) at his death in the Depression year of 1932 would have been unimportant to this remarkable man. More important to him was what he did with his money and how he influenced others to give. His son William remembers his father often asserting that large wealth must be regarded as being held in public trust.

He was born in Springfield, Illinois in a house one block west of Abraham Lincoln's home. Rosenwald's parents were German Jews who had migrated to America in the early 1850s. Julius's father, Samuel, worked in the early years at a men's clothing factory owned by the brothers of his wife Augusta Hammerslough. It was said that her uncle had specially fitted President Lincoln's extra long legs with a pair of pants. When the Hammerslough brothers moved to New York City, Samuel bought a haberdashery and men's clothing store business (and moved into a house across from the Lincolns).

At the age of seventeen, Julius went to apprentice with his uncles in New York City. He became friendly with Henry Goldman (later a founder of Goldman, Sachs) and Henry Morgenthau (future ambassador and father of Franklin D. Roosevelt's Treasury Secretary). Julius's initial efforts in New York and then Chicago to establish his own clothing businesses were moderately successful. In 1890 he married Augusta Nusbaum (they became the proud parents of five children). Augusta would play a crucial role in Julius's development as the leading philanthropist and retailer of his time. When he could least afford it, Julius impulsively donated $2,500 to a Jewish charity. Augusta supported him with the advice that he should never hesitate to give money. In the late 1890s, he became a merchant and expressed his life's ambition to earn fifteen thousand dollars a year: five for personal expenses, five for savings, and five for charity.

In 1895, Augusta's brother Aaron and Julius invested in an interesting venture, the new Sears, Roebuck and Co. The founder of the mail-order house was a sales and marketing visionary named Richard Sears. Although a pioneer in publicity, Sears was not an effective merchandiser. When Aaron and Julius each purchased their twenty-five percent interest in Sears (for $37,500 a piece, Julius's portion largely financed by a monied friend in New York), the business was in a shambles, the quality of goods inferior to store-bought goods and often misleadingly advertised. The opportunity for Rosenwald lay in making a great idea into a business that could grow efficiently, with customer confidence and proper business planning. Under Rosenwald's direction, Sears grew into a mammoth corporation servicing a customer who when not able to buy what was needed at the local store, instead of travelling far over poor roads, could simply reach for the Sears catalog and order by mail.

Sears had supplied his largely rural and small-town clientele, along with clothes and furnishings, firearms and patent medicines listed as perfect cures for most any ailment. Rosenwald discontinued the sale of handguns and potions, improved merchandise quality, and made sure that the catalog exactly depicted the goods that were available. Integrity and honesty, not gimmickry, proved simply good business. Americans learned they could rely on the Sears catalog, and it became a constant of American life.

A story often retold was of the Sunday school student who asked her teacher where the Ten Commandments came from. "Sears and Roebuck, of course," answered the teacher.

Rosenwald instituted other highly innovative and influential business practices, including using the principle of mass production (years before Henry Ford and other industrial giants). The money-back guarantee (including transportation charges both ways), use of the new parcel post, the first retail testing laboratory for sales products in the United States, the first automatic letter-opening machines in American industry, one of the earliest public offerings of a general merchandising company (arranged by his friends at Goldman, Sachs), as well as savings, profit sharing, stock plans, and health and recreational benefits for employees were all integral parts of Rosenwald's good business.

In the era before the income tax, Rosenwald, like such men as John Rockefeller and Andrew Carnegie, became wealthy beyond calculation. However, Rosenwald felt strongly (as had Baron Maurice Hirsch, Sir Moses Montefiore, and Jacob Schiff before him) that the life of a businessman was not worth living without civic responsibility.

Rosenwald contributed more than sixty-three million dollars to charity. The recipients of his gifts included, but were certainly not limited to, social settlements in Chicago slums, immigrant aid societies, agricultural research institutes, the University of Chicago and other prominent institutions of higher learning, the American Jewish Joint Distribution Committee (which helped Jews suffering from the ravages of the First World War, as well as Belgian, Armenian, Syrian, Serbian, and German victims—characteristically, Rosenwald offered a million dollars on condition that the Committee raise an additional nine million on a matching basis, thus becoming the leader in their first large campaign), Jewish organizations such as the American Jewish Committee, leading Jewish theological seminaries, and museums such as the Chicago Museum of Science and Industry (which he founded).

In addition to these contributions of money, Rosenwald developed novel concepts, for the time, of how to give. He opposed the idea of a perpetual endowment, the so-called dead hand of philanthropy, which dictated in perpetuity how gifts had to be spent. Trustees and directors must have discretion, he felt, to use principal as well as interest without restriction. His method of donating had a lasting and profound influence on the way charities receive and spend donations. He felt that money was best contributed preventively, that is, before a crisis occurred, not after, and that it was preferable to give so that others would follow his example with their giving.

Rosenwald's contributions of time and expertise often had as great and lasting an influence as his largess. He served with distinction on the Chicago Planning Commission, laying the design of modern Chicago. President Woodrow Wilson appointed him as a member of the Advisory Commission of the Council of National Defense led by Bernard Baruch. Rosenwald brought his retail know-how to the aid of the United States, playing a significant role in the outfitting of the nation's armies for war.

Following Lincoln's great model, perhaps the most remarkable and wonderful activity of Rosenwald's event-rich life was his support of education for young black people in the South. He financed the construction in the rural South of over more than two thousand rural schools, college libraries, and YMCA buildings for African-Americans. The schools became known as "Rosenwald schools." Although Rosenwald did not like contributing much to endowments (preferring that each generation take care of its own needs), he donated large sums to funds at black colleges such as Tuskegee Institute which became devoted to the best in higher education during an era of almost total segregation. Along with those of his friend Booker T. Washington and former neighbor Abraham Lincoln, Rosenwald's photograph adorned the walls of many schools and homes of grateful African-Americans.

60

Casimir Funk

(1884–1967)

Casimir Funk, the son of Polish Jews, was the discoverer of vitamins. Before Funk's original findings, James Lind in 1757 had shown the rich benefits of eating fruit to fight scurvy. Indeed, the British navy recognized in 1794 the usefulness of citrus juices by mandating their provision for lengthy sea voyages. At the end of the nineteenth and start of the twentieth century, scientists such as Bunge, Eijkman, Pekelharing, and Hopkins added to the general knowledge of nutrition with important observations and discoveries. Using mice or birds for study, they found that some

225

substances necessary for a complete diet must exist in milk, vegetables, and meat. Building on his predecessors' work, Casimir Funk discovered compounds in rice bran capable of curing beriberi in pigeons. He called the substance "vitamine."

Vita is the Latin word for life. "Amine" means chemical compounds with nitrogen. When it was discovered that every vitamin did not contain nitrogen, the original name was shortened by dropping its final *e*. Funk's original vitamine was later identified as vitamin B, a complex of multi-vitamins.

Funk's discovery was more influential than simply for its identification of a substance called the vitamin. Owing to the great influence of scientists such as Louis Pasteur and Paul Ehrlich, the medical community of the period focused solely on the ways infection caused disease. Funk's vitamin find shifted researchers' attention away from cure to effective means of prevention. His studies inspired legions of other investigations into nutrition and dietetics.

Young children could be raised with vitamins supplementing their everyday meals. They could be brought up with proper nutrition and have a chance to lead normal, healthy, productive lives. Minimum requirements of nutrition could be recommended by governmental health departments for the general welfare of the citizenry. Attention to proper nutrition changed how people ate and grew, why they would care about their diet, and whether they were what they should eat. Funk's remarkable paper "The Etiology of Deficiency Diseases," published in 1912 in the British *Journal of State Medicine*, and his book *The Vitamin* (1913, published in English in 1922) revolutionized biochemistry and medicine.

Although Funk felt that most important vitamins were found in a well-balanced diet, after him, food would never taste quite the same. Vitamin deficiencies could be caused, he wrote, by eating quantities of foods that have simply lost their potency. Food could be "devitalized" because of lengthy periods of storage or transport, the growing of plants in soil weak in mineral content, or just overcooking (the vegetables grandma fed you were probably boiled too long!). Vitamin supplements were necessary often to make up the nutritional difference because of mistakes in food processing, preparation, quantity, or just in the food itself.

Funk also stressed that many vitamins, not only one or a few, were required for good health. The savage food deficiency diseases, such as scurvy, beriberi, and rickets, were preventable if a person had sufficient intake of all the vitamins required, not just a few. Out of Funk's ideas came the MDA or minimum daily allowance of vitamins recommended by the U.S. government on every vitamin jar (and most cereal boxes).

Casimir was born in Warsaw to Jacques and Gustawa Zysan Funk. Jacques Funk was a respected dermatologist who influenced son Casimir's choice of biochemistry (instead of medicine) as his field. Biochemistry was then a growth field. He studied at the University in Berne, Switzerland, writing his doctoral thesis on a compound that would later be used as a substitute for a vital female hormone.

After research positions at the Pasteur Institute in Paris, the University of Berlin, and Wiesbaden Municipal Hospital, Funk in 1910 began to work at the Lister Institute of Preventive Medicine. It was at the Lister Institute that he identified the vitamin compound out of an incredibly small portion of rice bran. His discovery led later to the separation of thiamine.

International travels followed to the London Cancer Hospital (1913–15), research with two pharmaceutical companies in the United States (and becoming a U.S. citizen in 1920), at Cornell Medical College and Columbia University College of Physicians and Surgeons during and after the First World War, and in the 1920s to the State Institute of Hygiene in Warsaw (to work in a fourteen-room laboratory sponsored by the Rockefeller Foundation). Reacting to the growing fascist threat, Funk left Poland, first to Paris where he set up a private laboratory, calling it "Casa Biochemica," and then escaped and returned to America to work as a research consultant with another pharmaceutical company (many of his compounds became the first commercially available vitamins). After his groundbreaking work on vitamins, he made other important contributions to medical science, including the therapeutic use of sex hormones and the relation of diet to cancer.

61

George Gershwin

(1898–1937)

> George Gershwin died on July 11, 1937, but I don't
> have to believe it if I don't want to.
>
> —John O'Hara

Movies are made from stories such as George Gershwin's life
(and one was, *Rhapsody in Blue*, starring Robert Alda and Oscar
Levant). Gershwin at age nineteen sat down one night with a
childhood friend, Irving Caesar, and wrote *Swanee*. Al Jolson
picked up the song and made it into America's greatest hit of
1920. In his early twenties Gershwin had entered a select circle of

prominent American composers whom he would dominate until death from brain cancer at the age of thirty-eight.

Most of Gershwin's music is very familiar and is among the most often played of any composer. The *Rhapsody, Concerto in F, American in Paris, Porgy and Bess*, and the show and film tunes are as popular today as when they were first written. Gershwin insisted that a song had to be played over and over again to become popular, that is, "plugged." His music has survived countless repetitions, still filling concert halls and theaters with enthusiastic crowds (the 1992 Tony Award for Best Musical on Broadway went to the "new" Gershwin musical *Crazy for You*).

Gershwin's music is so attractive because it is so filled with sun and hope, yet often laced with a disarming melancholy. His tender melodies rise up from rich harmonic underpinnings, Jazz Age rhythms pulsating in his scores, missed beats and rapid-fire notes thrusting his brother Ira's lyrics almost ahead of the music. George brought the sounds of urban life, from the streets to the penthouses, into the concert hall, Broadway show, and opera theater. His personal amalgam of popular songwriting with African-American spirituals, Jewish cantorial singing, ragtime, swing jazz, and symphony heralded an age where, in colleague Cole Porter's words, "anything goes"—but only something expressive, moving, and abundantly musical.

The son of Morris (a leather worker) and Rose Gershovitz, Russian immigrants, George grew up in Brooklyn and the Lower East Side of Manhattan. While his older brother, Ira, could best be described as bookish, reading constantly and writing short, amusing pieces on contemporary mores, George was athletic, active, and vibrant. He was not a child prodigy, but in his teens displayed a growing aptitude for and interest in music. At fifteen George went to work as a song plugger on Tin Pan Alley, the area in the West 20s in Manhattan where most of the prominent music publishers of the time were situated. A song pounder sat at an upright piano all day in a small room plugging the publisher's newest releases to customers who wandered in. Sheet music was big business before radio and television made access to popular music easier. Gershwin learned quickly how and which music made the fastest and best impression. Never a conservatory student, he was trained in the tough competition of New York's musical marketplace. Gershwin's idols were Jerome Kern and

Irving Berlin. Indeed, George tried to work for the slightly older and brilliantly successful Berlin, who turned Gershwin down, urging him to write his own songs.

Swanee proved to be the biggest single hit of his songwriting career. Al Jolson's remarkably warm and energetic performance riveted audiences and made Gershwin a sought-after talent. When writing *I'll Build a Stairway to Paradise* and other songs for George White's *Scandals of 1922*, Gershwin met bandleader Paul Whiteman. Their meeting would have an enormous effect on the history of American music.

Gershwin was asked to write a composition for Whiteman's first jazz concert, intended to show serious music listeners that jazz was "respectable." On a train ride to the Boston tryout of his new (and to be unsuccessful) show, *Sweet Little Devil*, George was inspired by the rhythms of the rails to begin the composition of the *Rhapsody in Blue*. He completed the work in three weeks. Ferde Grofé, later the well-known composer of the *Grand Canyon Suite*, orchestrated the *Rhapsody* for Whiteman's jazz band. It is said that Ira titled the work after a visit to an art gallery. With its now famous opening clarinet glissando piercing the air, the *Rhapsody* with the composer at the piano made Paul Whiteman's "experiment in modern music" a historic event.

Gershwin's next show was *Lady, Be Good* starring Adele and Fred Astaire. *Fascinating Rhythm, Oh, Lady Be Good!, Half of It Dearie Blues* and *The Man I Love* (which incredibly was dropped from the show when it received a lukewarm response) were premiered in the musical comedy. Each show that followed had the same formula of boy meets girl, boy loses girl, boy gets girl, but also sparkling songs by George and partner Ira. These shows, including *Tip Toes, Oh, Kay!, Funny Face* (which contained Fred Astaire's first routine with high hat and tails), *Strike Up the Band*, and *Girl Crazy*, are now mostly forgotten, their books very much of the period. Songs that are standards today and usually played out of their original dramatic context first appeared in these Broadway musicals. *Sweet and Low-Down, That Certain Feeling, Do, Do, Do, Someone to Watch Over Me, 'S Wonderful, High Hat, Liza, Strike Up the Band, Embraceable You, Bidin' My Time, But Not For Me,* and *I Got Rhythm* stand alone now, apart from the frivolous stories that once contained them. The music beneath the titles of each of these songs has become an irrevocable part of American culture.

Just speak the titles, and you'll surely start singing them.

Between the production of the shows Gershwin continued to study harmony, counterpoint, and orchestration. In later years, Ira repeatedly asserted that his brother was a learned musicologist who in his early twenties was analyzing Arnold Schoenberg's scores and continually playing the piano works of Claude Debussy. Walter Damrosch, the conductor of the New York Symphony, commissioned the popular young Gershwin in 1925 to write a jazz symphony. Gershwin responded with the energetic and bluesy *Concerto in F*. The *Concerto*, even more than the *Rhapsody*, confirmed George's mastery of musical form and inventive design. The work's rhythms are so infectiously wild that one is rocked about, glad for the ride.

Similarly, his orchestral work *An American in Paris* in 1928 brought the cacophony of French taxicab horns into the concert hall. A lonely musical tour of Parisian streets, *An American* was a huge success, first performed by Damrosch's symphony, eventually by every major orchestra. At age thirty, Gershwin was the most famous and acclaimed composer in the world. His music began to have wide influence on composers as disparate as Ravel, Stravinsky, and Berg.

Of Thee I Sing, with a book by George S. Kaufman and Morrie Ryskind and lyrics by Ira, premiered in 1931 and won the Pulitzer Prize for *drama* (not for music!). The show targeted the U.S. government in a sarcastic lampoon of our most cherished institutions. *Who Cares? Love Is Sweeping the Country, Because, Because,* and *Of Thee I Sing (Baby)* were in critic Brooks Atkinson's words "funnier than the government, and not nearly so dangerous." The show's more complicated dramaturgy prepared Gershwin for his greatest challenge, the folk opera *Porgy and Bess*.

Porgy is quite simply the greatest stage work written by any American composer. Black life in the ghetto of Catfish Row was treated with love, clarity, and an innovative respect that still resounds with truth. Gershwin's music was no longer just Broadway show tunes or pseudo grand opera, but the music of the people, of real feelings, fears, lust, hope, something higher. As in most of his larger works, he brought all his musical experiences together in beautifully moving expression.

His remaining two years were spent in Hollywood writing more immortal songs (*They Can't Take That Away from Me, Let's Call the Whole Thing Off, They All Laughed, A Foggy Day (in London Town), Love Walked In,* and *Love Is Here to Stay*), dating gorgeous actresses (Simone Simon and the then Mrs. Charlie Chaplin, Paulette Goddard), suffering the tyrannical whims of producer Samuel Goldwyn, enjoying the company of his transplanted New York friends, and trying to make enough money so he could devote the rest of his life to serious composition. His death from a brain tumor before his thirty-ninth birthday was as great a tragedy as the early ends of Purcell, Mozart, Schubert, Mendelssohn, Chopin, and Bizet.

Many critics have noted (and some have demeaned) Gershwin's merger of popular and classical music. What he did, however, was not atypical of many of the great composers. The music of common people has its place in symphonic music along with grandiose utterances. The use by Aaron Copland and Elie Siegmeister of cowboy songs, Benjamin Britten of sea chanties, Sergei Prokofiev's Russian peasant music, Mexican folk tunes in orchestral works by Carlos Chávez and Silvestre Reveltuas, all find their roots in Gershwin's unique mixture.

The harmonies and rhythmic patterns of swing and jazz were also influenced by Gershwin's music. Notwithstanding the beautifully lyrical melodies and ingenious rhythms, his music seems to rise up first out of its harmonic structure. The development of jazz since Gershwin can largely be traced to the expansion and complication of harmony. Also, even before Benny Goodman's historic Carnegie Hall concert, Gershwin, along with Paul Whiteman, had shown the importance and artistic strength of jazz. For like Modest Moussorgsky (whose music is close to his black Russian soil) and George's great contemporary, Duke Ellington, Gershwin forever symbolizes the music of real American folks, expressed with sophistication, laughter, zest, and love.

62

Chaim Weizmann

(1874–1952)

First president of Israel, architect of the Balfour Declaration and the recognition of the Jewish homeland by President Truman, leading Zionist figure after Herzl, and distinguished scientist, Chaim Weizmann was one of the most influential Jews in history. As the third of a most disparate trio with David Ben-Gurion and Menachem Begin, Weizmann made use of his unique diplomatic skills to help bring about the birth of the Jewish state.

He had modest beginnings under tsarist rule. His father was a timber merchant with a taste for good literature. Despite Russian limitations on Jews securing a higher education, he journeyed to Berlin and Switzerland to study chemistry and earned a doctorate. While in school at Berlin Polytechnic, he learned of the efforts of Theodor Herzl. Herzl's brand of Zionism hit him "like a bolt out of the blue." At the age of twenty-four, in 1898, Weizmann attended the second Zionist congress.

At the turn of the century, Weizmann came to Edwardian England to teach biochemistry at Manchester University. In these years before the First World War, the British Empire was at its most powerful. Weizmann became enamored of English manners, aristocracy, and democratic form of government, becoming a citizen of the Crown in 1910.

After Herzl's death in 1904, Weizmann gradually became the leading voice of world Zionism. Unlike Herzl, who had talent only for world leaders but no sense for ordinary people, Weizmann was at ease in both worlds. Before the war, he sought the friendships of a dynamic generation of English statesmen, including the Conservatives David Lloyd-George, Arthur Balfour, and Winston Churchill, as well as Liberal member of Parliament Herbert Samuel. Weizmann also helped build grass roots support of the Zionist movement in the poor Jewish neighborhoods of London.

Weizmann also gained the trust of the British authorities with his production at the Admiralty's request of large quantities of a flammable ingredient of ammunition. This liquid acetone would greatly assist the British munitions effort during the war.

With the entry of Turkey on the side of Germany and Austria, Samuel and Weizmann saw an opening for British support of a Jewish homeland. They urged that France and England divide up a Middle East soon to be liberated from centuries of Ottoman domination.

On November 2, 1917, in a letter from Foreign Secretary Balfour to Lord Rothschild, president of the British Zionist Federation, His Majesty's Government viewed "with favour the establishment of a national home for the Jewish people" and promised to "use their best endeavors to facilitate the achievement of this object."

Later in the 1930s, in reaction to Arab and French objections, and frightened that Middle Eastern rulers would back Nazi Germany in the coming war, English officials gradually retreated from the Balfour Declaration, culminating in the notorious

White Paper of 1939 in which the British withdrew their support. Nevertheless, the theme of the Declaration was endorsed in 1922 by the League of Nations as a basis for the British Mandate over Palestine and led to the partitioning of the region by the United Nations after the Holocaust and the Second World War.

Between and for a short time even after the wars, Weizmann was the international voice of Zionism. In Palestine, however, Ben-Gurion, and later Begin, became the leaders of the Jewish national movement. However, it was Weizmann who secured the recognition of the United States of the birth of Israel in his secret meetings with Harry Truman.

Truman was incensed by the often rude and insistent demands of American Jewish organizations in 1948 that the United States support the creation of the Jewish state. The president's old friend and former business partner, Eddie Jacobson, a Jew from Kansas City, convinced Truman to talk with Weizmann. Jacobson's arranging for Truman to speak to Weizmann led directly to American recognition of Israel, the first country to do so (immediately followed by the Soviet Union). Weizmann left a profound impression on Truman, who quickly overrode powerful objections from Secretary of State George Marshall and his State Department that recognition would upset the Arabs and America's influence in the oil-rich Middle East. For the second time (thirty-one years after the Balfour Declaration), the old professor whom Truman called "Cham" had gained support for Israel from the world's greatest power.

Ben-Gurion asked Weizmann to become Israel's first president. Weizmann accepted the position, not realizing that it was a ceremonial post. When he died suddenly in 1952, Chaim Weizmann was remembered as one of the most influential fathers of modern Zion.

63

Franz Boas

(1858–1942)

The development of anthropology or the study of man as a modern science was begun, largely in the United States, by the German-born Franz Boas. Before Boas, anthropology was guided by theories of evolution and deductive reasoning. Nineteenth-century anthropologists thought cultures could be understood by first observing, then making certain assumptions based on limited facts and a good deal of pseudoscientific guessing, couched in colorful myth and fairy tales.

Boas urged instead that cultural scientists be more critical

236

and observant. They must note variations of behavior, peeling the external away layer by layer to reveal the inner core of truth. Boas's approach reflected the natural scientists of his day who assumed that behind real things lies structure. Only the outer shape of things change in relation to conditions in life. Boas combined these methods of "induction" (rather than deduction) to already developed evolutionary methods and thereby established anthropology as a contemporary science.

Born in Germany to a middle-class family, Franz showed interest at a young age in studying the customs of people from foreign lands. He concentrated at school first, however, in mathematics and physics, building his education on the abstract sciences. Influenced later by the eminent geographers and naturalists of his day, Boas the young scientist felt compelled to comprehend nature in the real world and the peoples who inhabit it.

His first expedition at the age of twenty-six was to the Arctic to study not only the peoples commonly known as Eskimos but also the geography of their lands. At great personal risk, Boas charted several hundred miles of coastline. He returned from the trip an anthropologist, convinced that geography was not the overriding force behind the evolution of a people that scientists then assumed it was. Rather, he asserted that the inner thoughts and mental development of peoples determined their behavior, not Darwinian theory.

When Boas returned to Germany, he was offered positions at a prominent museum and university in Berlin. However, he was disgusted with the unending anti-Semitism of German society. An opportunity arose to return to the peace of the Pacific Northwest and live with coastal Indian and Eskimo cultures, and he left quickly for the first of thirteen visits to the region.

After a series of poorly paying jobs in the United States, lecturing at Clark University and editing scientific journals, Boas became a curator at the American Museum of Natural History and a professor at Columbia University, both in New York. He remained at the museum for nine years and at Columbia for forty-two, training many of the preeminent anthropologists of the twentieth century, including Ruth Benedict and Margaret Mead.

In addition to teaching at the university, where he influenced generations of students, Boas continued throughout his career in countless texts, commentaries, monographs, and public lectures to urge the development of anthropology as a precise and vibrant science. He rigorously attacked the quasi-scientific assumptions of his day, insisting that research be conducted and conclusions reached only after strict adherence to careful analysis and controls. His approach, concerned with how societies change, not how they might have "evolved" up to a certain point, gave anthropologists a scientific basis upon which they could conduct their research. Boas asserted that scientists must observe what actually happens in cultures without imposing preconceived notions or prejudices. Do not bring yourself to others, but bring others to yourself, he repeatedly urged.

Research must be data intensive. The massive collection of facts is the only way of discovering how cultures are shaped and progress. The lives of peoples and the development of their cultures could not be explained by one grand evolutionary theory or urban psychology, but only by attention to the exact facts of their history.

Identifying variations in human behavior, Boas made clear, was the sure, systematic method of achieving an accurate understanding of culture. By reconstructing history and carefully analyzing each facet of a people's language, biological traits and social behavior, Boas's method of anthropology could give scientific answers to the questions of life.

64

Sabbatai Zevi

(1626–1676)

For a brief period in the mid-seventeenth century, almost half of world Jewry believed that at long last the Messiah had come. His name was Sabbatai Zevi.

Born and raised by a prosperous merchant family in Smyrna, this Turkish Jew was trained as a rabbi in the Sephardic tradition. He maniacally studied Jewish mystical writings and was known as a peculiar reclusive youth, given to swimming alone in the sea in cold weather, self-flagellation, and constant mood swings. But he had a certain charisma, handsome looks, an elegant, almost regal, bearing. At age twenty-eight, he was banished from Smyrna by its rabbis after uttering the phonetic name of God prohibited by the Bible from speech and declaring himself the Messiah.

Zevi wandered through Greece. In Salonika he decided to marry. There in the synagogue, he took the Torah as his bride. The Greek rabbis threw him out.

Journeying to Constantinople, he again caused controversy. In an odd ritual he mixed up the texts of several Jewish festivals in a blasphemous wild chant, blessing abominable acts forbidden by Jewish law. He was again cast out and returned to his home in Smyrna in a state of severe depression.

In 1662 he voyaged to Jerusalem. In a melancholic stupor, ravaged by imagined devils, he married a refugee from Poland, a young whore named Sarah, in imitation of the prophet Hosea (who also had married a prostitute). Sarah was an orphan of the Chmielnicki massacres which in 1648 and 1649 had cost the lives of over 100,000 Jewish men, women and children (almost a tenth of the total world Jewish population of the time). This incident, almost forgotten today, was as brutal in many ways as the Holocaust. A Ukrainian noble named Chmielnicki led raids against his Polish rulers, and threatened by the perceived economic strength of Eastern European Jewry, killed as many Jews as he could on the way. The period traumatized European Jews who had tragically and mistakenly believed that they would not be harmed if they quietly obeyed their Christian masters.

In 1665, Sabbatai Zevi learned of a young rabbi in Gaza, an exorcist, who was said to possess knowledge of the infinite and was capable of seeing straight into a man's soul. This rabbi, who became known as Nathan of Gaza or Nathan the Prophet, was skilled in the use of propaganda and became Zevi's ablest organizer and rabble-rouser. The combination of the psychotic, totally self-absorbed Zevi and the master propagandist Nathan proved to be potent.

Nathan insisted that Zevi was the Messiah. At first, Sabbatai did not believe him. They traveled together to holy places. Upon his return to Gaza, Zevi, most probably in a manic state, was consumed with a sense of overwhelming happiness. On May 31, 1665, with the support of his prophet, Nathan, Zevi declared himself the Messiah, King of the Jews.

In the coming weeks, he paraded about Gaza on a horse, reining in many supporters and designating apostles. Nathan soon issued a series of letters to European cities announcing the Messiah's appearance and calling for acts of repentance. Rumors spread about of miracles, of the Messiah's great powers, and of an army of ancient Israelites marching against and conquering Arabian cities.

Fifteen hundred years of oppression seemed over. The Chmielnicki massacres were reduced to a bad, evil memory. The light of Messianic fervor illumined centuries of darkness and fear. Jews everywhere, poor and rich, reacted with abandonment, unmitigated joy, mad frenzy. Juveniles were married and urged to procreate so that unborn souls remaining in the cosmos could find homes in babies' bodies. There was no time to waste, as the end of the world was here.

From a letter of Nathan of Gaza
to the Jews of Europe in 1665
showing the anointing of Zevi.

Sabbatai ventured through the Middle East, gathering the support of scholars along the way eager to see messianic predictions come true, meeting little opposition. Arriving back in Smyrna, he prayed in the synagogue during Hanukkah, singing a Castilian love song to a sacred scroll.

At the New Year, Zevi sailed to Constantinople and was immediately arrested as a subversive. Imprisoned in Gallipoli, albeit in royal style, he set up a court in exile, entertaining learned rabbis who left convinced of his divine state. In September, 1666, brought before the sultan in Constantinople Sabbatai Zevi was given the choice of conversion to Islam or summary execution. He immediately chose Islam and was given the name Mehmet Effendi and a royal pension for life. He lived in seclusion and died ten years later, followed shortly thereafter by Nathan.

Nathan spent his last years attempting to explain away in obscure kabbalistic reference why Zevi converted. It was necessary, Nathan explained, for the Messiah to go "undercover" in the gentile world to collect lost divine sparks. Most Jews reacted to the conversion with immense sadness and embarrassment at being duped. However, worship of this false Messiah was carried on by some for centuries. (Even into the twentieth century a sect in Greece continued to pray, in secret ceremonies, to Sabbatai Zevi.)

This odd and shameful episode had widespread effects on world Jewry. After him, Jews no longer felt totally isolated. Common people had their first taste of freedom since the beginning of the Diaspora. Zevi had unleashed the human passions which lay smothered beneath rabbinical law. The rise of ecstatic Hasidism, the liberating force of the Jewish Enlightenment which followed, and the aching desire to return to the homeland, Zion, originated in part in this most strange tale.

65

To the New York Philharmonic Symphony Society in deepest gratitude for giving me my great opportunity

Sincerely,
Leonard Bernstein

NYC—2/14/44

Leonard Bernstein

(1918–1990)

Conductor, composer, pianist, author, professor, television personality, Zionist, activist, scholar, producer, world-class raconteur—Leonard Bernstein was the most influential musician of the postwar era.

Aaron Copland, the enabler of American music, beloved of Bernstein, was surely a greater composer; David Diamond, one of his closest and oldest friends, was certainly a more eminent symphonist. Bernstein's devotion to their music acknowledged

243

this. Yet, again, greatness is not what this book is about. Through over forty-five years of whirlwind activity, Bernstein became a figure of such authority and charisma that at his death he was remembered in obituaries as a sort of monarch—the John Fitzgerald Kennedy of music. To understand his influence, one must separate out his activities.

Conducting student of Fritz Reiner and Serge Koussevitzky (the great Jewish conductors of the Chicago and Boston symphony orchestras), Bernstein rose to sudden fame in 1943 when he replaced the ailing Bruno Walter (another great Jewish conductor) as guest conductor of the New York Philharmonic on a nationally aired Sunday afternoon radio broadcast. Bernstein was just twenty-five years old.

The circumstances of this famous incident are in many ways symbolic of his career. After undergraduate studies at Harvard and graduate work at the Curtis Institute of Music in Philadelphia with Reiner, Bernstein ventured to Tanglewood in 1940, armed with references, to study conducting with Koussevitzky. Tanglewood, the summer home of the Boston Symphony since 1936, offered to Bernstein through its new Berkshire Music Center a pathway to fame. Rapidly becoming a pet pupil of Koussevitzsky, Bernstein combined the rigorous training he had received from Reiner with the flamboyance and feeling of Koussevitzky to secure a position as assistant conductor of the New York Philharmonic under the tutelage of the dictatorial Artur Rodzinski.

The offer to assist Rodzinski came quite unexpectedly. After leaving Tanglewood and the protection of his mentor Koussevitzky, Bernstein secured a twenty-five-dollar-a-week job with a pop music publisher transcribing jazz improvisations and writing popular arrangements under the name of Lenny Amber (Bernstein in English). Shortly thereafter, Rodzinski remembered having seen Bernstein rehearse at Tanglewood and offered him the assistant's job. The also unexpected substitution for Walter followed, and the short journey from the university to the conservatory, from music festival to Tin Pan Alley, to rising American conductor was complete.

Bernstein's ability to influence people to secure position and recognition never left him. His Horatio Alger–like vault to fame via live nationally broadcast radio and front-page headlines the morning after taught him the power of the media, a lesson he did not forget as he began to create his legend.

Bernstein was the first American to receive world attention as a conductor, clearing a path for later generations of Jewish American maestros such as Leonard Slatkin, James Levine, Michael Tilson Thomas, and Leon Botstein. In the early years his matinee-idol looks brought bobby-soxers to the concert hall yearning for the opportunity to touch his clothes as he fled into his car after a performance.

Simultaneous with his rise as star conductor, Bernstein was composing musical shows and symphonic works. During the Second World War he took advantage, like so many others, of Americans' patriotic interest in homegrown creations. His *Jeremiah* symphony and *Fancy Free* ballet (later adapted into the Broadway show *On the Town*) were composed during the same heady period as his celebrated debut with the Philharmonic. During these years he seemed to be everywhere.

From the late 1940s into the 1950s, Bernstein moved in what appear now to be inspired and coordinated strokes to consolidate his position in American music. After exciting but financially unprofitable years as the music director of the New York City Symphony, he taught at Tanglewood and at Brandeis University and guest-conducted with leading orchestras and opera houses from New York to Milan to Tel Aviv. After another successful New York–inspired musical, *Wonderful Town*, Bernstein tried film scoring and triumphed with *On the Waterfront*. His attack through operetta on McCarthyism, *Candide*, was a box office flop at first, then a cult favorite, and finally a recognized classic of sarcastic wit and intellect based on a well-meaning but disjunct play by Lillian Hellman.

In 1957 he collaborated with the great choreographer Jerome Robbins, the twenty-seven-year-old lyricist Stephen Sondheim, and the creator of *Gypsy*, Arthur Laurents, on a work that would transform musical theater forever, an adaptation of *Romeo and Juliet* set in New York's Hell's Kitchen, the unique *West Side Story*. This musical represents Bernstein's essence as a creative artist, what the world will best remember of him. "Broadway Lenny" had put it all together (at thirty-nine) in one fast-moving lyrical show, mixing social commentary, dramatic movement through Robbins's revolutionary ballet dancing, soaring lyrical melodies, pounding ethnic rhythms, and low comedy contrasted by high catharsis. The next year he became the music director of the Philharmonic.

He retired from the orchestra twelve years later to become its laureate conductor, freeing himself from administrative duties to pursue guest-conducting engagements throughout the world, most notably in Vienna, Jerusalem, and London, but always finding time to return most seasons to New York. As the years went by his ecstatic, athletic style of conducting produced increasingly more beautiful and profound results. He championed the works of American composers and introduced an ever-widening listening public to a special understanding of America's first truly great composer, Charles Ives, and the weltschmerz of Gustav Mahler (another greatly suffering Jewish composer-conductor whom Bernstein revered and to whom he was often compared).

Despite all these activities, some might say his greatest influence was on musical education. First on the *Omnibus* series and later as the star of the Philharmonic's own Young People's Concerts, he taught millions of viewers (probably more children than had ever heard music in the history of public concerts) the intricacies of Beethoven's *Fifth*, of jazz and orchestration. Most baby-boomer musicians today happily acknowledge that their primary musical influence was Bernstein's televised classroom. He made our garden grow.

Bernstein's desire to teach often expanded into a need to preach. His activism of behalf of civil rights yielded practical results in his hiring of minorities to play in his orchestra and bad publicity through Tom Wolfe's characterization of his fashionable dinner party for the Black Panthers as "radical chic." His production company, Amberson Productions, videotaped his performances and lectures for widespread commercial dissemination. Video performances were usually preceded by lengthy musical analyses, with Bernstein continuing his children's concert tradition of explaining the "why" of the work to be performed. He lectured at Harvard (of course the lecture was followed by books and tapes memorializing the talks), attempting to answer music's unanswerable questions. He sought through imaginative words to translate tones.

His later years took him on lengthy tours of the Orient,

Europe, and Latin America, exposing young and old in foreign lands to his special American way of dominating music and enthralling his audience. He championed causes such as AIDS while battling Republican administrations over what he perceived as increasing governmental threats of censorship. Bernstein, the Jew, conducted in Jerusalem during the 1967 War (a documentary celebrated this triumph) and also ironically Beethoven's *Ode to Joy* during 1989 in almost totally *Judenrein* Berlin as the Wall came tumbling down amid choral shouts of *"Freiheit!"*

Bernstein was never reluctant to tell the world through his careful manipulation of the media and musical materials, pop and symphonic, stage and screen, what or how he was feeling. He felt that if he wanted to tell us, we would want to know, and although some found his message overheated or superficial, most flocked to hear his prophecies. He did not want to simply conduct or simply compose or simply teach. He wanted us to want him do it all, all at once, so we would want more.

Bernstein taught the world that music could stand for something other than just notes. With blood, sweat, and often tears, he converted hordes of tone-deaf heathen into passionate music lovers, transfiguring popular stage shows into meaningful arenas of social thought and children's TV into fun orchestral play. His lasting influence on art may well be that conviction, expression, and love count in making the greatest music in this "best of all possible worlds."

66

Flavius Josephus

(ca. 38–ca. 100 C. E.)

It was known throughout the Roman Empire as the Jewish War. As the reign of Nero was ending in chaos, Jewish rebels, called Zealots, sensed a weakness in Roman strength and organized a revolt to end the empire's military occupation of Judea. The war that followed resulted in the deaths of hundreds of thousands of people and the destruction of the Second Temple in Jerusalem by Titus, son of the general Vespasian (soon to be crowned emperor). The official Roman history of this savage period was written by a participant, the Jewish general and traitor, Joseph ben Matthias, who took the Latin name Flavius Josephus in honor of his emperor's family.

Josephus's history is one of the most vivid works of literature from antiquity. Although his historical method and accuracy have been challenged for centuries, this account remains the most important record of the great revolt which together with the Bar Kokhba rebellion in 135 C.E. effectively ended the Jewish state until its resurrection in 1948 from the ashes of the Holocaust.

Josephus was born in Jerusalem to a family with royal roots, was well schooled in the Torah, and viewed himself as an authority in the oral law, sought out for his opinion and guidance. He spent three teenage years under the tutelage of a holy man, who may have been an Essene, a member of a sect practicing a rough, ascetic life in the wilderness (familiar to many from tales about John the Baptist).

On a visit to Rome at the age of twenty-six, seeking to free some Jewish priests, Josephus made the acquaintance of Nero's wife, Poppaea. Josephus was enthralled with Rome—and secured the priests' freedom. At this time he evidenced an ability to negotiate and free himself from a tight place which would later save his life and establish his fame.

When the Jewish War began in 66 C.E., Josephus was appointed commander of Galilee. He set about fortifying cities, preparing for the Roman onslaught. Regrettably, in what was a useless power play, the Jews fought each other almost as much as they fought the Romans. The Galilean leaders resented Josephus's appointment over them by the authorities in Jerusalem. When Vespasian arrived with his legions in 67 C.E., the Jews were unprepared for the relentless and professional Roman soldiers.

Vespasian's conquering advance slowly swept away all resistance in the Galilee. Josephus's troops fought their final battle in a town called Jotapata. When Jotapata fell, Josephus fled with forty survivors to a cave. The rebels decided to commit suicide together rather than be executed by the Romans or sold as slaves. They chose lots to decide who would kill whom and in what order. Josephus may have rigged the drawing as he and one other man were the only survivors brought before Vespasian and his son, Titus.

Vespasian ordered that Josephus be kept in the closest custody so that he could be brought to Nero in Rome at the earliest possible moment. Always quick on his feet, Josephus addressed Vespasian, enthusiastically predicting that the Roman general would become Caesar (the Talmud has Rabbi Johanan ben Zakkai doing the same thing!). Vespasian gradually began to believe the prediction, especially after the deaths in rapid succession of Nero's three hapless successors, and favored Josephus's advice. Josephus became an aide-de-camp of Vespasian and later of Titus, of special assistance at the siege of Jerusalem (Josephus was wounded while trying to convince the remaining rebels in Jerusalem to lay down their arms).

After Vespasian was crowned emperor by his troops and Titus had defeated the rebels and burned the Temple (stealing the master Torah scroll from the holiest of its chambers), Josephus was granted Roman citizenship and property. Seeking to warn all enemies of Rome of its invincible might, Vespasian commissioned Josephus to write an official eyewitness account of the Jewish War.

First written in Aramaic, the everyday tongue of Babylonian Jews, Josephus's *The Jewish War* was meant to threaten as much as inform. That version is lost. Josephus later translated the book into Greek, a version that served Vespasian's needs, legitimizing his merit (and that of his progeny) to be ruler of all men (despite his common birth).

Later in life, Josephus wrote *Jewish Antiquities,* an autobiography, and *Against Apion,* a defense against anti-Semitic writings. Although bitterly regarded by his people as a traitor, Josephus, when growing old and perhaps out of a deep guilt, defended Jewish tradition and the future of Judaism.

A Slavonic version of the *Antiquities* contains a famous passage about a certain Jesus of Nazareth. Over the centuries this passage was viewed by many in the Church as historical proof separate from the Bible of the existence of the Christ. However, most historians consider it a forgery of the third century when the Josephus manuscripts were in the hands of monks. Ironically, the works of Josephus were preserved for future readers primarily due to the commitment of the Roman Catholic Church to this passage, dubious though it may have been.

Josephus's work (particularly *The Jewish War*) greatly influenced the development of European art, drama, and fiction as an essential source of legend for Slavic-speaking peoples (heroic literature), Italian Renaissance painters (Mantegna), English dramatists, and Russian novelists.

67

Walter Benjamin

(1892–1940)

When he learned in 1940 of the suicide of his friend Walter Benjamin, Bertolt Brecht, the great playwright and collaborator of composer Kurt Weill, is reported to have said that this death was the first loss suffered by German literature at the hands of Hitler.

Walter Benjamin was a literary critic, journalist, activist, translator, and philosopher. He is best described by the French term *"homme de lettres,"* a man of letters. Rarely published during his lifetime, his writings were known only to a small circle of friends, some of whom had distinguished careers after the Second World War. Since the publication of some of his works in the 1950s, Benjamin's influence on contemporary perceptions of culture, history, metaphysics, and literature has grown exponentially. He is rightly viewed as one of the seminal thinkers of the twentieth century. His criticisms and viewpoints are often as illuminating for what they say as for how they are said. His paper "The Work of Art in the Age of Mechanical Reproduction" is among the most commonly referred to and influential cultural manifesto of contemporary writing. Benjamin's essays on Baudelaire, Kafka, Goethe, Leskov, Proust, and Brecht's epic theater continue to affect how modernist literature is understood and developed.

Benjamin's father was a well-to-do antique and collectible dealer. Walter inherited an ardor for collecting, obsessively wandering through used book shops, writing over and over again about his obsession. His parents were not religious. Assimilated German Jews living in bourgeois Berlin, Emil and Paula Benjamin sent Walter to progressive schools at home and in Freiburg and Munich. He became active in student movements. Before the slaughter of the First World War, many educated youths believed that solidarity through communal hiking and athletic activities would bring about cooperation and understanding. The war destroyed this optimism. Two of Walter's closest young friends, revolted by the world and the increasing jingoism of German youth, together committed suicide. Benjamin withdrew from association with youth groups, fled conscription into the army for school in Switzerland. During the war, he studied philosophy in Bern, returning to Germany in 1920. He attempted to secure a position teaching at the university in Frankfurt, but his thesis on German tragic drama was rejected.

During these early years Benjamin wrote essays on a wide variety of subjects, ranging from art criticism in German Romanticism, various literary figures such as Dostoyevsky and Goethe, and problems of language, to the role of the translator. He developed new concepts of literary criticism, whereby texts were viewed by themselves, the text for the text's sake alone, not in artificial contexts of culture or genre. Such criticism was undertaken as a form of expression. Indeed, criticism became for Benjamin a kind of philosophical investigation, though not a heavy Germanic philosophy based on Kant. Benjamin was creating something else, something ineffable, not easily pigeonholed.

His approach was profoundly Jewish, God-filled. Benjamin's writings sought the fundamental meaning underlying words, in essence, the theology of expression.

Walter Benjamin's essays often probe basic problems of communication and knowledge. We can only know the world through what is told to us. What is told to us is our world. What was written before our time was in a language peculiar to that time. To translate such older language into a language of our time requires that the original be capable of being said again. Yet, when a translation is made, the text becomes something far different from its origins. (Benjamin's translations of Proust's works were burned by the Nazis.)

Benjamin the revealer of stories was captivated by the storyteller Franz Kafka. Benjamin was one of the earliest critics to acknowledge the unique voice of the Czech Jewish novelist. Kafka, Benjamin believed, related experience through parable. Truth had to be foregone to be foretold.

Benjamin the Marxist was also greatly marked by his friend Brecht. He admired Brecht's fresh poetic voice. Brecht's art lay in the immediacy of his words, naked of any historical dressing, language disillusioned with any meaning other than its bare truth.

Benjamin the secular Jew was surely influenced by his friend Gerhard (later Gershom) Scholem, the masterful author, educator, and expert on Jewish mysticism who emigrated to Palestine in 1923. The magic of the sacred text, the holy character of words, entranced these men. To reveal the hidden meanings of words expressed in holy Scripture or epic drama was to make plain the presence of God.

Fleeing through France from the Nazis and Vichy French collaborators, Benjamin journeyed over the Pyrenees into the Catalan border town of Port Bou. The Spanish border patrol, learning of his arrival with a group of refugees, threatened to return him to France into the Gestapo's reach. One day earlier or later Benjamin would have been permitted to stay. In poor health from a weak heart and exhausted from his trek, Benjamin committed suicide. The site of his grave in Port Bou is not known. There is no memorial erected in his honor.

68

Louis Brandeis

(1856–1941)

Along with Benjamin Cardozo, Louis Dembitz Brandeis was the most influential Jewish jurist in American history. Cardozo's influence on the development of jurisprudence was probably greater than Brandeis's. Lawyers remain influenced by the beauty of Cardozo's legal writing and his attention to the part played by the courts in making law. Many of Cardozo's opinions, especially those made while he was chief judge of the New York State Court of Appeals, continue to affect the modern-day legal system. However, before Brandeis was a judge, he was a great lawyer, defender of the public interest, an important Zionist, and

254

a leader of the progressive politics that led to the elections of Woodrow Wilson and Franklin Delano Roosevelt. The first great Jewish lawyer in the United States and the first person of his religious faith to serve on the Supreme Court, Brandeis's example continues to work its powerful influence.

Born in Louisville, Kentucky four years before the Civil War into a cultured immigrant family from Bohemia, Brandeis learned the German spoken in his home and attended public school in Louisville. His father, Adolph, saw his grain business expand exponentially during the war and Reconstruction. In the early 1870s Adolph correctly predicted a slowdown in the abundant postwar economic boom (the depression of 1873), closed down his business, and moved the family back to Europe to visit relatives and enjoy the fruits of their prosperity. (He would later see fortune come and go—Louis was to show in his career a similar degree of discernment, but a more heightened frugality.) Brandeis attended the Annen Realschule in Dresden, Germany, incorporating the discipline of Teutonic thinking and logic while at the same time reacting with discomfort to the rigidity and oppression of the pedagogy.

Returning to the United States in 1873, Louis did find a place of learning totally to his liking—Harvard Law School. Brandeis was one of the earliest law students (and its first prominent success) to benefit from the rigors of the form of study called the "case method" (initiated at Harvard by Christopher C. Langdell). Pupils learned the law by studying its evolution in actual court cases. Brandeis fell in love with legal studies, reading so much and so intensely that he hurt his vision. Graduating with the highest grades in his class, Brandeis founded his own law firm with a classmate, Samuel D. Warren, son of wealthy industrialists and intimately connected to Boston's upper-class or Brahmin society.

Warren & Brandeis quickly became a success. Brandeis's analytical skills, incomparable ability to digest and interpret complex fact patterns, wide knowledge of business, and keen understanding of people ensured his involvement in what was then the cutting edge of the legal profession. In the age of the Robber Barons, America was losing its soul in a too rapid industrialization. The fast accumulation of personal wealth was deemed more important than the public good.

Brandeis built an early career as an activist lawyer on top of a lucrative practice representing wealthy families and institutions. Known popularly as the "People's Attorney," he spent most of his time taking on public interest cases for no fee, pro bono. Yet he continued to bring in sufficient commercial clientele (serviced by his partners) to warrant the princely draw for that time of $100,000 a year. The cases included the granting of transportation and utility franchises, regulation of the insurance industry and the development of savings bank life insurance available to all at nominal charge, defending the State of Oregon in its enforcement of a ten-hour work day, wrongdoings in the Interior Department, and the settling of labor unrest. He created a form of written argument listing general principles first, then pages of supporting facts. This became known as the "Brandeis brief" and revolutionized litigation.

Brandeis viewed his activism as an attempt, ultimately conservative in its approach, to restore a balance to America's democracy. Unfettered control of every walk of life by big business diminished the Jeffersonian ideal of democracy Brandeis cherished. Every small man must have his say. Brandeis took on unpopular causes as his way of righting the balance.

In 1912 he met another great reformer, Woodrow Wilson, who had just received the Democratic nomination for president. Their meeting at Sea Girt, New Jersey, was widely publicized, the controversial Jewish lawyer from Boston, "more Brahmin than the Brahmins," endorsing the stern Protestant scholar. Although Wilson at the time had strong ideas about social justice, his economic program was vague, not thought through. Brandeis filled Wilson with ideas of social reform serving as the great regulator of business growth. Wilson's New Freedom for America was to be built based on morality, not just on making money (how the Harding-Coolidge-Hoover years were to prove him wrong!).

When Wilson was elected, Brandeis was passed over as too controversial to be attorney general or secretary of commerce. But he continued to work as an unpaid adviser to Wilson, guiding the early administration in its formation of the Federal Reserve System and the Federal Trade Commission.

Brandeis never practiced his religion. Just before the First World War, however, he began to equate Zionism with being a good American. Brandeis assumed that Jewish tradition mandated that a renewed Jewish Zion could only be a democracy like the United States. He opposed Jewish leaders such as Jacob Schiff who believed that an American could not be loyal to his country and still be a Zionist. Brandeis's developing leadership role in the American Zionist movement led to creation of the American Jewish Congress. To have America's greatest Jewish lawyer actively behind American Zionism gave the movement in its difficult early years a much-needed legitimacy.

When presidents before Wilson nominated Supreme Court justices, their recommendations largely met with little or no opposition in the Senate. In 1916 Wilson proposed Brandeis to the Court and thereby unleashed a furious fight. Brandeis's integrity and progressive politics were viciously attacked at the hearings of the Senate Judiciary Committee. Prominent conservatives such as former president Taft could not accept that a Jew could become a Supreme Court justice.

Wilson prevailed, however, and Brandeis was confirmed by the Senate by a 47 to 22 vote, the first Jewish Supreme Court justice, whose appointment opened the door for future Jewish justices Cardozo, Frankfurter, Goldberg, Fortas, and Ginsburg.

Early in his tenure, Brandeis established what has become a tradition on the Court. Rejecting the use of a permanent secretary, he chose each year a recent graduate (chosen by his friend, Professor Felix Frankfurter) from Harvard Law School as an apprentice. Future secretary of state Dean Acheson was one such assistant.

Brandeis's career on the Court was a continuation of his progressivism. He felt deeply that the Court was too often preoccupied with property rights to the deprivation of personal freedoms, such as privacy. Brandeis believed his opinions should not only persuade but should instruct and guide. Possessing a broad and detailed knowledge of American business, Brandeis was able to give his opinions, many in dissent with his friend the great justice Oliver Wendell Holmes, a profound resonance. Brandeis was one of the first great modern justices not to rely solely on a narrow interpretation of the law, but to develop his opinions after sensitive investigation and accumulation of facts, seeing the law as an active and growing part of life, the "living" law, relevant to all.

69

Emile Berliner

(1851–1929)

No Jewish inventor has yet equaled the greatness of men such as Bell, Edison, or Ford. None has developed to date, in inventor Gordon Gould's words, "one you don't quite see." However, there have been many Jewish inventors who have transformed impractical innovations into useful tools, immensely improving mankind's quality of life in the process.

Emile Berliner did not invent the phonograph; Thomas Alva Edison did. Ten years after Edison's invention of a tinfoil recording cylinder machine, however, Berliner created the gramophone, replacing Edison's cylinder with a flat disk made of zinc.

Berliner also did not invent the telephone. Alexander Graham Bell is commonly credited with that invention. However, Berliner sought to improve the clarity and amplification of transmitted sound. He thus invented a kind of loose-contact telephone transmitter, which Berliner called the "microphone." He also developed the induction coil, improving the telephone's performance. Because of Berliner's improvements (and original creation of the microphone), the telephone became more than just a gadget, but instead an efficient method of mass communication capable of sending sounds over long distances. And later refinements made the microphone an integral part of public speaking, broadcasting, and recording.

Berliner was born and studied in Wolfenbüttel, Germany, near Hanover. When he was nineteen, he emigrated to the United States, settling, after a short stay in New York, in Washington, D.C. While working as a clerk, salesman, and then as an assistant in a chemical lab analyzing sugar, Berliner studied electricity and acoustical science.

In 1876, he began to fiddle at home with Bell's brand new design for the telephone. To make Bell's invention useful, its poor sound quality and low amplitude had to be improved. Fashioning a loudspeaker out of a soap box, Berliner assembled a crude microphone. With the addition of an induction coil, the telephone was transformed into a convenient and useful means of communication. The rights to his improvement were snatched up by the Bell Telephone Company. Berliner was then hired as chief electrical instruments inspector for Bell.

In 1887, Berliner developed the gramophone and flat disk for recording sound. Berliner's invention of a flat disk proved that the primary agent distorting the sound generated from Edison's hand-rotated cylinders was gravity. Sound waves fixed with shellac onto a flat disk, however, successfully captured sound. In addition, Berliner invented the method of reproducing copies from a master recording, now commonly known as "duping." Berliner's patent was purchased by the Victor Talking Machine Company, serving as the model of a multimillion-dollar industry. "His Master's Voice" was Berliner's.

Berliner continued dabbling in many fields, later experimenting in aviation (inventing the revolving cylindered light engine and erecting a helicopter at about the same time as Igor

Sikorsky, the man commonly credited with the invention), public hygiene, and improving the quality of milk production. Berliner also led national efforts in fighting tuberculosis and supported the construction of the Hebrew University of Jerusalem.

Other Jewish inventors include, but cannot be limited to, the list being so long: Abraham ibn Ezra (astrolabe for navigators), Levi ben Gershon (the "Jacob's staff," a quadrant used by Columbus), Nahum Solomon (thin-spoked wheel and the first safety bicycle), Leopold Mannes and Leopold Godowsky, Jr. (Kodachrome color process), Peter Carl Goldmark (color television and the long-playing record), Jacob Rabinow (mail-sorting machines), Harold Rosen (geosynchronous satellites), and of course John Von Neumann (most of the basic features of the modern computer, such as its central processing unit, memory-storage capabilities, and the use of binary numbers and serial processing).

70

Sarah Bernhardt

(1844–1923)

No figure greater represents *la belle époque*, the beautiful era of late nineteenth-century France, than the actress Sarah Bernhardt. The Divine Sarah, as she was known, was the greatest performer of her age, and like Caruso in opera or Chaplin in the movies, became for actors, directors, and playwrights who witnessed her talents their source and inspiration. During her lifetime there were certainly other great theatrical figures such as the actresses Rachel and Eleonora Duse, and the playwrights Sardou, Wilde, Ibsen, Rostand, and Shaw. But none of them had Sarah's worldwide influence.

Her mother, Youle Bernard, was a Dutch Jew who fled a middle-class life in Amsterdam with her sister Rosine for adventure on the continent. The sisters wandered through European capitals, finally settling in Paris, supporting themselves through prostitution. Youle's first pregnancy resulted in the birth of twins who died in infancy. One year later, in 1844, her little girl, Sarah (then Rosine), was born, daughter of an unknown father.

A seamstress by day, Youle was at night a well-regarded courtesan. Her salon attracted some of the most prominent figures of Parisian society, such as the writer Dumas père (whose son would supply Sarah with her greatest role, *Camille*) and the composer Rossini. Although Sarah was generally kept away during her early years at convent school, Youle brought her back in her teens to join the family profession. Sarah, however, desired first to become a nun, but soon realized that she would be better at playing the part (and many others). A school production had exposed her to the freedoms of the stage. It is suggested in correspondence and memoirs of her life that she flirted with older men who visited Youle and, without necessarily sexual relations, secured their devotion and support. With the help of the Duc de Morny, she gained a place at the age of sixteen in the Paris Conservatory where she studied with the most famous acting teachers of the time.

The connections she made at the Conservatory and through her mother led to a position at the illustrious Comédie Française, France's national theater. She made little impression on her audiences and irritated her fellow actors by allowing her kid sister, Regine, to tag along backstage and at private celebrations. Sarah's contract was terminated after six months.

She supported herself with liaisons until the Gymnase, a fashionable theater in Paris, hired her to understudy its leading ladies. Her time at the Gymnase was also uneventful except for giving birth at twenty to her only son, Maurice.

Sarah continued to support her increasingly lavish lifestyle not on the stage but in bed. The young Sarah was remarkably beautiful with dark smooth skin and penetrating eyes. She was soon noticed by the great woman writer George Sand, who sponsored the young actress at the Odéon, the experimental theater located on the Parisian Left Bank. In contemporary plays of Sand, Alexandre Dumas fils, and Victor Hugo, *"la petite*

Sarah," as she was initially called, became a star.

Though no longer needing to rely solely on the life of the courtesan to support herself, Sarah drifted from one well-heeled lover to the next. Returning to the Comédie ten years after her termination, she took up with its leading man, Mounet-Sully, with whom she would appear countless times.

Her success would however be tainted by tragedy. Her sister Regine died at the age of eighteen of tuberculosis, a dissipated whore. In a bizarre attempt to compete with Regine, Sarah began to sleep in a coffin—a morbid exercise which fascinated and repelled all of Paris. She seemed constantly to be in search of new sensations and new emotions.

By her early thirties she had already become a legend and was desired by countless men. Victor Hugo, William and Henry James, the composer Tchaikovsky, the artists Gustave Doré and Georges Clairin, were enamored of her. Later in her life she would inspire the writers Mark Twain, D.H. Lawrence, and Edmond Rostand, and her portrait would earn an honored place on the wall of the office of Sigmund Freud. On her trip to England with the Comédie Française, Sarah won the adoration of Oscar Wilde. With Sarah as his muse, twelve years later he wrote his infamous *Salomé*. Her success in London was astounding and catapulted her to international recognition.

She resigned from the Comédie, founded her own acting company, and set out to tour the New World. Her voyage to America in 1880 received wide press coverage. Before she landed in New York, Sarah saved a woman from falling downstairs when the ship suddenly tilted. She had rescued Mary Todd Lincoln, a fate not appreciated much by the president's forlorn widow.

In New York, Sarah appeared in seven classic roles twenty-seven times in twenty-seven days; visited Thomas Alva Edison at his laboratory in New Jersey and made her first gramophone recording with lines from Racine's *Phaedre* which concluded with the inventor merrily singing *Yankee Doodle Dandy*; and in Boston communed with the poets Oliver Wendell Holmes and Henry Wadsworth Longfellow. In six packed months she earned a million dollars, the glamour of her personality (to use Oscar Wilde's words) overwhelming her American audiences.

She would return to the United States several more times with rich success. Her trip to Italy inspired the young Eleonora

Duse to act and to Russia inflamed Anton Chekhov to virulent literary attack.

Back in Paris, during most of the 1880s, Sarah scored her greatest successes with Sardou's *Fédora, Théodora,* and *La Tosca*. With these plays Sardou established the Bernhardt style, which would mark acting well into the silent-film era.

In the 1890s she went on a worldwide tour which lasted much of the decade. She met the composer Reynaldo Hahn, whose lover Marcel Proust would immortalize Sarah in his immense novel *Remembrance of Things Past*. She stole Duse's lover, the great Italian writer Gabriele D'Annunzio, opened and closed two theaters, in her fifties performed the title role of *Hamlet*, and with writer Emile Zola publicly supported Captain Alfred Dreyfus against vicious anti-Semitism.

Her remaining years were spent in declining health. The amputation of her right leg after an accident did not prevent her however from performing for French troops during the First World War or again traveling to remote parts of America on yet another tour. She lived long enough to be captured permanently in early silent films, her broad theatrical gestures in keeping with the contemporary acting style. Tens of thousands lined the streets of Paris to view her funeral cortege. France's regal star had become immortal.

Sarah's influence lies not only in her immeasurable development of the art of acting, but also in the continuing fascination with the life she led and the great artists she inspired. Her tours throughout Europe and America brought classical and modern drama to people who had never experienced theater, moving individuals and institutions to commit greater resources to the writing and acting of plays. Her transformation of melodrama somehow into great art inspired artists like Puccini (who adapted Sardou's *La Tosca* in 1900 into his popular opera) and Proust, and actors like La Duse and John Gielgud. Sarah's art and life serve today as an emblem of the beauties and splendor of her age, before its obliteration forever in the madness of world war.

71

Levi Strauss

(1829–1902)

When American tourists traveled to the Soviet Union before its collapse, they were often asked by merchandise-starved Russians to trade blue jeans for vodka. "Levi's! Levi's!" were desperately sought, a kind of status symbol, liberty expressed in a pair of denims.

No other piece of apparel signifies America so much. To people everywhere jeans mean cowboys, the Old West, horses, saddles, rugged individualism. Even people who cannot try on the stars and stripes can sport a pair of pale blue pants and feel free.

Born in Buttenheim, near the German-Austrian border in the Bavarian Alps, Lob Strauss was a peddler of dry goods for most of his early life. With his mother and two sisters, Vösila and Maila, in 1847 Lob emigrated to America to join his two step-brothers, Louis and Jonas, in New York. At the docks in New York Harbor Lob became Levi, and as legend has it, the most famous name in the history of the clothing business was born.

How Levi created the first pair of jeans is also legendary. Sometime in the middle 1850s, during California's gold rush, Levi was peddling in mining towns, hard-living places with exotic names like El Dorado. One day a rough hewn miner approached Levi and asked what was for sale. Levi offered to sell a tent. The miner did not want a tent, but said he could use some strong pants that would not easily rip. Seizing the moment (and his customer), Levi measured the miner and promised rugged clothing made to order. Levi found a tailor in a nearby mining town (after some difficulty, good tailors not being in much demand in the hills), and had the tailor fashion a sturdy pair of pants out of the tent canvas. The pants had large pockets that could hold gold nuggets and tools. The miner was pleased, and Levi had a six-dollar sale (in gold dust!). The word about "those pants of Levi's" spread through the camps quickly, becoming a miners' fashion rage.

By the 1860s, Levi had changed the fabric of his pants to denim, a cloth imported from de Nimes, France (thus their name). Aided by his stepbrothers' manufacturing capabilities in New York, men throughout the United States in every walk of life (not just miners) began to wear Levi's pants.

Levi Strauss & Co., the first and most famous jeans manu-facturer in the world, developed out of a family business. Levi, with his stepbrothers on the East Coast and brothers-in-law David Stern and William Sahlein in San Francisco (and their children), created the company that would initially popularize tough clothing for the workingman, then later casual wear for both sexes.

The family sold wholesale as well as retail, developing a transatlantic business. With factories on both coasts, a fast distribution network, and salesmen journeying to remote towns not laden with dry goods but efficiently selling from their catalog, Levi Strauss & Co. grew quickly. When a customer suggested a way of making the pants stronger at the rise and in the crotch, the rivet stitch was invented. The customer, Jacob Davis, a tailor, was recruited and became the company's first foreman in charge of production. At the beginning the rivets were made of copper. After mothers and schoolmarms complained that the copper rivets were scratching furniture at home and in school, Levi exchanged the rivets for strong thread. The company also developed its well-known trademark orange stitches on the back pocket and the beloved patch depicting two horses attempting to tear apart a pair of Levi's. No self-respecting Levi's wearer could ever remove that patch. It became (along with the Levi's logo initiated in the 1930s) the longest-lasting symbol in fashion history.

Levi Strauss brought his sister's sons into the business. The company remained in family control well into the twentieth century. Levi became a well-regarded philanthropist, supporting in particular the study of Judaism at the University of California. Sensitive to the distribution needs of a national company with factories on the Atlantic and the Pacific coasts, as a member of the San Francisco Board of Trade, he lobbied diligently for the creation of a canal in Central America. Around the time of his death, the Panama Canal became a reality.

He remains a role model not only for his Horatio Alger tale, but for his ability to develop a uniquely American enterprise. Especially in the United States and England, Jews have continued to predominate in the "rag" or *shmatte* trade. Contemporary designers such as Ralph Lauren still find esthetic inspiration in the Wild West of Levi Strauss's California.

72

Nahmanides

(1195–1270)

Known as the Ramban (an acronym) or Nahmanides of Gerona, Spain, Rabbi Moses ben Nahman was perhaps the greatest Jewish scholar of the thirteenth century. His commentary on the Pentateuch, the Five Books of Moses, is a classic of biblical scholarship. He also tried in vain to defend the works of Maimonides against claims of heresy.

Yet Nahmanides' lasting influence on world history is derived from his involvement in one of the most troubling events of all time, the Disputation at Barcelona in 1263. Upon the order of the king of Aragon, Nahmanides debated a converted Jew (probably from southern France) named Pablo Christiani in public on the relative merits of Judaism and Christianity. Nahmanides' account of the debate led to a charge of blasphemy and his banishment. In exile in the Holy Land, he helped to revive a poor and dwindling Jewish community.

The idea of a public debate on the two religions was conceived by Catholic priests who sought to convert the Jews en masse by defeating before their eyes their greatest rabbi and spiritual leader. The Church typically imposed strict limitations on what a Jewish debater could say. The outcome of each debate was preordained. Brutal punishment for not going along with the prepared script was always threatened. The debate between Christiani and Nahmanides is the best known and was the most influential of these tragic encounters.

King James of Aragon respected Nahmanides, often consulting him on matters of state. Most probably on the urgings of Dominican priests, James forced Nahmanides into the debate.

In a room filled with bishops and royalty, the participants were asked simple questions not simply answered. Was Jesus the Messiah, was he divine, was the Messiah yet to come, was the Messiah a man, not a god, and who practiced the one true faith and was guided by the only correct law, Jews or Christians?

But the debate was not rigged this time. King James had given Nahmanides permission to speak freely, without fear of retribution.

Christiani argued that sections of the Talmud confirmed that the Messiah had come. Jesus, Pablo urged, was both god and man, dying on the Cross to atone for all the sins of humanity. By Jesus' intercession on earth, Judaism had lost its reason to be, and was therefore not valid. Jews must be guided by the one true faith, belief in the Christ.

Nahmanides carefully refuted Christiani's Talmudic references. The Ramban noted that Christianity was basically illogical. Jesus could not have been the Messiah, for he did not bring peace to the world, did not confirm the fundamental prophecy uttered by the prophet Isaiah ("Nation shall not lift up sword against nation, neither shall they learn war any more"). Imperial Rome had gone into decay after accepting Christianity. Jesus' death was followed by over a thousand years of great savagery and blood, often committed in his name. Christians, praying to the Prince of Peace, had "shed more blood than all other peoples."

The debate dragged on for four days.

Nahmanides noted that Jews and Christians were divided by the question of Jesus' divinity. Jewish tradition had no place for belief in a Messiah as god. No man could be a god. Only God was God. Why would the Almighty create out of a human mother a baby who would grow up only to be betrayed by his brethren and executed horribly, then resurrect him and bring him back home again? Nahmanides told the King that he would never have believed such a story if he had heard it for the first time as an adult. Only through indoctrination since birth would someone believe such a tale.

As to which law was still binding, Nahmanides urged that the Torah remained valid as the world had not changed. Mankind needed God's guidance.

Unable to tolerate Nahmanides' free speaking, the priests halted the debate in its fourth day. The King, a rather remarkable man for his time, rewarded Nahmanides with a cash prize for his efforts, angering the priests to fever pitch. Nahmanides published an account of the debate. Despite the protection granted the rabbi by the King, the Dominicans enlisted the aid of the Pope and sought to try Nahmanides for blasphemy. With the probable help of King James, Nahmanides fled to safe haven in Jerusalem. The Barcelona debate hardened the Church's position against the Jews, leading directly to the horrors of the Spanish Inquisition.

Although there were other great debates between Jews and Christians over the centuries, including those between Moses Mendelssohn and Johann Lavater or Martin Buber and Karl Ludwig Schmidt, the Disputation of 1263 displayed how far apart people remain when intolerance restrains their ability to communicate with understanding. Of course, whether one believes in the divinity of Jesus or not is a matter of faith, and matters of faith must always be respected and cherished by everyone. However, people have repeatedly shown their inability to respect each other's beliefs (religious or not) as if such respect would be to deny their own existence. The Disputation at Barcelona was but another tragic example of man's failure to listen when blinded by hate. Many historians have dated the fall of Spanish culture and political dominance to the expulsion of the Jews from Spain in 1492.

73

Menachem Begin
(1913–1992)

Political figures are often chastised for their lack of conviction. All they seem interested in is power and glory. Menachem Wolfovitch Begin, however, was totally and consistently convinced of his beliefs. A follower of Vladimir Jabotinsky, the founder of the Zionist Revisionist organization and a believer in armed struggle as the only way to create the Jewish homeland, Begin first led Betar, the European Jabotinsky youth movement, and in 1940s Palestine, Irgun Zvai Leumi, the clandestine terrorist group battling British colonial rule. His militaristic activities led directly to the resistance by Jews of oppression first in Europe and later in the Middle East.

The Irgun functioned alongside Yitzak Shamir's rival group, the Stern Gang, as a brutally aggressive counterpoint to the more conventional, but no less dynamic and crucial, Haganah or regular forces, led by David Ben-Gurion. Without Begin's covert actions, the State of Israel might not have been established in 1948.

Out of the remnants of the Irgun, Begin built a political party into a major force in Israeli government. As prime minister, he exchanged land for peace with the Egyptians, sharing the Nobel Peace Prize with the dynamic and courageous President Anwar el-Sadat. Begin fostered the construction of settlements on lands captured in the 1967 and 1973 Arab conflicts, considering them part of the biblical Israel. He was unable however to calm the savage tensions with the country's other Arab neighbors, leading to a costly war in Lebanon which reached to the bloody streets of Beirut.

Menachem Begin grew up in a household which treasured the idea of the Jewish Zion. Born in Brest, a part of Poland still part of tsarist Russia before the First World War, Begin was exposed by his father, Dov Zeev Begin, a merchant, to the Jewish "heretics" or nationalists. The young boy exhibited a remarkable talent for public speaking, giving his first oration at the age of ten in Hebrew and Yiddish. He joined Betar at fifteen and soon learned how to handle weapons. Within ten years he not only held a law degree from Warsaw University, but was also the head of the seventy-thousand-strong Betar movement.

Fleeing the approaching Germans in 1939, Begin left Warsaw for Vilna, the great mythical capital of Yiddish and Talmudic learning, then occupied by the Soviets. The Russians arrested him, accused him of being a Zionist and British spy, and sentenced him to Siberia. His wife of a year, Aliza, traveled to Palestine, hoping to pave the way for Menachem after his liberation. He survived a brutal incarceration to be freed in 1941 in a general release by the Russians of over a million Polish prisoners. Begin then joined the Free Polish Army, found his sister, made his way to Iran and then Palestine. Both of his parents had been killed by the Nazis. Begin often imagined his father going to his death praising the name of the Lord and singing his beloved *Hatikvah*, the Slovak folk song that would become the national anthem of Israel. Dov's son never forgot his father's teachings that the Jewish people would not travel, go, or come but would *return* to their homeland. To return after thousands of years of dispersion in foreign lands was a right given to the Jews in eternity.

For a short time in Palestine, Begin served in the British army as an interpreter. By 1943, however, he assumed the leadership of the Irgun and went into hiding to fight the British. By 1946 Begin had a price on his head of first eight then fifty thousand dollars. "Grim, bespectacled Menachem Begin" was a target of an intensive manhunt resulting from such terrorist tactics as executing captured British officers in retaliation for the deaths of Irgun operatives in British jails. The most famous incident, however, was the blowing up of a wing of the King David Hotel in Jerusalem. The explosion killed ninety people, including many British officers and some Arab and Jewish workers. A more infamous incident was the attack by Irgun forces on the Arab village of Deir Yassin. Two hundred men, women and children died in the assault. Two months later, Ben-Gurion, furious at the Irgun activities and fearful of civil war, directed the Haganah to fire on Irgun forces on board a cargo ship laden with arms and ammunition.

Menahem Begin while a university student in Poland.

From the creation of the State of Israel in 1948 until he became prime minister twenty-nine years later, Begin led the loyal opposition to the Labor governments of David Ben-Gurion, Levi Eshkol, Golda Meir, and Yitzhak Rabin. Attracting many Sephardic or Oriental Jews to his side, he built a potent political party grounded not in socialist and liberal ideals, but in orthodox religious beliefs and biblical ideology. To Prime Minister Begin, the West Bank captured in the 1967 war with the Arabs was the Judea and Samaria of the Old Testament. It was the government's obligation to the faithful to establish settlements on this land, a controversial decision opposed by many in the Labor party and condemned at the United Nations. Begin told the world that Israel did not need anyone's blessings for its acts—it was legitimate because it existed.

However, the deserts of the Sinai peninsula were not part of the greater Israel of the Bible. When President Sadat indicated his willingness to trade peace for land, Begin was waiting, eager to negotiate. With the able assistance of President Jimmy Carter, after sixteen months of difficult talks, the Camp David accords were signed on March 26, 1979. Peace with Egypt was at last achieved.

Yet the rest of the Arab world would not let the Israelis live in peace. Every terrorist attack was responded to severely. When he felt Israel's vital security interests were threatened, Begin's response was immediate. In 1981 the prime minister ordered the bombing of the Iraqi reactor outside of Baghdad, halting Saddam Hussein's atomic weapon research for many years. (For this strike, Begin was widely criticized. But think of how Desert Storm might have ended in 1991 if Saddam had the bomb!)

Begin annexed the Golan Heights, also captured in the 1967 War. He changed the unit of currency from the Israeli pound to the shekel, the coin used by the ancient Israelites. Under his direction the Israeli Parliament or Knesset declared Jerusalem, undivided, the capital of the nation, for all eternity.

After Sadat's assassination, relations with Egypt cooled, particularly after the invasion of Lebanon in 1982 by the Israeli army. Relying largely on the advice of his defense minister, Ariel Sharon, Begin directed the routing out of terrorist bases just over the border. The Lebanon War dragged on for months, bringing the Israelis to the outskirts of Beirut and into an occupation no one really wanted. When hundreds of people were massacred in the Palestinian refugee camps at Sabra and Shatila by Lebanese Christian militia, the Israeli military was roundly damned as responsible for not securely guarding the victims.

Begin's medical problems, his wife's death in 1982, and his despair over the futility of the Lebanese conflict led to his resignation in 1983. Until his death in 1992 he lived a reclusive life, rarely venturing out of his home, usually only to visit his wife's grave or attend a family function. At his death he was praised as the guerilla fighter who made peace with Egypt and defended his homeland, never wavering from his beliefs.

It is, of course, too soon to totally judge Begin's effect on the history of the world and the Middle East. However, Menachem Begin made it clear that never again would his people be dictated to by the world; they would determine their own destiny, no matter what anyone thought. This fighter for Zion and creator of a powerful political movement was an elegant speaker who dressed formally and took everything personally. He could not, would not, separate his beliefs from his feelings. Begin made extreme statements for extreme purposes. The world had to know quite clearly what he meant and why he meant what he said. His message is unmistakable and forever—Israel, the nation of survivors, is here to stay. Without Begin's courage at Camp David, Prime Minister Rabin and Defense Minister Shimon Peres would not have been able to begin negotiations in 1993 with Yasir Arafat and the Palestine Liberation Organization.

74

Anna Freud

(1895–1982)

Anna Freud was born in 1895, the youngest of Sigmund and Martha Freud's six children. Her birth coincided with father Sigmund's revolutionary discovery of the meaning of dreams, the lynchpin of his psychoanalytic theory. She grew up to become her father's constant companion, assistant, and creative heir. With Melanie Klein, Anna Freud is widely regarded as the cofounder of psychoanalytic child psychology.

Like her father, Anna drew on the experiences of her childhood to develop her psychoanalytic theories. Although she was raised by her mother, Martha, and her aunt, Minna Bernays, her nanny, a Catholic nursemaid named Josefine Cihlarz, became what she would later call her "primary caretaker" or "psychological mother." Once while at a fair in Vienna, the little Anna got lost. She bypassed her mother and aunt, who were plainly in sight, only to feel comforted when at last she rested in the arms of her beloved Josefine.

Sigmund Freud had a special feeling for his youngest child, whom he nicknamed in the Viennese fashion "Annerl." She was to become the closest companion of his life (Anna never married), his personal assistant and secretary, the Cordelia to his King Lear, his Antigone. Under his strong influence, Anna in her late teens presented papers to the Vienna Psycho-Analytical Society (her first paper was on beating fantasies and daydreams), was analyzed on Sigmund's couch, and began to practice psychotherapy.

In the early 1920s she established a seminar on child behavior, the *Kinderseminar,* which proved to be a seminal force in the training of well-known child analysts. These analysts included Erik Erikson, Dorothy Burlingham, Margaret Mahler, and others who in turn would teach several generations of students.

At this time the schism between two different theories of child analysis arose (and still divides many). The so-called British school, founded by Melanie Klein, applied established concepts of adult psychoanalysis to children without modification. Anna Freud's "Continental" brand of child psychology urged an approach more tailored to children's development.

Anna also spent the years between the two world wars assisting her father in perfecting his theories. Her study of the psychology of the ego, how our conscious defends itself from danger, has had lasting impact.

After the Anschluss, the Nazi invasion of Austria, in 1938, the Freud family fled to England. Sigmund died of cancer the following year. Anna and Burlingham began the Hampstead Child-Therapy Course and Clinic in England, which developed out of a nursery, started during the Second World War, for children separated from their parents or who had lost their homes during the bombings. The two women used their experiences at the Hampstead War Nursery to develop the new field of psychoanalytic child psychology, using original diagnostic tools in treating children, including the influential developmental profile.

Although she spent much of her professional life expanding and refining her father's theories, Anna Freud also developed new approaches to the understanding of child development. Her concepts were derived not only from theoretical but also from clinical study.

Anna Freud's profound concern with the best interests of children led her in the 1960s to develop at the Yale Law School guidelines for adoption, child custody, and divorce proceedings based on psychoanalytic research and clinical practice. Largely due to her influence, American courts now consider the importance of the *psychological* parent in adjudicating family disputes.

75

Queen Esther

(Fifth century B.C.E.)

Some historians say she never existed. She was not noble but common (and a foreigner). The Greek historian Herodotus relates that King Xerxes (Ahasuerus in the Bible) married one "Amnestris" (close however in sound—a Babylonian Esther?). There is no mention of Esther in other ancient texts, except, of course, in the Scriptures and several holy scrolls.

Whether or not she lived, her story, celebrated annually on

the festival of Purim, has instructed mankind for twenty-five hundred years. To hate people just because they are different is the most debased action, a sin only to be punished by the blackness of death.

The story of Esther is not only about anti-Semitism. It is a deceptively simple tale, almost a fable, in which good triumphs over evil through the wits of a great man and the charm and extraordinary courage of a beautiful woman. For centuries imaginative scholars have pondered the hidden meanings of the story.

Having either banished or killed his Queen Vashti for failing to dance naked for his friends, Ahasuerus sought a new consort from the young women of his realm. Esther became Ahasuerus's favorite, a queen of all Babylon. Mordecai, Esther's uncle, saved the king from murderous plotters. Haman, the Amalekite, rose to become prime minister. Insulted by Mordecai's failure to bow, Haman convinced the king that there was a people in their midst, the captured Israelites, who obeyed their own laws, spoke their own language, ignored the rule of Ahasuerus, and that, therefore, they must die, must all be massacred. Esther, urged on by Mordecai and at enormous personal risk, gave a series of banquets for the king and Haman. She captured the full attention of her sovereign who ordered a royal tribute to Mordecai (for his uncovering of the plotters' attempted coup) and granted Esther's wish to halt Haman's genocidal plot before it could start. Haman replaced Mordecai at the gallows and a bloodbath of Haman's family and supporters followed, Old Testament retribution taken for the attempted annihilation of His chosen people.

We should always be reminded by the events of history since Esther that there was no courageous queen to save the Jewish multitudes from oppression and slaughter during the Roman wars, the Crusades, the Spanish Inquisition, the Chmielnicki massacres in Poland, the Russian pogroms, or the Nazi Holocaust. Titus, the Crusaders, Torquemada, the tsars, and Hitler did not heed the lesson taught by the Esther story to humanity. During their tyranny there was no ingenious palace intrigue to protect countless innocents from brutality. But their evil did play itself out, their initial triumphs shattered after exposure to the cold reality of a people forever unwilling to recognize an idol other than their one true God.

The absence of any reference to a deity in the Esther story was noticed by the Jewish sages. In the midst of great oppression Jews have often asked why God did not reveal Himself to save His people, to show some sign of His favor. The Talmudic commentator Rashi noted that when Esther lived there was a holy eclipse, that God retreated from human affairs, but still motivated and permitted people to suffer their own consequences.

Elie Wiesel, the profoundly humane novelist and voice for justice, in his *Sages and Dreamers* feels anguish when recounting Esther's tale. He finds the story enchanting in its naiveté, but is troubled by the many meanings of the plot and the motivations of the characters. To Wiesel the story of Purim is not simply about persecution. Rather, he celebrates its call to our memory. We must always remember what it is about and learn from its message to preserve our future.

After the expulsion from Spain in 1492, Jews in the ghettoes of Europe continually asked themselves why their people did not stand up to the cruelty of the Inquisition. Mordecai did not bow to Haman. Yet the rabbis reminded them that Mordecai advised Esther to conceal her Jewish origin. Purim with all its giddy happiness and drunken revelry carried a potent message. Haman had sought to destroy all Jews. As the Jews had been scattered throughout the Babylonian Empire, making them easier to prey upon, so were they scattered throughout Europe during the Diaspora. One of the prime reasons for the founding of the State of Israel was to unify the Jewish people in their own homeland, never again to be prey for the Hamans of Berlin or St. Petersburg.

Today, Esther's message must be understood by all peoples. Whether Armenians are marched into death by Turks, Cambodians stripped of their dignity and eliminated in killing fields, or South Africans robbed of their futures in vicious apartheid, Haman is still with us.

76

Martin Buber

(1878–1965)

David Ben-Gurion, the first prime minister of Israel, called Martin Buber "a metaphysical entity in his own class, a true man of the spirit." Born in Vienna during the reign of Emperor Franz Josef; trained in Austria, Switzerland, and Germany; a professor of higher learning at universities in Frankfurt and Jerusalem; Zionist; journalist; theologian; expert on Hasidism; patron saint to Jewish and Christian intellectuals; biblical scholar; political leader—Mordecai Martin Buber, as he was known to Israelis, was the foremost Jewish philosopher of the twentieth century. At his death the great writer and teacher Abraham Joshua Heschel described Buber's "very being" as his "greatest contribution." His distinguished biographer, Maurice Friedman, noted that Buber dealt with "meaninglessness, sustaining in the darkness the living substance of faith." He was a man beloved.

Buber's greatest gift to mankind was his concept of dialogue. Born more out of religious feeling than abstract philosophy, Buber's expressive book *I and Thou* (1923) set forth how man relates to his world. He presented two forms of relationships, I-Thou and I-It. The I-Thou relationship is the only truly open means of communication. Everything seen or felt, spoken or heard, is mutual, interconnected, there. It is a true dialogue "spoken with the whole being." The I-It nexus has none of these attributes. It is restricted to the object, never a true dialogue, closed. The quantity of technical knowledge is increased materially through the I-It relation. I-It is not necessarily evil, but is selfish in its accumulation of data. The I-It relationship spawns knowledge, but I-Thou is purest revelation.

Buber's philosophy of dialogue led to his "Hebrew Humanism," which stressed the divine role of the Jewish people among nations. When they communicate wholly with and directly to each other and with the "Eternal Thou," God, people have realized what is holy in their everyday lives. In the heat of factional hatred, Jews and Arabs must work out their problems for the common good, liberated through understanding to develop as they individually wish. Buber's politics of cooperation and understanding with Israel's Arab neighbors was controversial during his time, but has been proven correct by history.

He came from a background of commitment and scholarship. Buber was raised by his grandfather, Solomon Buber, a notable rabbinic scholar. After studies in Vienna, Leipzig, Zurich, and Berlin, Buber became an active Zionist. He attended the third Zionist congress in 1898 and became known as a proponent of education to promulgate Zionist ideals. For a brief time he served as editor of the Zionist weekly *Die Welt*, resigning when his ideas on cultural development were rejected by the more politically minded followers of Theodor Herzl. Buber then founded a Jewish publication society and began the study of Hasidism.

He was first drawn to the ecstatic Hasidic movement by its colorful folk tales and rich history. His *Tales of Rabbi Nachman* (1906) and *The Legend of the Baal-Shem* (1908) are literary classics.

Buber was the first to bring to world attention the beauties and majesty of the mystical wonders of the early Hasids. Later in *For the Sake of Heaven* (1941), *Hasidism and Modern Man* (1943), and *The Origin and Meaning of Hasidism* (1945), Buber would shift his attention from legend to its relevance in contemporary life.

After the exhilaration of the first Hasidic retellings, Buber was prepared to return to public life. In a time of rapid assimilation in Germany he gave lectures to students on returning to Jewish life, influencing a generation (and most notably, the philosopher Franz Rosenzweig). Although supportive of the national war movement, Buber created a Jewish National Committee to help Jewish people in countries in Eastern Europe under German occupation. At this time Buber also began to preach his special brand of Hebrew Humanism. He stressed the importance of creating a society in Palestine committed to ideals of sharing, peace, and life-giving values. His friend Gustav Landauer, the minister of culture and education in the Bavarian Socialist Republic after the First World War, shared many of Buber's thoughts. Landauer however was assassinated by counterrevolutionary soldiers. During the 1920s idealistic German politics were rapidly consumed by the madness of Nazi tyranny.

With his colleague Rosenzweig, Buber's main literary output in the 1920s consisted of a new German translation of the Bible. They viewed the Bible as an oral history which had lost its immediacy in earlier pedantic settings. Completed after Rosenzweig's death by Buber in 1961, the translation is vibrant and directly immediate. For Buber, the reader is never an object to be manipulated by the author, but someone to join with in the celebration of revelatory history.

Buber's productive work as professor of Jewish religion and ethics at the University of Frankfurt was terminated when the Nazis seized power in 1933. Jews throughout Germany were restricted from attending public schools. In a period of progressively vicious racial and religious prohibitions, Buber served as director of a bureau for Jewish education in Germany. He traveled throughout the country, often at great personal risk, an inspiring symbol of spiritual strength and resistance.

In 1938 Buber emigrated to Palestine, just escaping the horrors of the Holocaust. He was named professor of social philosophy at the Hebrew University, where he taught until 1951.

Buber remained active in Israeli political and cultural affairs until his death in 1965, often espousing unfashionable views based on his unique ethical values.

For some he remains a kind of master of Jewish existentialism. Perhaps his most important influence on the non-Jewish world was his profound affect on leading Protestant theologians such as Reinhold Niebuhr, Paul Tillich, and Karl Barth. Buber, more a universal philosopher than just a Jewish thinker, was admired for his view that the relationship of I to the Eternal Thou favors a life of dialogue, faith as an active, not passive, participation and oneness with God, in everything we do.

77

Jonas Salk

(b. 1914)

Until the 1950s, the disease had been the scourge of young people, savagely attacking, rendering strong muscles flaccid, causing sudden painful paralysis and often death. Poliomyelitis, commonly known as polio, is a crippling, potentially deadly sickness which during the epidemic of 1952, for example, killed 3,300 persons out of the 57,626 stricken.

Amid great publicity, acclaim, and controversy, during the 1950s a handful of scientists, led by Jonas Salk and Albert Sabin, using conflicting methods and in almost virulent opposition to each other, developed vaccines that have largely eradicated polio

286

from the industrial world. The discovery of a vaccine for polio improved forever the health of society. Children could grow up and run about their homes, yards, and schools, free from what was a common, brutally debilitating illness.

Under the auspices of the National Foundation for Infantile Paralysis, Salk, a researcher at the University of Pittsburgh medical school, announced in 1953 the creation of a dead virus serum which when needle-injected immunized its recipient against contracting polio. Salk's announcement preceded by seven years the introduction by Sabin of an oral live virus vaccine that became most widely used and has proven extremely effective in fighting polio.

However, it was Salk's declaration that galvanized the medical community into doing something definitive and lasting to end this awful plague. To prove his point that the vaccine was safe, Salk first injected himself, his wife, and their three sons. Evidence was soon established that the serum was effective in warding off the virus. The serum was then used on children crippled with polio and at an institution for the retarded. Such methods of experimentation would today most probably be illegal. In 1954 the Foundation (now called the March of Dimes) sponsored a mass test of the vaccine on almost two million schoolchildren. By 1955, the vaccine was proven fit for use and was the accepted form of vaccination until the establishment of the oral Sabin serum in 1960.

Salk was born in New York City, the oldest son of a garment center worker. He was an exceptional student at the City University of New York and later in graduate school at New York University medical school. Salk also studied with and worked in Michigan for the eminent virologist Thomas Francis Jr., with whom he helped develop one of the early commercial vaccines against the flu.

In 1947 Salk joined the research staff at the University of Pittsburgh, which was to be the site of his great discovery. He continued to develop vaccines to fight influenza, but was drawn to preventing the spread of polio. Two years later, Dr. John Enders received the Nobel Prize for growing in his Harvard laboratory polio virus in a test tube containing monkey tissues. Enders' findings proved an effective means of mass-producing the viral strains required for the creation of Salk's vaccine.

Three types of polio viruses were identified. After growing these strains in Enders' test tube environment, Salk killed them with formaldehyde. Developing a vaccine from the mixture, he injected sufficient amounts of the dead virus serum in his patients to achieve immunity.

Salk's vaccine made him internationally famous. Proceeds from the vaccine were used to improve its potency and in other medical research. To further the cause of science and the humanities, he also established the Salk Institute in La Jolla, California in 1963. Salk served as director of the Institute until 1985. Thereafter he conducted experiments on a dead virus vaccine for AIDS, seeking to bring to the battle against this dread disease the same multinational forces he had directed in the development of the polio serum.

78

Jerome Robbins

(b. 1918)

In 1935 a young dancer named Jerome Rabinowitz applied for a scholarship at the School of American Ballet run by George Balanchine—and was summarily rejected by a secretary.

Born in New York City to Harry and Lena (Rips) Rabinowitz and raised in Weehawken, New Jersey, Jerome Robbins became (without the early overwhelming pressure of Balanchine's presence) one of the most influential choreographers in modern history.

Active in both Broadway musicals and classical ballet, Robbins developed an eclectic style immediately recognizable for its rhythmic clarity and angular form. A fierce ballet master, Robbins elicited seemingly perfect performances from his dancers, the geometric shapes of his choreography sharply realized. Agnes De Mille once remarked that Jerome Robbins brought to dance a kind of American colloquialism, as if the streets ran into the stage. Whether working with composer Leonard Bernstein on *Fancy Free* or *West Side Story* or at George Balanchine's New York City Ballet on *Dances at a Gathering,* based on piano music by Chopin, Robbins added remarkably original masterpieces to the ballet and theatrical repertoire. In an interview with *The New York Times* in 1990, Robbins expressed wonder at how each of his ballets, composed over a then thirty-five-year period, retains "its own character, colors and spines—its own center."

He developed out of a milieu common to the experience of children of immigrant parents. Harry and Lena had left the fearful pogroms of Russia like so many others for security in America. Settling in Weehawken, Harry worked in a delicatessen and later manufactured corsets. Jerome's older sister, Sonya, interested him in studying dance. Jerome was not a child prodigy, coming to dance studies as a teenager. After graduation from high school and one year at college at New York University, Robbins put aside a business career and concentrated on dance.

He studied with masters of almost every dance discipline including ballet (with Antony Tudor), interpretive, modern, Oriental, and Spanish dance. Robbins studied acting and worked winters in the chorus of many Broadway shows and summers (like so many Jewish boys of his generation) in the mountains (Camp Tamiment in Pennsylvania).

In 1940, the young professional dancer was hired by the newly formed Ballet Theatre (later known as American Ballet Theatre or ABT to its fans). In 1942 Robbins portrayed the title role in Igor Stravinsky's classic ballet *Petrouchka,* dancing into immediate stardom.

In the remarkable year of 1944, Robbins and his contemporary Bernstein created *Fancy Free.* Considered a period piece today for its Second World War setting and casual theme (on leave from naval duty, three sailors go out on the town trying to meet girls), the work was a smash. Appealing to the patriotism of the time, *Fancy Free* was highly influential, not only through its music and everyday story, but also for dance that easily combined popular and classical styles with wit and brilliance.

Bernstein and Robbins were so elated with their success that they enlisted the book and lyrics writing team of Betty Comden and Adolph Green to expand the ballet into a Broadway show. For the first time as a creator, Robbins stepped out of the classical ballet world into popular culture. His creative cross-fertilization would immeasurably and permanently influence both worlds. Three days before the end of 1944, on December 28, *On the Town* opened, marking New York forever as "a helluva town."

Through 1965, Robbins worked almost simultaneously on Broadway and in ballet. His classical ballets such as *Interplay* (music by Morton Gould) and *Facsimile* (again Bernstein) were juxtaposed with pathbreaking dance direction for popular Broadway shows such as Phil Silvers' *High Button Shoes* (featuring a take-off on Mack Sennett silent comedies and for which Robbins won his first Tony award).

Robbins joined Balanchine's infant New York City Ballet in 1948 as associate artistic director. In Robbins, the great Russian choreographer Balanchine (apart from Robbins and a very few others, the most influential choreographer in history), found an American version of himself (but not quite, Robbins always being his own man), a business partner, and a collaborator with whom he could develop many of the great ballets that now form the basis of much of the repertoire. With Balanchine, Robbins was also participating in a prominent setting in a virtual renaissance of dance in America. New companies sprouted up and flourished like corn in Kansas in June. It was a period to create and to set an unforgettable standard.

While dancing such roles as the Prodigal Son for Balanchine (until at thirty-four he gave up prancing about, as he called it), Robbins continued to choreograph many Broadway shows. After working on Irving Berlin's *Call Me Madam* with the irrepressible Ethel Merman (they would do it again on *Gypsy*), Robbins' most impressive theatrical work of the early 1950s was his creation of the Siamese court and their unusual presentation of *Uncle Tom's Cabin* by Harriet Beecher Stowe (pronounced "Stowah" in the play) in Rodgers and Hammerstein's immortal *The King and I*.

Also during this fertile period, Robbins developed and choreographed Mary Martin's *Peter Pan* with a deliciously wicked Cyril Ritchard as Captain Hook. The television version of *Peter Pan* continues to delight children with its flights of fancy, magical choreography in the air. With a precocious Bob Fosse, Robbins directed *Bells Are Ringing* starring the effervescent Jewish comedienne Judy Holliday. After directing Aaron Copland's *The Tender Land* at the City Opera, Robbins began his collaboration with Bernstein, Stephen Sondheim, Arthur Laurents, and Harold Prince that would permanently change American theater, *West Side Story.*

West Side Story, aided by Bernstein's aggressively lyrical score and Sondheim's youthful poetry, used dance as the underlying force moving the drama to its tragic and cathartic conclusion. No other musical play before it had so incorporated dance into its organism, influencing profoundly the later creations of Fosse, Michael Bennett, and Tommy Tune.

Robbins followed *West Side Story* with astonishingly deft work on *Gypsy* (initially not a hit, but probably the work most respected by the professionals in the business) and the worldwide success of *Fiddler on the Roof* (a sentimental yet clearheaded retelling of the stories by Sholem Aleichem about Tevye the milkman and his wife and many daughters).

With the City Ballet in the early 1950s, Robbins developed major works, including *The Guests, Age of Anxiety* (to Bern-

Jerome Robbins demonstrating before a class.

stein's symphony), *The Cage* (a story of female insects gobbling up males), and *Fanfare*. In 1958, Robbins organized his own company, Ballets, USA, touring internationally (and not without controversy—he was considered somewhat "far out" during these years). Among his productions was a wondrous retelling of Vaslav Nijinsky's *Afternoon of a Faun.*

Robbins returned to the Ballet Theatre with a colossal and highly acclaimed production of Igor Stravinsky's *Les Noces*. Working simultaneously and then exclusively with the City Ballet, Robbins composed the masterworks of his maturity, *Dances at a Gathering, The Goldberg Variations, Watermill, Scherzo Fantastique, Mother Goose, The Four Seasons, Glass Pieces,* and *Ives, Songs,* among several others.

The production in 1989 of *Jerome Robbins' Broadway,* a seventeen-number compilation of his greatest dances from thirty-five years of shows, was a hit, confirming his continuing influence on American dance and theater. Although Robbins had turned to classical ballet after *Fiddler,* his dazzling theatrical work retained its fresh appeal and vibrancy. With De Mille and Bennett, Robbins is America's greatest dance master, its particularly jazzy soul arresting our consciousness with ecstatic visions of young people dancing in joy and sorrow, geometric shapes made personal by the interaction of flesh and form.

79

Henry Kissinger

(b. 1923)

Surely one of the most controversial Americans of the second half of the twentieth century, Henry Kissinger guided his country's foreign policy through the escalation of and then the withdrawal from the Vietnam War, the invasion of Cambodia, the opening to China, and detente with the Soviet Union. Except for Haym Salomon, and more than Judah Benjamin, Bernard Baruch, or Henry Morgenthau, Kissinger was the most influential Jewish political figure in United States history. Many have argued that his activities were not the most beneficial.

Heinz Alfred Kissinger was born in Fürth, Germany during the early years of the Weimar Republic. His father, Louis, was a schoolteacher, proud to be German, intellectual, quietly dignified. Louis's wife, Paula, evidently transmitted her wit and practical approach to their shy, studious son.

The Nazis came to power when Heinz was ten. Kissinger's profound mistrust of people and his sad, dark view of human history were surely grounded in a youth spent in segregated Jewish religious schools, unable to go to soccer matches for fear of beatings by fascist thugs, fleeing with his parents to safety in New York before the Holocaust engulfed his remaining family. Settling in the German-Jewish neighborhood of Washington Heights at the northern tip of Manhattan, Heinz became Henry, attended George Washington High School and then City College.

The Second World War interrupted his education, but provided remarkable opportunities and life experiences. A U.S. Army officer, Fritz Kraemer, vigorously anti-Nazi but of German extraction, recognized Kissinger's special talents and brilliance and relieved him from infantry duties, letting him use his mind for more suitable work in counterintelligence. Kissinger's wartime life as a general's assistant and later the administrator of the German city of Krefeld exposed him to American government and military practice (and won him the Bronze Star).

When he returned to the States from the war, Kissinger enrolled at Harvard. Under the tutelage of another powerful man, Professor William Yandell Elliot, Kissinger studied philosophy and history. Even early on, he established a reputation for grandiose statements and a verbose, leaden way with words. His senior thesis on the meaning of history broke all Cambridge records for length and depth.

His career at Harvard was exemplary and formed the basis for later success in diplomacy. As a graduate student he founded the Harvard International Seminar, to which were invited many future leaders (his later close ties with Japan's Yasuhiro Nakasone, Valéry Giscard d'Estaing of France, and Israel's Yigal Allon date from this period). Kissinger also created a journal called *Confluence*, enlisting such contributors as Hannah Arendt, John Kenneth Galbraith, Paul Nitze, and McGeorge Bundy.

Kissinger's doctoral dissertation, not surprisingly, was about Prince Metternich and the making of the post-Napoleonic peace.

For Dr. Kissinger, the problems of peace after Waterloo mirrored the era of Cold War. While others were devising nuclear test ban concepts, he was contemplating the Realpolitik of Metternich and Viscount Castlereagh of 1812–22. The Harvard professor thrilled to Metternich's vision of diplomacy as rooted in the limitations of personality. Kissinger also admired Bismarck, the Iron Chancellor of Prussia, who so humiliated the French while unifying his country into a world power. Kissinger preferred Bismarck's view that foreign policy must be based not on feelings but on the weight of military, economic, and political strength.

Before his appointment in 1968 as national security adviser to President Richard Nixon, Kissinger built up his base of influence at Harvard with an appointment to the Center for International Affairs Defense Studies Program (where he developed academic theories of arms control), by writing a best-seller on the tactical use of nuclear weapons (which first attracted Nixon's attention to Dr. Kissinger), at the Council on Foreign Relations (creating ideas of fighting limited nuclear wars—the so-called flexible response theory—and graduated deterrence), and as special consultant to the perennial presidential candidate, Governor Nelson Rockefeller of New York (for whom Kissinger suggested a new, open policy toward then hated China).

Henry Cabot Lodge recommended Kissinger to Nixon, who had read the professor's books and journal articles. Nixon and Kissinger, two highly emotional and introverted men, would for five tumultuous years run American foreign policy out of the White House, circumventing the State Department at every turn. Both men apparently felt that they lacked the support of the American people for Lyndon Johnson's war policies. During their tenure, foreign policy decision making was closed to public view, relying more often than not on deceit and obstruction. Both felt that the Vietnam War could not be won, but that an American presence in the area assured an honorable peace. Most important, peace "with honor" (vain words to the millions of Cambodians and Vietnamese still to die) would prove America to be the credible and reliable defender of freedom it had represented itself to be.

Kissinger's great influence on American foreign policy thereafter was his view (first clearly stated during the Vietnam conflict) that before our country engaged in any major foreign effort, the long-range effect of that effort must first be under-stood and agreed to by as many citizens as possible. He felt that the great tragedy of the Johnson administration was its failure to identify those long-term goals.

The Nixon-Kissinger reliance on power coupled with cred-ibility proved effective in the opening to China. Nixon's historic visit to China was probably the most important and intelligent American foreign policy maneuver since the Truman administra-tion's Marshall Plan. However, the frigid realism of Kissinger's worldview led to a power-driven diplomacy unmarked by Ameri-can idealism and morality. Kissinger viewed foreign relations only for its effect on the balance of power and influence, not as an agent for good or for American values.

His personality and ideals led to a unique style of negotia-tion which was rapidly dubbed "shuttle diplomacy." His paranoia and fear of American public opinion resulted in the fourteen-month secret bombing of Cambodia, the vicious Christmas bombing of Hanoi, and the creation of the "Plumbers' Unit" to ferret out the source of State Department leaks. His denial of his Jewish identity (Nixon never forgot Kissinger's religion and referred to him on the notorious White House tapes as "my Jew boy") may have partially led him to delay aid to Israel during the Yom Kippur War (until Nixon, threatened by the modest Soviet airlift to Syria, ordered military supplies rushed to the Israelis).

Although Kissinger would grant Nixon other great successes in the first Strategic Arms Limitation Talks (SALT I) and the signing of a peace treaty with North Vietnam (the war would still drag on until the American withdrawal in 1975 despite Kissinger's assumption of duties as the first Jewish secretary of state and the award of the Nobel Peace Prize), their legacy remains disturbing. Many of their policies reflected their personalities. Seemingly brilliant in strategy and tactics, both men failed to identify and support human rights movements founded in open, democratic values that their basically authoritarian personalities could not understand. The secretive Kissinger also did not give press conferences for most of Nixon's first term for fear that the press would mock his rough German accent and call him "Dr. Strangelove."

A survivor of Nazi persecution, Kissinger sought order, but often at the expense of American values and ethics. The secret war followed by the invasion of Cambodia widened the Vietnam conflict, leaving a power vacuum which the murderous Khmer Rouge filled with bloody terror and killing fields.

Kissinger too often failed to comprehend the importance of local political and ethnic trends, supporting the shah of Iran, for example, to guard U.S. power interests while ignoring the burgeoning Islamic fundamentalist movement of Ayatollah Khomeini.

Kissinger was the first European-style practitioner of official American diplomacy. His ice-cold realism led to the highly influential view that American foreign power had its limits. Detente with the Soviets meant, more often than not, cooperation brought about through grand strategies of restraint and threat. Kissinger's clear expression of balance-of-power thinking, despite being alien to an open democracy, remains highly influential and controversial.

80

Wilhelm Steinitz

(ca. 1835–1900)

Before Bobby Fischer, Boris Spassky, Samuel Reshevsky, Saviely Tartakower, Akiba Rubinstein, and Emanuel Lasker, the greatest—and the first—Jewish chess champion was the irascible, mean-tempered Wilhelm Steinitz. Lasker remains probably the most successful chess master of all time, Tartakower one of its greatest teachers, and Fischer the man who made chess into a worldwide fad. Steinitz, however, was the first chess player to be recognized as a world champion, is widely regarded as the founder of the principles of modern chess, and was the first to give the game a truly international prominence.

He was born in Prague, studied the Talmud as a young boy, and journeyed to Vienna in his early twenties. Forsaking mathematics classes, Steinitz played chess wherever he could. Representing Austria at an English tournament in 1862, he remained in London, earning his living playing chess. In 1866, Steinitz fought the great Adolph Anderssen, master of the so-called cut-and-thrust style, a romantic in the grand manner. Steinitz prevailed, eight games to Anderssen's six. As Anderssen was then widely revered as the world's best player, Steinitz concluded, and wildly shouted, that he had become the world champion. Steinitz never hesitated to make it clear just who he was. Claiming to hold the title for twenty-eight years, Steinitz took off much of the period to perfect new ideas, resuming play at tournaments but holding off championship matches until he was sure of his refined technique.

His rivals, before Lasker, were Zukertort and Chigorin. Mikhail Chigorin is widely regarded as the beloved founder of Russian chess, still a revered figure. Riga born, German speaking Johannes Zukertort was a cultured man, a skilled musician and linguist. Both could not have been more different from Steinitz. He was perhaps the most disliked man in chess history. Nothing could be so trivial that it would not cause the great Steinitz to erupt. His colleagues simply hated to be near him.

Although Steinitz seemed to enjoy being personally revolting, he made it a rule to play "against the board," not the player. Chess was an abstract science. The feelings and motivations of one's opponent, Steinitz urged, were unimportant. What occurred on the chess board however, was paramount.

Opponents came to fear not just his explosive temper, but even more his relentless defense and inevitable attack. For over two decades, most players could not fathom what he was doing. Steinitz threw out the romantic notion that being inventive was what counted most. He lay in ambush for the fashionably swift, king-sided invasions of his competitors. Steinitz developed highly influential defense strategies, accumulating tiny advantages to prepare for a final, brutal onslaught. In many ways Steinitz symbolized the end of chess as chivalrous sport, much as Ulysses S. Grant had shown that modern warfare would not permit gallants such as J.E.B. Stuart to survive. Steinitz proved that success could only follow from sure advantage. For him, every piece assumed importance. Every unit could kill. His theories of close, defensible positions profoundly changed the game.

Steinitz popularized his methods by writing an influential chess treatise and by editing and contributing to an internationally distributed chess magazine (Lasker would follow Steinitz's example and write the standard book on the game). After dominating British chess for almost twenty years, in 1883, Steinitz ventured to the United States, sure he would become rich. However, Americans had little interest in playing chess (Harold C. Schonberg in his informative *Grandmasters of Chess* recounts that in all of Wyoming of the day there was only "one Chessist" to be found), and Steinitz could barely make a living. Yet he was able to drum up interest in 1886 in a championship rematch against Zukertort. The match was played over several weeks in three cities, and even more than the exploits of New Orleans–born Paul Morphy (the greatest American chess player of the generation before Steinitz), aroused intense American interest in chess (Steinitz's later match against Chigorin did much the same for the Russians). Steinitz, of course, humiliated Zukertort (leading, some would say, to Zukertort's rapid deterioration thereafter and then death two years later).

In 1894, the twenty-five-year-old Emmanuel Lasker, the son of a German Jewish cantor, trounced Steinitz, then fifty-eight, and captured his title. Steinitz continued to play, however, contributing gems to the chess literature. By 1899, he had lost his edge in the game and gone mad, was cloistered in an insane asylum on Ward's Island in New York City, and died broke in 1900. Lasker, fearful that he too could die penniless like Steinitz, made it a point never to defend his championship except for the highest possible stakes. The huge fees paid chess masters to this day stem from Steinitz's sorry checkmate.

81 *Arthur Miller*

(b. 1915)

Theater is a form of entertainment designed to bring people together into a public place for a common experience. The ancient Greeks used theater as a forum for deeply felt sadness and laughter. Gods and the noble rulers of the earth were portrayed in epic tragedies and hysterical comedies, catharsis achieved through crying and giggling. Over the centuries, theater has meant different things to succeeding generations, from a casual passing of time to a religious happening. Some of Shakespeare, and later, much of Ibsen and Strindberg, was preoccupied with social issues, man's relationship to others in his society, to those he loves, to himself.

302

Arthur Miller, born in New York City in 1915, has been the most prominent proponent in the twentieth century of a theater of the concerned. In realistic plays that artfully toy with time to often fantastic effect, Miller has striven to create what he called a "drama of the whole man."

How do any of us stay true to ourselves and good to the ones we love, faced with the hopeless daily grind of making a living in the world? How does our work life work on our life? Why do people suddenly go mad, reveling in hate and oppression? When must the victim stand up to the victimizer? Can we repair the damage we do to each other and ourselves?

All of these (and many more) questions are asked by Miller. His plays often answer with unbearable but true-to-life gloom. That Miller has demanded our response makes his work influential, for his theater is never a passing fancy (perverting Ira Gershwin's words, if Gibraltar tumbles, it will fall on us). There is nothing easy about Miller's work, except for the exceptionally accessible way his words fall on our ears. He has said that to be a good playwright one must write hearing people speaking. Miller's characters mostly seem to be real people revealing their thoughts to us through their words and actions. The drama is in their predicament, revealed by themselves or by what they do.

Willy Loman, protagonist of the masterpiece *Death of a Salesman: Certain Private Conversations in Two Acts and a Requiem,* is Miller's greatest, and most representative, character. First produced in 1949 to great acclaim with an exciting cast (Lee J. Cobb, Mildred Dunnock, and Arthur Kennedy) directed by Elia Kazan, *Salesman* won the Pulitzer Prize and other awards. The play has been produced in countless languages and countries, including a highly regarded production in Chinese directed by the author. It is surely the best-known and most influential play yet written by a Jewish playwright.

Willy Loman is a universal symbol and one of the greatest figures in the history of tragedy. He is important not only for the pity we feel for him but also for what his story reveals about our capitalist society. Willy believes deeply in the American dream. If you work hard, play by the rules, keep up your friendly contacts, you will succeed. But Miller shows how Loman's life has been a tragic farce. Willy does not even know he is lying to himself (that is, until his suicide at the play's end). His outgoing nature turns people off, he cannot sell much anymore, and he keeps a woman other than his faithful wife stashed away for his business trips. Only by destroying himself for life insurance money can he beat the system that owned him and repair the damage done to his family.

In *Salesman*, Miller freed drama from the restrictions of convention and reality. The time values and psychological emphases of the drama of Ibsen and Strindberg are extended and refashioned in Miller's play. We are drawn into Willy's mind and world by brilliantly shaped structure and poignant language.

Before *Salesman*, Miller wrote plays while an undergraduate at the University of Michigan, then for the Federal Theatre project, and on CBS and NBC radio workshops. His first successful Broadway play, *All My Sons* (like *Salesman* also about a father and two sons), is a raw, imperfect, yet stirring prelude to his greatest work. Miller used many of the techniques learned in radio in *Salesman* and later plays to alter audiences' expectations and perceptions of time.

Arthur Miller testifying before the House Un-American Activities Committee in 1956.

The Crucible, first produced in 1953 in New York, was Miller's response to the McCarthy era. Saddened by the naming of names before the House Un-American Activities Committee (HUAC) by his friend and colleague Kazan and by the atrocities committed in the name of freedom by Senator Joseph McCarthy, Miller wrote a play about the Salem witch trials of 1692. When one thinks about those dark years, Miller was extraordinarily courageous and squarely in the best American tradition of resistance to tyranny. Miller points out in his excellent autobiography, *Timebends,* that the HUAC hearings were designed as a peculiar, almost religious, rite. The accused was expected to name comrades in the Communist party and then, after the accusations were made, the committee would absolve the witness of all sins, freeing the accuser to return to Main Street America. *The Crucible* reminds us that personal dignity and fighting against those who would degrade us are essential if we are to retain our humanity.

Miller's other plays, such as *A Memory of Two Mondays, A View from the Bridge, After the Fall, Incident at Vichy, The Price,* and *The American Clock,* and the screenplays *The Misfits* and *Playing for Time,* examine many of the themes first explored in *Salesman* and *The Crucible.* The two works most famously identified with his second wife, Marilyn Monroe, are *The Misfits* and *After the Fall. The Misfits* starred Monroe with Clark Gable (in his last film), Montgomery Clift, Eli Wallach, and Thelma Ritter, and directed by John Huston. A critical and box office failure when it opened, *The Misfits* is now considered a great film for its unyielding examination of desperation, unfulfilled dreams, and the need for love. *After the Fall* remains controversial (largely because of the immense affection audiences still have for Marilyn), but it is a model of technical brilliance, the action taking place "in the mind, thought, and memory" of Quentin, the lead character many think is Arthur Miller. *After the Fall* is not conventional theater and its examination of Quentin's relationship with Maggie (Marilyn?) and himself is troubling and relentless.

Miller's work will continue far into the future to guide playwrights in the emotional and formal ways Ibsen and Strindberg moved him. His probing identification of mankind's most troubling aspects must remain with us to warn of what we can do to each other and then finally to ourselves.

82

Daniel Mendoza

(1764–1836)

Daniel Mendoza, a British Jew of Portuguese origin, was the first great Jewish sports champion and a seminal figure in the development of scientific boxing. Holding the undefeated British boxing crown from 1789 until 1795, Mendoza was feared as much for his fast hands as for his remarkable use of the entire boxing ring.

Prior to Mendoza, prizefights were won by the biggest and the strongest. Huge louts would pummel each other with bare knuckles round after round until only the most powerful, with the longest wind and the heaviest jaw, remained standing.

Mendoza was a small man by boxing standards, weighing 160 pounds with a height of five feet seven inches. To compensate for his size, he developed a system of guarding his face and body, stepping from side to side and using his innovative straight left hand to expert advantage. Mendoza's pugilistic skills were so impressive and consistent that despite his weight and height disadvantage, he cut a bloody swath for many years through his less intelligent and clumsier opponents.

Dubbed the "Light of Israel" by his contemporaries, Mendoza reinvented boxing as a sport in which strategy, not slugging, would rule. Like every other smart boxer since, Mendoza was soundly criticized by some as being cowardly, unable to trade punch for punch with other fighters. His attention to the manner of holding one's hands and the artful direction of punches would influence another Jewish boxer, Dutch Sam, at the turn of the nineteenth century, to develop the uppercut. After a successful boxing tour of Ireland, Mendoza founded a school for boxers which would serve as the foundation for the development of many great Irish champions.

Mendoza came from Aldgate in London's East End, the toughest and poorest neighborhood in England's capital city. After his initial fights were won by the slimmest of margins, he sought to develop a winning combination of protection and aggression, retreating when danger came too near and closing in with his superior boxing skills when he noted an advantage. As Joe Frazier would be bested twice in three fights by Muhammad Ali—surely one of the greatest boxers of all time—Mendoza's great rival, Richard Humphries, or the "Gentleman Boxer," "done the Jew," as he would later remark, in a twenty-nine-round fight, only to be roundly defeated by Mendoza in their second and third fights (which lasted only fifty-two and fifteen minutes, respectively).

Mendoza lost his championship when his flowing hair was yanked in a bout in 1795 by another "Gentleman," Jim Jackson, who held the Jewish champion's head in a tight lock and then pummeled him mercilessly. Mendoza attempted comebacks at ages forty-two and fifty-six (two hundred years before George Foreman!) to mixed results.

Mendoza died at the age of seventy-two, having revolutionized prizefighting with his concepts of scientific boxing, especially among amateur athletes. Not until "Gentleman Jim" Corbett would there be his equal.

Other Jewish boxing champions include Abe Attell, the world featherweight champion from 1901 to 1912, Jackie Berg (Judah Bergman), the junior welterweight champion in the early 1930s, Battling Levinsky, the king of the light heavyweight division during the First World War, the extraordinarily colorful light heavyweight champion "Slapsie" Maxie Rosenbloom, Barney Ross (Barnet Rasofsky), lightweight and junior welterweight champion during the Depression, and the true heir to Mendoza, the great Benny Leonard (Benjamin Leiner), who was the smartest boxer, greatest lightweight champion, and possessed the most remarkable scientific skills in boxing history. Like Mendoza, all these champions and many other Jewish fighters (similar to their Irish, Italian, black, and Hispanic brethren) pursued boxing as their route of escape from oppression, poverty, and persecution. Jewish boxers such as Mendoza and Leonard brought original techniques and approaches to boxing, enduring in their influence.

83

Stephen Sondheim

(b. 1930)

Bit by bit,
Putting it together...
Piece by piece—
Only way to make a work of art.
Every moment makes a
contribution,
Every little detail plays a part.
Having just the vision's no solution,
Everything depends on execution:
Putting it together—
That's what counts.*

* Permission granted by Tommy Valando Publishing Group Inc., ©1984 Revelation Music
Publishing Corporation/Rilting Music Inc., A Tommy Valando Publication.

Selling his work to contributors at a museum cocktail party, George, an artist, intensely reminds us that "art isn't easy." Vision is not the solution; "everything depends on execution." One's work is sold "drink by drink," "dot by dot," "shot by shot," "piece by piece," "mink by mink." *Sunday in the Park with George* brings us into the world of the artist as few, if any, stage works have before. Stephen Sondheim's musical is about process, how the creative person starts a work, pieces it together, makes something out of many things—some related, others conflicting, the whole more or sometimes less than its parts—after which the public reacts to or ignores it.

Unlike that of most of the other figures in this book, Sondheim's life thankfully is still a work in progress. While the influences of the others are in most cases clearly evident, Sondheim's prospective impact on musical theater can at best be a guess. Some might argue that although Sondheim is a great figure, he is so unique, like Gershwin, that influence is beside the point.

In every musical he has written since *A Funny Thing Happened on the Way to the Forum,* Sondheim has toyed with concepts and ideas, wandered down new paths, attempted to reflect our fears or glorify our follies. He has repeatedly said that he cannot write a song away from a dramatic context. A song simply cannot be imagined without thinking where the character will be onstage, how he will move, to whom he is reacting, and why he is singing, rather than talking or shouting or just being quiet. Sondheim's concentration on the theater in musicals rather than just the show has enriched his work (while also mystifying those who come to Broadway only for dinner and a night out). *Sunday in the Park with George* and *Sweeney Todd, The Demon Barber of Fleet Street* pull audiences in with contrasts of low comedy and high drama, quasi-operatic arias side by side with musical comedy skits, the music propelled by the finest lyrics Sondheim himself can fashion.

Remarkably, this man of the theater writes along with his dramatic music the most exemplary lyrics. Sondheim's work reflects an encyclopedic knowledge of the history of lyric writing. His verses often combine many styles. He can switch from a delicate, almost poetic manner to brassy burlesque all in the same song (sometimes the same line). His lyrics have been favorably compared to the poetry of E.E. Cummings and other modernist poets. To develop character and dramatic progression, Sondheim will choose unusually expressive ways to portray emotions and thoughts. For example, the juvenile lead in *Sweeney Todd* sings not that he loves his Johanna but that he "feels" her. In his New York musical *Company*, which examines in brilliant detail the relationships of contemporary men and women, the hustle of city streets and the parallel tensions of its inhabitants are portrayed in the restless song *Another Hundred People*—a rush of concentrated energy and sharply etched feeling.

The inner worlds and rhymes of Sondheim's words are mirrored in melodies and rhythms sustained by pulsating accompaniments always mandated by theatrical impulse. Like his lyrics, his music sensitively reacts and exists only to develop the drama. Sondheim can compose in many popular styles, although his music often has a neoclassical irony and edge not usually encountered on Broadway.

Sondheim's first attempt to write a show was, as for Jerome Kern, at school. Sondheim brought the score to his friend's father, the renowned lyricist Oscar Hammerstein, a neighbor near the Sondheims' summer home in Bucks County, Pennsylvania. The teenage Sondheim was sure Hammerstein would immediately seize the work for production on the Great White Way and therefore asked the older man to review the show on a professional level. The next day, Hammerstein tore the work apart, distilling in a few hours much of his theatrical experience in a sharp tutorial. Hammerstein became a mentor to Sondheim. The young composer also studied theory with the influential Princeton professor Milton Babbitt, a disciple of Arnold Schoenberg and a learned and affectionately humorous man.

Although his first musical as an adult, *Saturday Night,* failed to gain sufficient backers for production, Sondheim began to make a name for himself. After a brief stint writing scripts for the 1950s television show *Topper,* Sondheim, age twenty-seven, was asked to write the lyrics for a new musical to be produced by, among others, Harold Prince, directed and choreographed by Jerome Robbins, book by Arthur Laurents, and music by Leonard Bernstein. First called *East Side Story,* then *Gang Way,* *West Side Story* began a new era in the history of the Broadway musical. Sondheim considered himself a composer first and foremost and did not, after an audition with the charismatic maestro, wish to submerge his ego in that great ocean called Bernstein. Hammerstein advised Sondheim that the experience would be well worth it. However, his separation from the composition of music for the show may have affected Sondheim's best theatrical impulses. He noted later that some of his lyrics were inappropriate for the characters. The complex inner rhymes of *I Feel Pretty*, for example, do not fit a young, inexperienced immigrant girl. Although well received by the critics, the show was not a box-office success. Only when the film was produced did the producers and creators reap financial reward and widespread acclaim. The musical, theatrically propelled by dynamic modern dance, soaring melody, and sharp lyrics, remains compelling, a contemporary Romeo and Juliet tale—cool and hot.

His next musical, *Gypsy*, featured Sondheim's tart lyrics, the abundant music of Jules Styne, and the towering presence of Ethel Merman. Incredibly, *Gypsy*, like *West Side Story*, was not a financial success, achieving classic status only in its many revivals. The lyrics for *Rose's Turn*, Merman's revealing soliliquy, remain a model of penetrating insight and revelation. (Sondheim would write lyrics for just one other collaborator, Richard Rodgers, in *Do I Hear a Waltz?*—disastrously.)

Sondheim's other shows of the early 1960s, *Forum* and the short-lived cult classic *Anyone Can Whistle*, were his first mature and individual turns on the musical comedy form. *Forum*, based on the wild tales of Plautus, the ancient Roman humorist, featured a brilliant cast led by the insanely funny and uncontrollable Zero Mostel.

After the unpleasant diversion with Richard Rodgers, Sondheim developed *Company*. The work, which opened in 1970, is less a straight play than a series of small character vignettes, building relentlessly to reveal the desperate and unhappy souls of urban-dwelling marrieds. The strong plot line of the Rodgers and Hammerstein musical form was discarded for a searing dissection of modern life.

No other musical has become such a cult favorite as his next show. *Follies* examined the lives of aging actresses through elaborate production and arias laced with nostalgia and pastiche. Sondheim unravels his characters through the imagery, sounds, and styles of his great forebears, Gershwin, Berlin, Kern, and others, while expanding his range of expression and psychological unveiling.

His most popular musical, *A Little Night Music* (the English translation of Mozart's *Eine Kleine Nachtmusik*), based on a film of Ingmar Bergman, followed. In this grand work, Sondheim attempted to merge in waltz time the insightful methods of character disclosure developed in his previous works with a more conventional linear plot. *Pacific Overtures*, his tribute to Kabuki theater, displayed a broader mastery of musical texture and formal design, but was not a commercial success.

First in *Sweeney* with Hal Prince and then in the musicals produced with James Lapine—*Sunday in the Park with George, Into the Woods*, and *Passion*—Sondheim achieved a total mastery of a new and entertaining art form, not quite Broadway show or operetta but somewhere in between (or beyond). These works, like George Gershwin's *Porgy and Bess*, elevated the contemporary American musical to new and higher artistic levels.

Sondheim has been criticized for the lack of "memorable" tunes in his shows. Audiences do not leave the theater humming his songs. Others have noted that the "difficulty" of some of his music has alienated many from American musical theater and provided an opening to the spectacular productions of Andrew Lloyd Webber.

Despite these criticisms, no future composer or lyricist writer can create a musical or opera without absorbing Sondheim's immaculately conceived works. Like his friend Leonard Bernstein, he is a great teacher and observer, imploring us to remember that "children and art" are what really matter in this world, that we should not make so much drama, should avoid sentimentality for its own sake, and feel more.

84

Emma Goldman

(1869–1940)

Known as "Red Emma" to millions of Americans before the First World War, she was at that time the most feared woman in the United States. An anarchist and one of the founders of the women's rights movement, Emma Goldman, a Jewish immigrant from Russia, preached free love, assassination, women's liberation (before and after the right to vote was granted), aggressive opposition to the draft and oppressive capitalists, and birth control. She developed twentieth-century feminism out of Victorian constraints toward what she called "true emancipation," the freedom of the self after political rights and equality are achieved. She was the greatest agitator of the 1900s before Lenin,

314

and despite a small number of writings, left an enduring brand on the role of women and men in our society.

Unlike many later feminists', her unique ideas did not develop from only intellectual brilliance. Emma's ideology grew straight from her troubling, active, and colorful life, fleeing an abusive father in Russia, toiling in sweatshops, planning the execution of a great industrialist, editing an anarchist journal, nursing the sick, and loving men much older and much younger who captivated her mind and stirred her sexuality.

Goldman considered marriage a kind of murder (Margaret Sanger, the influential Christian feminist and birth-control advocate, compared it to suicide). But Emma could not live without men, and unlike many radical feminists she insisted that women's lives would only improve if there was more common ground with men. Not only did men have to change the way they viewed women, they also had to change their views about fatherhood and the mother's role in the family. Men could work and be fathers at the same time. Why couldn't women too?

Despite a disastrous early marriage to a factory worker in Rochester (Emma married not for love but to have sex, only to discover that her husband was impotent and a gambler), she was attracted to men all her life. The image of Emma Goldman as a frumpy matron with intense eyes glaring through spectacles was belied by a woman who was careful about her dress, insisting always that to be a feminist did not mean one could not be beautiful. A feminist should have fun. When her longtime friend and short-time live-in lover Alexander "Sasha" Berkman chastised her for bringing home cut flowers for the table, she threw him out of their otherwise drab apartment, screaming that to be a revolutionary and worker did not mean that one had to be denied a little beauty.

When steel magnate Henry Clay Frick (later the founder of New York's Frick Collection) ordered hired thugs to shoot at striking workers, she plotted his assassination with Sasha. He wounded Frick, Emma went into hiding (she had not accompanied Sasha due to an involvement with another man), and Sasha was given a twenty-five-year sentence. Emma began to make a series of incendiary speeches, and after a famous harangue in Union Square in New York City was arrested and incarcerated for one year for inciting rebellion.

In the prison infirmary she attended the sick, and taken with nursing, upon her release (and with the support of another lover, Edward Brady) left for Vienna to study nursing (attending some classes taught by Dr. Sigmund Freud). She returned a year later to find herself disillusioned with her radical friends. What they said did not seem to be relevant anymore.

Giving up nursing (and Brady), Emma opened a beauty parlor, specializing in applying head and neck massages. She started a journal called *Mother Earth,* dedicated to freeing the earth for all individuals. Her anarchist background merged with her feminist concerns. She examined why women are different from men and how their differences could be understood. Emma insisted that examining these differences should not demean a woman or make her less than a man.

She began a well-publicized relationship with an ugly doctor named Ben Reitman who spent much of his professional time assisting the unemployed. Known as the "King of the Hobos," his free love match with the "Queen of the Anarchists" made amusing reading for those seeking to ridicule Emma's activism.

Yet despite her active social and professional life, she toured America speaking in over three dozen cities, spreading her particular mixture of anarchism and women's rights. By 1910 she was the leading anarchist and feminist in America and had published essays setting forth her beliefs.

After Sasha was released from prison, in 1919 they organized an anti-draft organization, the No-Conscription League, to fight U.S. involvement in the First World War. Both Emma and Sasha were arrested for their activities and deported from the country. She was never during her lifetime permitted to return to America, and wandered through Europe and Canada for her last twenty-one years. Initially taken with the Russian Revolution, Emma became disgusted with Lenin's tsarist tactics. The revolution in reality was a hoax and just another power play.

Emma Goldman's lasting influence is not for her political involvements but rather for her active role along other pioneering women such as Sanger, Florence Nightingale, Emily Davies, Josephine Butler, Elizabeth Blackwell, and Caroline Norton, who in Margaret Forster's words were significant sisters at the grassroots of active feminism in the nineteenth and early twentieth centuries.

85

Sir Moses Montefiore
(1784–1885)

Ritual murder, the alleged ceremonial killing of Christians and the drinking of their blood by Jewish perpetrators, is a libel that is more than eight centuries old. The first claim of ritual murder against the Jews was made in 1144 in Norwich, England. As no dead person could be found to justify the crime, no retaliation was sought. However, in 1255 in the town of Lincoln, a Christian boy named Hugh, missing for three weeks, was found dead in a cesspool. Jews of the town and Jewish guests visiting there for a wedding were accused of kidnapping the boy, fattening him up for ten days with sweet food, then brutally murdering him in a mad ritual of crucifixion and bloodletting. Nineteen Jews were lynched by a mob. The blood libel, as it became known, was copied, becoming a widespread method of persecution for generations of anti-Semites.

In the same England some six hundred years later, Moses Montefiore, the son of Italian Jewish immigrants, became a prosperous stockbroker (as brother-in-law of Nathan Rothschild) and then confidant of Queen Victoria. In 1840, Sir Moses led the first international effort in Jewish history to protest an example of anti-Semitism, the vicious Damascus blood libel. Organizing a group from the leading western nations, Montefiore was successful in securing the release of most of the Jews wrongly imprisoned for a crime they did not commit (two had died from the brutal Syrian torture).

After retiring at a young age from successful military and business careers, Montefiore devoted his many remaining years to the improvement of Jewish life throughout the world. Although many of his triumphs proved to be short-lived, Sir Moses set an example that was emulated by Benjamin Disraeli and succeeding Jewish leaders. It was possible for a Jew not only to compete in international finance (the Rothschilds had made this plain), but also in world politics and diplomacy. With the help of enlightened modern nations such as democratic England, Jews could take care of their own.

Montefiore was born in Leghorn, Italy. His parents visited London when he was small, and remained. Young Moses gained his first business experience as an apprentice to wholesale grocers. He became a stockbroker, known as one of the twelve "Jew brokers" of London, worked for and then (through marriage to Judith Cohen, who later as Mrs. Montefiore would write the first book of guidelines for social behavior in the English language, a precursor of Emily Post) befriended Nathan Rothschild, served in the Surrey Militia, carried dispatches at the Battle of Navarino, and then at the age of forty began his true calling, the saving of Jews worldwide from oppression.

In his early years he was not an observant Jew. However, in 1827 after the first of seven visits to Palestine, Montefiore began to revel in ritual, building his own synagogue on his estate and including in his entourage wherever he went a shohet or ritual slaughterer. Ironically, the man who would be most instrumental in the fight against the accusation of ritual murder knew from daily living the positive values behind the strict observance of Jewish law.

Many (including Paul Johnson in his *History of the Jews*) have described Montefiore as the last of the so-called shtadtlanim, respectable Jews whose high social and business standing allowed them to undertake international diplomacy on behalf of persecuted Jewry. His friendship with Queen Victoria began when she was a young girl (in 1837 the Queen knighted Sir Moses, who served then as the first Jewish sheriff of London). Johnson feels her pronounced sympathy for Jewish history and culture arose out of a high regard for Montefiore.

Another important British leader (first secretary of war under Wellington, then foreign secretary with Grey, Melbourne, and Russell, and finally prime minister of England), Viscount Palmerston, believed that helping the Jews return to Palestine would hasten the return of the Messiah. Palmerston was for many decades a great supporter of Jewish causes. Montefiore secured Palmerston's aid in creating a coalition of European nations (with the support of President Martin Van Buren of the United States) in securing the release of imprisoned Jews falsely accused of murdering and drinking the blood of a Capuchin friar. The Damascus affair was an early edition of the infamous Dreyfus case of France, but more a matter of international power politics than only old-fashioned anti-Semitism. The French, seeking to dominate the Middle East, were viciously encouraging the libel and attempting to suppress any investigation. A prominent French-Jewish lawyer, Adolphe Crémieux, opposed his government's cynical position and allied himself with Montefiore. With the support of Palmerston and the English government, Montefiore and Crémieux convinced the Syrian ruler, Mehmet Ali, to free the tortured prisoners and avert an international crisis.

Over the next forty years Montefiore continued to use his influence in the British Foreign Office in combating anti-Semitism. Many of his good faith attempts had, in the end, negligible results. In the Mortara case, a young Jewish Italian boy was kidnaped by Catholics seeking to convert him to Christianity. Montefiore protested to Pope Pius IX and the Italian government without success (the boy, Edgardo Mortara, became a pious Christian, took the name of Pius from the Pope, and ended a

professor of theology and canon in Rome). In 1863, supported by
the British Foreign Office, Montefiore convinced the sultan of
Morocco to warrant the safety of Moroccan Jews. Yet when Sir
Moses had returned to England, the Sultan withdrew his decree,
plunging Moroccan Jewry into decades more of persecution.

Despite the fleeting achievements of Montefiore's campaigns, he was an important symbol to Jews and Gentiles.
Oppression had to be fought, preferably by diplomacy, but always
vigorously. Jews learned from Montefiore that they could organize into powerful groups devoted to bettering their people. The
support Zionists later received from England's Lord Balfour and
others for the formation of a Jewish state was surely helped by the
dignified example of one of the greatest Victorians, Sir Moses
Montefiore.

86

Yitzhak Rabin

(1922–1995)

It is said that Yitzhak Rabin, not much of a singer and peeking at the words on a crib sheet, sang the peace song "Shir la Shalom" at a peace rally his last night in Tel Aviv's Kings of Israel square. Minutes after the Saturday night rally ended, Yigal Amir shot and killed him. Many Israelis long certain of their nation's purpose (despite the constant stress of terrorism and war) felt in their deep sadness—and perhaps for the first time—a gnawing doubt about the future of the Jewish people. A Jew had killed a Jew, a forbidden act had occurred, and in the House of Israel the illusion of inner peace was shattered, conceivably for many years to come.

There were some who wrote that at that time in Israeli history Rabin's death somehow defined him and his people. Like the murder of John Fitzgerald Kennedy, Rabin's assassination was viewed as a seminal event rather than as merely the act of a fanatic. The killing certainly revealed that modern Israel contained many of the same divisions as had ancient Judea in the time of the Roman Wars. Historians pointed out that the fall of Jerusalem in 70 C.E. was as much due to deep schisms in Judean society as it was to the overwhelming force of Titus's legions. Pharisees were fighting Zealots who were murdering Sadduccees. Similar strains were noticed in modern-day Israel: right-wing religious groups were supposedly poised to return to the ancient kingdoms of Judea and Samaria a messianic theocracy, in violent opposition to more secular and contemporary ideas.

Yet, these historical perspectives voiced when the world was in shock ignored who indeed Rabin was. Never just a politician, like the great Israeli founders, Ben-Gurion, Weizmann, Eshkol, Meir, and Eban, Rabin was the first "sabra," a native-born Israeli, to become prime minister of his country. He could be blunt in attitude, "typically Israeli," some said, a Middle Eastern Hebrew Everyman, fond of cigarettes and Scotch, distrustful of ornate speech, cautious, never willing to jump at anything, maybe to some a plodder, to others careful to a fault, courageous, a soldier-statesman, a born leader. In many ways Rabin was Israel.

Born in Jerusalem in 1922, he attended an agricultural school in Galilee. At the age of nineteen, during the Second World War, Rabin joined the Palmach, the select strike force of the Haganah, the precursor to Israel's defense forces of today. In 1945 he led a raid to free two hundred Jewish immigrants held by British authorities in a camp south of Haifa. Captured by the British in mid-1946, Rabin was imprisoned in Gaza for six months, but was released by the beginning of 1947 in time to help lead the defense of Jerusalem in Israel's War of Independence. The hero of Leon Uris's *Exodus,* Ari ben Canaan, is said to have been based partly on the Rabin of this period. Appointed deputy commander of the Palmach, Rabin led the Har-El Brigade in the War of Independence. In maneuvers essential to the conduct of the war, his unit, although unsuccessful in taking all of Jerusalem, maintained vital supply links between the capital city and the coast.

The War of Independence not only brought him fame and

the thanks of his people but also a wife, Leah Schlossberg, who had served in his battalion during the fighting. Leah, the mother of their son and daughter, would be at his side through triumph, political setbacks, more triumphs, and then the final tragedy.

After study at the British Staff College in Camberley, England, Rabin slowly rose through the Israeli armed forces to become chief of staff in 1964. Widely recognized in 1967 as the architect with Moshe Dayan of Israel's crushing defeat of Egypt, Jordan, and Syria in the Six-Day War (and the liberation of the Old City of Jerusalem), Rabin retired from the army and was appointed in 1968 to his first nonmilitary position, ambassador to the United States. In 1973 he returned to Israel, entered politics, and was appointed by Prime Minister Golda Meir to her cabinet as Minister of Labor. After Meir's resignation due to the alleged lack of readiness of the defense forces in the Yom Kippur War of 1973, Rabin became prime minister in May 1974. He negotiated and signed the Egyptian-Israeli disengagement agreement of 1975 and led his country in 1976 (with his defense minister and sometime rival Shimon Peres) through the daring Entebbe raid in Africa, which freed over one hundred hostages held at the airport by Palestinian terrorists. The following year a succession of scandals, including reports that his wife had violated Israeli currency laws, forced his resignation. Peres became prime minister, and Rabin's brilliant and patriotic career was seemingly at an end.

Yet the country needed him, and by 1984 Rabin was named minister of defense in the Labor-Likud coalition government led at various times by Peres and Yitzhak Shamir. Rabin administered Israel's withdrawal from Prime Minister Menachem Begin's devastating occupation of southern Lebanon and reacted firmly to the Palestinian uprisings known as the *intifada*.

In 1992 partly due to his hard-line actions against the *intifada* and to Peres's soft support within their party, Rabin again became the Labor leader. Later that year, Labor defeated Likud in national elections, and Rabin once again became prime minister. In 1993, after a year of secret negotiations in Sweden (largely run by Peres), Rabin reluctantly shook the hand of Yasir Arafat and signed a self-rule agreement with the Palestine Liberation Organization (PLO) on the White House lawn before a gracious President Bill Clinton and an incredulous world. It was an amazing turnaround for an old soldier like Rabin, who had seen so many comrades perish in battles with the Arabs, but he viewed it as the only way to peace. Building on the accomplishments of Begin with the Egyptians, the practical leader Rabin looked at all the alternatives, and despite his emotions and caution, he gave peace a chance by settling with the PLO. This decision, affecting so many people, not only in the Mideast but also throughout the world, led to his murder by a right-wing religious Jew opposed to peace.

At the state funeral for the great fallen leader, Prime Minister Peres read the words of that song of peace sung haltingly by Rabin just minutes before his end. Those words bear repeating and must never be forgotten in times of peace and of terror:

> Let the sun rise, the morning shine,
> The most righteous prayer will not bring us back.
> Who is the one whose light has been extinguished
> And buried in the earth?
> Bitter tears will not wake him, will not bring him back.
> No song of praise or victory will avail us.
> Therefore, sing only a song of peace.
> Don't whisper a prayer—
>   sing aloud a song of peace.

87

Boris Pasternak

(1890–1960)

"His spirit pervaded our whole house," wrote the Russian poet and novelist Pasternak of his family's friend and mentor, Count Leo Tolstoy. The spirit of Tolstoy, it can be truly said, of caring for humanity, tolerance, compassion, of a profound understanding of motivations and hopes, survived in Russia through the black nights of the Stalinist terror in Boris Pasternak.

To the West he is remembered largely for his last major work, the novel *Dr. Zhivago* (and mostly due to the David Lean film). Russians, however, glorify his life for the great poetry written during the golden age of Vladimir Mayakovsky and

325

Sergei Yesenin after the Revolution of 1917 and later during the years of oppression and reconstruction after the Second World War.

Awarded the Nobel Prize for literature in 1958 for his life's work culminating in *Zhivago*, Pasternak was forced to renounce the award, fearful of being cast out of Russia by the government. Although publicly defeated by the authorities, Pasternak, like his compatriot the composer Dmitri Shostakovich, remains a potent symbol of the force of artistic truth and courage in the shadow of the bitterest tyranny. Almost all of his poetry and the novel *Zhivago* endure through an irrepressible lyricism and humanity.

Pasternak grew up in Odessa and Moscow, the son of Rosa Kaufman, a concert pianist (and student of the influential Russian Jewish pianist and composer Anton Rubinstein) who had given up her promising career for her family, and Leonid Pasternak, a respected post-Impressionist painter and illustrator (notably for Tolstoy's *Resurrection*). In addition to the Tolstoys, his parents were friendly with the great musicians, composers, novelists, and poets of the time including Sergei Rachmaninoff, Aleksandr Scriabin, and Rainer Maria Rilke.

Pasternak first thought he would be a composer. During one notable summer, his family rented a house next door to Scriabin's. Pasternak was intoxicated by the color-rich harmonies and ecstatic melodies wafting across the lawn from his illustrious neighbor's house. On long walks with his father and Scriabin, he absorbed the reactions of the two fine artists to nature and listened carefully to their disparate views on eternal issues. Scriabin encouraged Boris to compose and urged him to leave the easy study of law for philosophy. While studying philosophy at the University of Marburg in Germany, Boris fell in love for the first time and began writing verses.

Pasternak was a witness to some of the most important events of twentieth-century Russian history. During a demonstration in 1905 during the first Russian revolution, he received a blow from a Cossack on horseback (later recounted in *Dr. Zhivago*). He also ventured with his father in 1910 to the railway station at Astapovo to view the body of Tolstoy, who had died the night before.

Prior to the First World War, Pasternak aligned himself with a group of writers called "Centrifuge." In literary battles carried out in cafes and city squares, young authors belonging to groups called Futurists, Symbolists, and Imagists imitated in art the civil strife then raging in Russian's streets between Bolsheviks, Whites, Mensheviks, and Anarchists. Pasternak became friendly with Mayakovsky and acquainted with the peasant's poet, the mercurial Yesenin (future husband of Isadora Duncan). Both Mayakovsky and Yesenin were carried away by revolutionary fervor. Pasternak, however, due to what he called his slow-moving mind, could not get caught up in the revolutionary bathos. Neither did he follow his parents to Berlin when they emigrated in the early 1920s, frustrated with a deteriorating life in Russia. Pasternak felt the need to remain in his beloved Russia. Repelled by the human carnage of the Revolution and its oppressive aftermath, Yesenin and later Mayakovsky committed suicide. Pasternak meanwhile continued his steady and sensitive examination of the human condition.

His early prose and poetry have an almost translucent quality. Unlike the bombast of his revolutionary friends, this work shows the influence of his musical upbringing, a charming, quiet lyricism, clearly and simply expressed, but always highly sophisticated.

He chose to pass quietly through the years of Stalinist madness, first as a librarian and then as a translator. His translations of Shakespeare were widely performed throughout the Soviet Union.

In 1934, Stalin declared a literary manifesto, demanding total control over all literature, directing writers how to think. Only socialist realism, the praising of collective work and the Great Leader Stalin, was rewarded. Free thought expressed in a personal manner was damned. Vicious purges destroyed great spirits. While many of his friends fell, Pasternak met the woman whom he would later call "Lara" in *Zhivago*, crediting her with saving him from the numbing desperation of those dark years.

During the Second World War, Pasternak started to write poetry once more, first, to avoid censorship, on patriotic themes, then more personally. When Stalin again imposed literary controls after the war through his flunky Andrei Zhdanov, Pasternak resumed translating. He continued to work secretly, however, on a novel about a poet, a novel that ended in poetry. This epic was about a doctor who grew up in tsarist comfort, wrote poems, was witness to a great war and a violent revolution, fell in love with a mysterious woman, rekindling his poetic flame, and perished in the Soviet wasteland. Although Pasternak wrote autobiographical prose, *Zhivago* was in many ways his own story.

His great contemporary, the Russian poet Anna Akhmatova, observed that Pasternak always exhibited a childlike vision. He did not promote his "self" like the revolutionary poets Mayakovsky and Yesenin. Lyricism should never be confused with or used in defense of history. A poetry rising out of the unconscious, tempered with sensitive, almost luminous feeling, will surely outlast the Gulag, the purges, the denunciations. As Tolstoy had once remarked to Boris's father, Leonid, all money, property, empires are fated to disappear, but if art contains the smallest grain of truth, it cannot die.

88

Harry Houdini

(1874–1926)

The great playwright and critic George Bernard Shaw once quipped that alongside Jesus and Sherlock Holmes, Harry Houdini was one of the three most famous people in world history (Shaw's ranking of Houdini with a fictional and biblical figure seems curiously appropriate). For a little over a dozen years around the time of the First World War, Shaw's quip may just have been true.

Harry Houdini, death-defying "Self-Liberator," legendary "Maker of Miracles," "World's Champion Gaol Breaker and King of Locks," was the greatest showman in a golden age of showmen, a hugely popular entertainer, a pioneer of mass entertainment and the artful use of self-promotion. Like P.T. Barnum, John L. Sullivan, Enrico Caruso, and Sarah Bernhardt in their fields, Houdini was the undisputed and unique master of his craft, an awe inspiring escape artist, a celebrity and acclaimed hero wherever he journeyed.

A rabbi's son, Houdini was born in Pest, across the river from Buda in Hungary's capital. He shared a remarkable birth year with Winston Churchill, Arnold Schoenberg, Chaim Weizmann, Charles Ives, Herbert Hoover, Somerset Maugham, Guglielmo Marconi, Gertrude Stein, and Robert Frost. Houdini's real name was Erik Weisz, which he changed to Ehrich Weiss after the family emigrated to Wisconsin (his father had answered an advertisement—a small town called Appleton needed a rabbi).

While other boys were playing catch or catching frogs, young Ehrich was escaping from locks or practicing dangerous stunts on his backyard trapeze bar set. He was fascinated with magicians and the wandering circus acts that visited the town. Ehrich studied magic from books and pamphlets and emulated the great nineteenth-century illusionist Robert Houdin, a French master famous as an ambassador, author, and conjuror of eternal secrets and mysteries.

Rabbi Weiss was a harsh, disagreeable man who lost his job in Appleton after alienating his tiny congregation. The family moved to Milwaukee to a desperate poverty. Ehrich ran away from home when he was twelve to seek his fortune as a performer. Rejecting his natural father, he became the son of Houdin, adding an *i* and transforming himself, as if by magic, into Houdini. First with a friend and then later with his brother Theo (dubbed "Dash"), the Brothers Houdini worked at fairs, in dime museums, medicine shows, morality plays, and on boardwalks.

In the 1890s he met his bride, Bess, while appearing in Coney Island. He split with Dash (who prospered, but always in his brother's shadow, as "Hardeen") and formed an act with his wife as The Houdinis. From an older performer they purchased a rigged trunk out of which husband and wife would alternatively disappear and reappear, hands free or shackled, in magical "Metamorphosis."

Wherever they played, Houdini studied with locksmiths, determined to learn every combination and mechanical construction. By giving locks directed blows, hiding picklocks in his body, contorting his body into awful positions, or dislocating his unusually loose joints, Houdini learned how to free himself from every handcuff or straitjacket.

He became a headliner by challenging the authorities in every town on the vaudeville circuit. Houdini promised to pay a large sum to anyone who could lock him up—and hold him captive. At the turn of the century he traveled to Europe, where neither Scotland Yard, the Polizei of Prussia and Bavaria, nor the secret police of Tsar Nicholas could hold the "Handcuff King." Every time they tried, he escaped. His fame first grew slowly, then sensationally. After being thrown manacled in a crate into the East River, Houdini rose up out of the waters free to perform (to sold-out audiences) at Hammerstein's Roof Garden.

When his act became too well-known, he developed new, sensational routines to thrill his fans, like the Milk Can and Chinese Water Torture Cell (placed upside down, left to drown, able only through what seemed superhuman exertion to release himself from sure death). He toured throughout Europe, Canada, and the United States, gathering immense public attention, the most famous performer in the world.

The death of his mother in 1913 threw him into a profound depression. Houdini became obsessed with conquering death. He was buried alive, digging his way up out of the smothering earth. Seeking to speak with his deceased mother, Houdini sought the company of eminent spiritualists, one of them Sherlock Holmes's creator, Sir Arthur Conan Doyle. At the same time Houdini led a crusade against charlatans trafficking in the sorrows of the bereaved with fake séances and bogus raisings of the dead.

After patriotic duty entertaining the troops during the First World War, a brief silent movie career and new acts (such as The Disappearing Elephant) could not rekindle the kind of widespread adulation he had developed earlier. When he died in 1926 from peritonitis caused by a blow to the stomach from a misguided fan, Houdini's star had already been eclipsed by film stars Charlie Chaplin, Rudolph Valentino, and Douglas Fairbanks, in an era with little patience for the escape artist's complex and slow-moving acts. Houdini had left Bess and certain friends coded messages he promised to utter to them from the afterlife. No supernatural sightings, however, were ever made of Harry Houdini, ghost.

Apart from a continued importance to magicians and escape artists, Houdini was the first great popular superstar to use the media to gain the broadest possible acceptance. Through his manipulation of the press, giving the public increasingly sensational performances, and wrapping it all up in a pseudoartistry, Houdini created mass entertainment. What he did, the astounding escapes from icy rivers, formidable jails, or locked containers, remains remarkable. How he commanded the public's attention, locking the masses in his powerful vise, releasing his audiences only at the last possible moment when death seemed ready to pounce, was extraordinary and appeared inhuman. That an immigrant boy, an itinerant rabbi's son, was able to accomplish by his wits and superlative athletic skills what Harry Houdini did, is both an American success story and a Jewish fairy tale. Houdini symbolized his people's unnatural ability to survive, even when faced with no way out.

89

Edward Bernays

(1891–1995)

> He who molds public opinion is more powerful than
> he who makes laws.   —Abraham Lincoln

Edward L. Bernays, nephew of Sigmund Freud (the founder of psychoanalysis), is generally recognized as the father of public relations. Eager to differentiate his field from press agentry, Bernays had friend H. L. Mencken define "public relations" in a book on the American language as "a vocation applied by a social scientist who advises a client or employer on the social attitudes and actions to take to win the support of the public upon whom the viability of the client or employer depends." With pioneers such as Ivy Lee, Carl Byoir, and John Hill, Bernays helped mold contemporary opinion in the twentieth century, exercising a greater influence on culture than many of the politicians and corporations he represented.

Throughout his extraordinarily long career, Bernays sought to gain for the field of public relations the same professional attitude and ethical standards commonly assumed of attorneys or architects. Bernays wished to be known as a "counsel on public relations." Such counsel was a professional adviser who out of a profound understanding of people's motivations guided public opinion.

Edward Bernays was public relations counselor for, among many others, the Ballet Russe of Sergei Diaghilev, the Metropolitan Opera, Enrico Caruso, Procter and Gamble, President Calvin Coolidge (loosening up his image by inviting vaudeville stars to the White House), Henry Ford, Conde Nast Publications, David Sarnoff of NBC, William Paley of CBS, Mack Trucks (influencing the construction of the first interstate highways that united the country economically), United Fruit (bananas), America Tobacco, United Brewers Association (bringing beer out of the taverns into supermarkets and the home), the National Association for the Advancement of Colored People (NAACP), the American Civil Liberties Union (ACLU), and Columbia University. Bernays's activities for these organizations and individuals revolutionized the American way of life and mass communications. Bernays also lived to see (and outlived) totalitarian regimes such as Dr. Joseph Goebbels' Nazi propaganda machine steal many of his techniques of social persuasion for sinister purposes.

Bernays's family tree was as impressive as the people he guided during his many years. His mother was Sigmund Freud's sister, Anna (Freud) Bernays, his first cousin, Sigmund's daughter, the great child psychologist Anna Freud, and his daughter Anne Bernays, a marvelous novelist and wife of Justin Kaplan, Pulitzer Prize-winning author (of most notably a unique biography of Walt Whitman).

Born in the Vienna of his uncle Sigmund, Edward was raised in New York City from the age of one. His father was a prosperous grain merchant. Edward attended public school and Cornell University's College of Agriculture (perhaps to please his father).

He realized early that what he did best was to influence people. Of all the people in this book about influence, Bernays was the only one to earn a living from his ability to make people react. He was of course not the most influential Jew of all time, but he was perhaps the most successful Jewish person in modern times whose profession was engineered and intended to influence others.

His first try at public relations was assisting an actor produce a play about sexually transmitted disease, surely then prohibited subject matter. Bernays was able to make the play a sell-out by promising participating civic leaders that their attendance and sponsorship (which drew crowds) would support needed sex education.

During the First World War, Bernays publicized theatrical events (mostly ballet and opera). Volunteering to aid the American war effort, he joined President Wilson's Office of War Information. During the Paris peace conference that followed the Armistice, Bernays composed propaganda extolling the virtues of America's role in "the war to end all wars."

With his wife-to-be, Doris Fleischman, Bernays founded his own office of what he first called "publicity direction" and then later "public relations counsel." Always basing his advice on sound, detailed research, Bernays's practice flourished. His most famous early campaigns were on behalf of a hairnet manufacturer, Venida, and P&G's Ivory soap. Bernays used public opinions of, for example, safety (working women in factories with long hair constrained in hairnets were less likely to get hurt than others who exposed their bobbed haircuts to machinery) or education (a national competition for kids sculpting figures out of Ivory soap established the product as an American staple).

Bernays became a national figure in 1929 when he orchestrated the fiftieth anniversary of Thomas Edison's inventing electric light. Sponsored by Henry Ford in Dearborn, Michigan, in attendance were the elderly genius inventor himself as well as President Hoover, Madame Marie Curie, and John D. Rockefeller.

Bernays's book *Crystalizing Public Opinion,* published in 1923, was the first and most influential book in the history of public relations. In the same year Bernays became the first person to teach a course in his field, lecturing at New York University.

90

Leopold Auer

(1845–1930)

For many Jews with talent in the nineteenth and early twentieth centuries, pursuing a life in music was the only way to escape the ghetto. Leopold Auer, the great violinist and greater teacher of the violin, was a beacon of hope and pride for little Jewish boys with the last names of Elman, Zimbalist, Heifetz, and Milstein and for many others desiring to escape a life of persecution. Auer established the line of violinists who have dominated string playing for over one hundred years. More than any other instrumentalist in history, Auer set standards of interpretation and technique which continue today to dominate music making and pedagogy.

Auer also represents the incredible ascendancy of Jewish instrumentalists from Felix Mendelssohn, Joseph Joachim, and Anton Rubinstein during the nineteenth century through Josef Hofmann, Joseph Lhevinne, Leopold Godowsky, Wanda Landowska, and Artur Schnabel in the early part of the twentieth, into more recent times with Artur Rubinstein, Joseph Szigeti, Rudolf Serkin, Vladimir Horowitz, Benny Goodman, Emanuel Feuermann, David Oistrakh, Yehudi Menuhin, Isaac Stern, Mstislav Rostropovich, Vladimir Ashkenazy, Itzhak Perlman, and Murray Perahia.

Auer was born in Hungary, the son of a housepainter. He showed an early aptitude for music, but did not receive formal training on the violin at the Budapest Conservatory until he was eight. Studies followed in Vienna and then with Joseph Joachim in Hanover. Joachim, a Jew and childhood friend of the great German composer Johannes Brahms, was in many ways a precursor of Auer. Like Auer, he collaborated with and inspired well-known composers to create important orchestral and chamber works. He also taught prominent musicians who passed on to further generations his pure, classical interpretive approach.

Joachim arranged for Auer to debut at age nineteen with the Leipzig Gewandhaus orchestra, at that time one of the most prominent showcases for musical artists. Positions followed as concertmaster with orchestras in Düsseldorf and Hamburg. He met and played with the great Russian Jewish pianist and composer Anton Rubinstein in London, which led to Rubinstein's recommending Auer in 1868 to succeed Henri Wieniawski as violin professor at the St. Petersburg Conservatory and as court violinist to the tsar. Auer remained in Russia for forty-nine years.

Auer's almost half century in Russia coincided with the awakening of Russian music after centuries of neglect. With the liberation of the serfs at about the same time Auer arrived in Russia, its society and industry began to modernize. A Russian school of composers including Modest Moussorgsky, Nicolai Rimsky-Korsakov, Aleksander Borodin, and the very individual Peter Ilyich Tchaikovsky produced nationalist works of great rhythmic force and lyric beauty. Tchaikovsky would dedicate his violin concerto to Auer (only to face Auer's rejection of the work as awkward and overwritten); Auer later saw his error and edited and performed the masterpiece.

His first student to grab world attention was Mischa Elman. Elman became a model for young Jewish boys who also as if by magic wanted to perform before the tsar. Auer's most famous pupil was Jascha Heifetz, generally regarded, like Niccolò Paganini earlier, as the greatest violinist of his century. Auer inculcated in his students (who were usually well trained and prepared for Auer's finishing lessons) a unique sense of style and interpretation, as well as a method of gripping their bows that became known as the "Russian bow grip."

Fleeing the Russian Revolution, Auer came in 1917 to America where he taught a new generation of string players at the famed Curtis Institute in Philadelphia. Auer's incredible legacy of friendships with the greatest composers and musicians of his time, including Franz Liszt, Gioacchino Rossini, Hector Berlioz, Brahms, Tchaikovsky, Aleksander Glazunov, Henri Vieuxtemps, Johann and Richard Strauss, and many others was passed on to his students with taste and intensity.

Auer died in Germany in 1930 at the age of eighty-five. His wish that he be buried in the United States was fulfilled with his internment at the Ferncliff Mausoleum in Hartsdale, New York.

Auer's influence can still be heard when listening to most of the great orchestras and string players of Europe and America. Virtuosity reined in always by the best taste, sentimentality directed by clear expression, and rich, pure line never bled dry, are musical attributes sought by most musicians today and ultimately derived from Auer's great teaching.

91

Groucho Marx

(1890–1977)

Whatever it is, I'm against it!

Whether Groucho Marx was professor Quincy Adams Wagstaff, explorer captain Jeffrey T. Spalding, impresario Otis B. Driftwood, quack doctor Hackenbush, or dictator Rufus T. Firefly—Julius Henry Marx, brother of Leonard (Chico), Arthur (Harpo), Milton (Gummo), and Herbert (Zeppo), was the most influential comedian in the world after Charlie Chaplin.

Groucho's unique combination of comedic gifts—physical movement, verbal insult, political wit, slapstick, burlesque, and expert delivery—inspired generations of performers. His immense talents assaulted and overwhelmed audiences. Groucho simply did not and could not let up. Think of comedians after him (and think also of the importance of comedy in our lives), and you will recognize their (and our) debt to him. Many comedians before and since have had greater individual skills than Groucho: the grace of Chaplin and Buster Keaton, the slapstick of Jackie Gleason, Milton Berle, and Lucille Ball, the subversive battery of Lenny Bruce, Jackie Mason, and Richard Pryor, the intellectual fancies of Sid Caesar and Woody Allen, the unrelenting mania of Mel Brooks, Jonathan Winters, and Robin Williams. Yet, Groucho had it all. We still are astonished by the artistry and force of his movies. We watch these old films over and over again, with their creaky plots, dated supporting casts and locales, never tiring of them. We cannot stop laughing, because Groucho and his brothers *won't let us stop.*

Raised on the Upper East Side of Manhattan in the poor streets of Yorkville by an Alsatian-born tailor and his stagestruck wife, Minnie, Julius and his brothers were pushed into show business—in order to eat. Most people do not realize that the Marx Brothers were in their late thirties and early forties when they first appeared in movies. Before their breakthrough success in 1929 with *The Cocoanuts,* the brothers had been on the road for twenty-five years, appearing in theaters on the vaudeville circuit, seedy hotels, and even brothels.

As their act developed, they used carefully thought-through scripts as diving boards into uncharted seas of improvisational mirth. Famous writers like George S. Kaufman, Morrie Ryskind, and S.J. Perelman, skilled in the fast pace of vaudeville and Broadway comedy, wrote for the brothers. Kaufman in particular was often frustrated with Groucho's repeated inclination to warp the playwright's lines into wackier and often funnier lingo.

Groucho's career began in variety shows and ended in the 1970s at Carnegie Hall and on television talk shows. More than four generations of fans reveled in his zany antics. The appeal of his comedy remains unaffected by the passing years. Usually, comedy is rooted in contemporary events and cultural mores. Audiences often fail to react to what was thought in an earlier day to be hilarious. For example, we do not respond to Fatty Arbuckle and Harold Lloyd as our forebears did. Some comedians remain "classic" and "perfect" to us (Chaplin, Keaton, Fields, Caesar, Gleason, Lucy), but many are so wedded to their era that with its passing they become dated. Groucho, however, still teaches us how to think like him and how to really insult, not with just slightly unpleasant jibes, but with shattering, shredding jolts of sarcasm. Yet his humor is shaped with such great timing and taste that it always seems inoffensive.

The best extant source of Groucho's art are the movies the Brothers made for Paramount and M-G-M during the Depression of the 1930s. *Duck Soup* is perhaps their greatest movie, containing no fussy romantic subplots, but in the context of rising fascism in Europe, just uninterrupted political chaos. *A Night at the Opera* does to *Il Trovatore* what countless operagoers

Groucho Marx appearing in *Horse Feathers* (1932) with Thelma Todd.

have been powerless to do but would have loved to try. Whether right-wing dictatorship or grand opera, retail capitalism (*The Big Store*) or higher education (*Horse Feathers*), institutions are easy (and appropriate) targets. They must be exposed for their tyranny, stupidity, arrogance, petulance, and downright cussedness. Idiot leaders should be kicked in the pants not once, but at least several times. When Chaplin and Mickey Mouse lost their early bitter, vicious side, they became less funny to us (but much sweeter and safer). Except in the last few movies, the Marx Brothers never halted their frontal attack on authority, their ridiculous rush at every symbol we don't hold dear.

When Groucho slides up to the knees of that imposing dowager of considerable means, Margaret Dumont, screaming "Can't you see what I'm trying to tell you? I love you. Why don't you marry me?", he is not only making himself look quite ludicrous (and attempting for profit and lascivious fun a rather bald and bold seduction), but making incredible fun of romance. These dashes at Dumont recur often, contrasting with the boring love stories that studios of the period insisted films must contain (again, with the notable exception of *Duck Soup*). When Groucho dances across hotel furniture with blond bombshell Thelma Todd (and winds up hiding in her closet), he's not interested in money. Groucho's love try with Thelma comes straight out of Roman farce (full of raunchy glances and sexual suggestions). This scene was quite daring for its time. It still titillates us.

Groucho never forgot his immigrant roots. Just recall his amazing dialogues with brother Chico, firing rapidly at each other a cultural mishmash of ethnic puns and asides. "Why a duck?" becomes "viaduct"; "down by the levees" a reference to the Jewish neighborhood; and contractual parties of the first and second part are edited out literally by ripping documents apart. In his old age Groucho objected to the ethnic humor of comedians like Myron Cohen, on the grounds that their approach demeaned the Jewish people. Yet to many, Groucho's method of delivery, loose-limbed strides, cigar smoking, large mustache, old-fashioned dress, and general "misdemeanor" were all representative of the quick-thinking, fast-talking, wisecracking Jew. Unlike the Three Stooges, Groucho did not have to physically attack to overwhelm. In the well-worn Jewish tradition of inquiry and subversive humor, Groucho overwhelmed by the power of his wits. He would live to see his brand of subversion appropriated by 1960s radicals. Hippies Abbie Hoffman and Jerry Rubin often seemed more influenced by father Groucho than comrade Karl.

During the 1950s and early 1960s, Groucho's television show *You Bet Your Life* brought his personal brand of insult into America's living rooms. In an era marked by conformity and postwar prosperity, the elder Groucho used the conventional game show format as a pulpit. No age group, profession, sex, or celebrity escaped his glare. The talk show gave him the opportunity in a commercial setting to dispense with plot, scenery, physical action, his brothers' antics, love stories, and institutions and to concentrate on his greatest love, using words perfectly inflected and timed to make people laugh, blush, and always learn.

92

Man Ray

(1890–1976)

Born Emmanuel Radnitsky in 1890 in Philadelphia, Man Ray was one of the most influential artistic figures of the twentieth century. Photographer, painter, sculptor, philosopher, writer, collagist, and creator of objects of art—Man Ray was a leader of the Dada-Surrealists who dominated European art in the 1920s and continue today to influence every field of art. With his compatriot in creativity and lifelong friend the great French painter Marcel Duchamp, Man Ray created a kind of anti-art. He found artistic meanings and sardonic humor in commonplace things seemingly thrown together in a haphazard way yet always with a serious purpose afoot.

344

Self portrait.

Son of a Jewish immigrant vest maker, Emmanuel was raised in Brooklyn. When he graduated from Boys' High, he accepted the award for best English student (a copy of Walt Whitman's *Leaves of Grass*) wearing an unconventionally bright red shirt. Just after the turn of the century, New York was slowly starting to become home to important artists such as those of the "Ashcan School," an indigenous form of social realism depicting urban scenes in an almost pre-Cubist style. Man Ray was also exposed to great European art of the period, viewing works by Auguste Rodin and others at the 291 Gallery of the American Jewish creative pioneer Alfred Stieglitz, an innovative photographer, supporter of the latest artistic trends, and the future husband of the American painter Georgia O'Keeffe. Hours were also spent at the massive Brooklyn Museum carefully studying its Old Masters collection. Although Man Ray would be at the vanguard of one of the most truly avant-garde artistic movements in history, he remained devoted to tradition and its discipline.

On February 17, 1913 the International Exhibition of Modern Art, commonly known as the Armory Show, opened in New York. The Armory Show exhibited works of the Ashcan School as well as paintings by Paul Cézanne, André Derain, Francis Picabia,

Constantin Brancusi, Georges Braque, and Pablo Picasso. But the work that aroused the greatest controversy was Duchamp's *Nude Descending a Staircase*. The painting was an attempt to end the reliance on representing nature in realistic forms. Rather, the nude was painted in almost falling slats of wood; others called them saddlebags. Duchamp viewed these forms as containing "an expression of time and space through the abstract presentation of motion." Man Ray was overwhelmed by the thoughts and talents exposed at the Armory.

Soon thereafter at a mutual friend's house, Man Ray met Duchamp for the first time as they squared off against each other in a tennis match. They began sharing ideas, molding each other's visions of what art should be and do. At about the same time, a movement in Europe reacting savagely to the carnage of the First World War burst forth in Switzerland, led by the Rumanian Jewish poet, Tristan Tzara (born Sami Rosenstock in Bucharest). Thumbing their noses at the world, the Dadaists sought to liberate artistic expression from all rules. Anything was possible and doable; nihilism reigned. Dada ("yes, yes") had its roots in cabaret, gaily ridiculing accepted values. Duchamp, Ray, and Picabia joined together in the United States to create a group later called the New York Dadaists. Examples of their artistic decisions at this time include Duchamp selecting a urinal and Ray choosing nonreflecting mirrors or buttons that did not start anything when pressed as objects of art. Man Ray also started to experiment with a simple Brownie camera, first photographing his Cubist-style paintings, then creating portraits. He began to photograph what he did not wish to paint. Sheets blowing in the wind on a backyard clothesline created meaningful forms and movements. Portraits could be taken by shooting the camera over one's shoulder, photographing the subject when least aware.

Unable to support himself and escaping an unhappy marriage, Ray left New York in 1921 for Paris, where he made his home for most of the next fifty years. Emmanuel, the free spirit, transformed himself into the expatriate artist, Man Ray. Aligning himself with both Tzara and the poet André Breton, the promoter of the new art form, Surrealism, Man Ray quickly impressed influential artists and critics with his virtuosic and varied abilities. Surrealism became the rage in Paris as artists applied the psychological discoveries of Freud to artistic expression. The

Surrealists believed that the fantasies of the unconscious world possessed a reality more important than real life. Only in tapping the unconscious could one's imagination be made free.

Dada had in its fierce anger and rebellion a destructive streak. Surrealism, on the other hand, was a more positive movement seeking to liberate expression by revealing man's deepest and most hidden emotions. Like Dada, all reason and morality was eschewed. But for the Dadaists, the rebellion *was* the art (Groucho Marx's later chant "whatever it is, I'm against it!" was a popularization of Dada). In sharp contrast, the Surrealists wanted to create great art out of their greatest fantasies—usually based on realistic forms.

Man Ray's contribution to the art world of this period was his combination of Dada with Surrealism filtered through a uniquely American imagination. He created objects of new artistic expression, like attaching a photograph of an eye to a metronome or using utensils as male and female forms. While Man Ray considered his painting to be his true serious work, his photographs and experimental filmmaking brought him the greatest exposure. His short films incited riots. Yet he became the favored photographer of the great artistic figures of his time. His photos of fashion models liberated commercial photography from traditional constraints. The broad expression found in commercial advertising today largely owes its freedom to Man Ray. Experimenting with the photographic process itself, he perfected photogenic drawings or what he called "rayographs." Playing with the effect of light on exposed film by moving objects on and off a developing photo, Man Ray created a new art form of amazing subtlety and spontaneity. After him, there would never again be any limits to what a photographer could do.

93

Henrietta Szold

(1860–1945)

Her biographer, Irving Fineman, dubbed her a "woman of valor." Henrietta Szold, the founder of Hadassah, the women's Zionist organization, and a leading force in the development of social and child welfare, was an exemplary Jewish woman in a long line of impressive Jewish women stretching from Rebecca, Deborah, and Esther in ancient times to Golda Meir and Betty Friedan in the twentieth century. Like them, Henrietta Szold overcame the severe restraints imposed on women to change society in ways that perhaps only a Jewish woman could. Szold's importance and influence lies not only in her great deeds (and

348

there were many, compressed into a relatively short time frame despite her long life), but in her remarkably inspiring and selfless example.

Henrietta Szold was somewhat similar to other reformers of her day, but also something more. Before John Dewey, Szold lectured and developed new methods of education, for example, establishing night schools for Russian immigrants. During the same era when Jane Addams was providing social services to the needy in Chicago, Szold created welfare programs in Palestine to help Arabs and Jews alike where there had been no aid whatsoever before. With Florence Nightingale as her example, Szold introduced contemporary nursing care in impoverished areas of the Holy Land, conquering superstition and medieval medical practices.

Born in Baltimore at the beginning of the American Civil War to German-speaking Hungarian-born parents, Henrietta's earliest memory was witnessing President Lincoln's funeral cortege passing through her town. Her father, Rabbi Benjamin Szold, was the religious leader of their community, a stern, scholarly man. The family conversed in German, the language of cultured Jews of the time. Henrietta, the eldest of six girls, was a substitute mother for her sisters and her father's best "son" and assistant. She grew up in a comfortable yet sheltered religious environment, encountering anti-Semitism only from the taunts of children in the streets.

Her life was relatively staid until her late forties. She lived the role of the cultured, educated, yet socially committed old maid, doting on her father and devoted to public causes. Szold taught in public and religious schools, lectured on educational topics, translated, edited, and wrote articles for Jewish publications, became an editor at the prestigious Jewish Publication Society, and, most important, in her early maturity established a night school for Russian immigrants. The school was a trailblazing enterprise during years when the downtrodden masses newly arrived in America were largely forgotten, abused, resented. When she learned of the horrors of pogroms in Russia, government-sanctioned persecution, she was stirred her to greater action on behalf of her people.

Citing Theodor Herzl's example and inspired by a visit to the Alt-Neu Shul in Prague, Szold organized a circle of Jewish women to meet as a discussion group interested in Zionist activities. The first meeting of what she called Hadassah, the Hebrew for Esther, took place at Temple Emanu-El in New York City in 1912 with a talk "illustrated by stereopticon views" of Palestine. Hadassah was founded for many of the same reasons as the suffragette movements of the period. Women simply wanted to take part in the great issues of their day. These Jewish women would not tolerate being separated from pursuing Zionist ideals. Hadassah or the Women's Zionist Organization of America became one of the most important philanthropic and socially committed volunteer groups in modern history.

After the death of her father and a sour love affair with a prominent Jewish scholar ten years her junior, Szold traveled to the Middle East to attempt to help transform Palestine into a place where women could prosper. She organized women's societies for public welfare, established a training school for nurses, and founded the famed Hadassah Hospital in Jerusalem. Elected in 1931 to the National Council of the General Assembly of the Knesset, the Jewish autonomous ruling body, Szold served as a virtual clearinghouse for social service activities in Palestine. Her name became internationally synonymous with the providing of health and child care. Influential methods of family casework were developed under her auspices. In her final years, she helped many Jewish children flee Nazi hatred to Palestine, made the words "Youth Aliyah" or immigration of young people into the land her clarion call. The old maid had become the "Mother of Israel."

94

Benny Goodman

(1909–1986)

Popularly known as the King of Swing (and to musicians of his era simply by his initials "BG"), Benny Goodman was more than a great clarinetist and bandleader. BG developed ensembles known for their remarkable cohesion and integration (musically as well as racially). He had enormous societal influence by placing black musicians in his bands at a time of intense bigotry and segregation. Goodman commissioned important compositions from the greatest composers of his time, including Béla Bártok, Paul Hindemith, and Aaron Copland, as well as performing and

351

recording works of Leonard Bernstein, Igor Stravinsky, Johannes Brahms, Carl Maria von Weber, and many others. His solo virtuosity set a standard for clarinetists to emulate. As a touring artist, BG introduced his unique classical swing to Asian and Russian audiences, bringing his special way of making jazz to international prominence.

Benjamin Goodman was born in Chicago, Illinois on May 30, 1909. His parents were Eastern European immigrants who brought their three sons to synagogue for special musical programs. The smallest of three boys, Benny, was given the clarinet to play because it was lighter than the trumpet and tuba given to his bigger brothers. His real studies began at age twelve when he studied with the first clarinetist of the Chicago Symphony Orchestra. The great jazz musician would always be marked by the rigorous classical training he received in his teens. This training separated him from many of the jazz musicians of his era, several of whom were self-taught, educated in what was quite literally a school of hard knocks, one-night engagements in small towns and taverns. Also in his early teens, BG played in many local dance bands, meeting several important jazz artists such as the great cornet player Bix Beiderbecke.

Influenced by the New Orleans players who voyaged up to the Windy City on party boats, Goodman's playing gained the maturity and variety necessary for him to venture to and compete first in Los Angeles and then in New York. For the first five years of the Depression (1929–1934), Goodman freelanced in New York City, establishing himself as a force in popular music. Freelance work during this period included playing in Broadway show pit orchestras, radio shows, and recording sessions. The first-night audience in 1930 of George Gershwin's musical *Girl Crazy* witnessed not only the ingenue Ginger Rogers and the debut of Ethel Merman belting *I Got Rhythm*, but a pit band consisting of future jazz greats Jimmy Dorsey, Jack Teagarden, Glenn Miller, Red Nichols, Gene Krupa, and Benny Goodman. Imagine what it must have sounded like!

In 1933 Goodman met the young John Hammond, an independently wealthy jazz promoter and critic, a meeting which would prove pivotal in the history of American popular music (and in Goodman's life—he would marry Hammond's sister). Hammond helped guide Goodman's professional development and assemble jazzmen for his ensembles. More and more, these players were African-American. A year later, BG put together his first permanent band. He hired important arrangers such as the genius Fletcher Henderson and Benny Carter to develop new styles of orchestration, set in vibrant jazz rhythms people started to call "swing." Whole sections of instruments played as one. A new period of musical arrangements had begun.

Professional musicians were not only "sent" by Goodman's band but also dazzled by its precision, drive, and musicianship. When the band played at the Palomar Ballroom in Los Angeles during August 1935, the swing era was in full swing. It was music that one could dance to, listen to, swing to; it was so technically outstanding, one could not resist it. BG's band included many great musicians, black and white, many who would go on to create their own bands. Ziggy Elman, Harry James, Lionel Hampton, Teddy Wilson, Gene Krupa, Bunny Berigan, Dick Haymes, Patti Page, Peggy Lee and Charlie Christian were some of the great names who regularly appeared with the Goodman band.

Benny Goodman shown on the cover of sheet music.

At the same time Goodman was electrifying radio and ballroom audiences with his amazing band, he decided to form chamber jazz ensembles to apply in a smaller, more intimate setting many of the techniques and styles first attempted with his large group. First as a trio with drummer Krupa and pianist Wilson, then as a quartet with vibraphonist Hampton (and later as a sextet or septet or whatever), Goodman's combos pioneered an improvisatory style of jazz playing which led directly to the bebop revolution of the postwar era.

BG's use of the elegant stylist Teddy Wilson as his pianist was the first national example of integration in popular music. When Lionel Hampton later joined the ensemble, it was not a matter of another black musician playing with whites, but rather the addition of the most brilliant vibes player around. Over ten years before baseball or the army were integrated, Benny Goodman's bands used the best players regardless of race.

Goodman also broke down the barriers as to what was the proper venue for musical performance. In 1938 he brought his band to Carnegie Hall. This fabulous concert was recorded to great acclaim, bobby-soxers dancing in the aisles, classical music's bastion of elite culture brought down to earth and then sent soaring.

The Second World War broke the spell of swing on the American public. Swing music had helped release young people from the sadness of the Depression. The war turned the musical mood first to patriotism, then to smooth-sounding vocal music, tied more to the ballad than to instrumental jazz. New jazz artists appeared, such as Charlie Parker and Dizzy Gillespie, creating music that was more esoteric and intellectual, music that only one's mind could dance to.

Goodman's reaction was to retreat from pop music into performing classical repertoire. He was the first great jazz artist to cross over successfully, and serves as a model to this day for artists such as trumpeter Wynton Marsalis and flutist James Galway who perform with ease in many styles. Racial and musical barriers simply did not exist for the gracious virtuoso Benny Goodman. Only superb musicianship mattered.

95

MAIN SQUEEZE
At-2. Steven Spielberg
made Jaws at 27, in 1975,
Close Encounters ('77),
Raiders (with Lucas in
'81), and E.T. ('82), whose
star Spielberg called "a
squashy little mensh."
Next?

SCREEN

Steven Spielberg
(b. 1947)

His films have been seen by more people than any other director's. No other director has made so many movies as consistently entertaining and as action-packed. Perhaps only Walt Disney exhibited greater talent than Steven Spielberg in appealing to the widest possible audience. Spielberg's entertainments have worldwide appeal. His films have been dubbed into over a dozen languages, and to most of the world today represent the best in American cinema.

Spielberg is a member of an extraordinary generation of directors. With Martin Scorsese, Francis Ford Coppola, Oliver Stone, and George Lucas, Spielberg (the only Jewish director in

355

this premier group) has dominated commercial filmmaking in the United States since the overwhelming success in 1975 of his shark-infested *Jaws*.

As a teenager, Spielberg studied Alfred Hitchcock at work. Like the English master, Spielberg shares an uncanny ability to draw his audience right into the action on screen. Many people have likened the feeling of watching his films to riding a roller coaster. Indeed, among the most popular attractions at both Disney World and Universal Studios amusement parks are the *Indiana Jones Stunt Spectacular* and the *Jaws* and *E.T. the Extra-Terrestrial* rides.

Academic critics have criticized not only Spielberg's melodramatic instincts, but also his sentimentality. The poignancy of many scenes in *The Color Purple* undermines such criticism. His "gushiness" is sometimes so appropriate, telling, and comforting.

Spielberg relates his talents with a kind of boyish amazement. When things in his films appear to be beautiful or awesome, this great director just sits the camera back and lets his audience gape. In *Jurassic Park* (the second-biggest grossing film in history, right behind *E.T.*), a genetically bred brachiosaur is viewed, roaring up on its hind legs, stretching to munch on the top leaves of a gigantic tree. This colossal sight confirms for the viewer Spielberg's genius for the image aptly framed. More often than most filmmakers, he conveys precisely what he intends with the sharpest clarity and the most thrilling majesty.

There is always a wonderful sense of place in his films. The brutality of a marauding Great White stalking its human prey is more horrible for being starkly set in the clear light and warm ocean spray of Cape Cod in summer. *Indiana Jones and the Temple of Doom* is more thrilling for its placement in the overheated locales of gangster-plagued Shanghai and a lushly green India burned into dust by religious fanaticism. *E.T.*, a benevolent and unique creature from outer space, meets his match in a wide-eyed boy who lives in a house with his mother and brother and little sister, on a street in a development of houses all looking the same, in suburban sprawl. The spaceman meets the boy who has no space. A ride on a bike through the air releases both from the confines of childhood and society.

Strangely, like some other great film directors, Spielberg's films do not have memorable screenplays. What characters say in his movies is not so easily remembered. What remains most vivid is his mastery of visual imagery. He tells grand stories with grand cinematic gestures, John Williams's proud music triumphantly moving the story along. In this, Spielberg is closest to the half-Jewish Soviet director Sergei Eisenstein. Eisenstein was certainly Spielberg's direct precursor in the use of broadly shaped visual imagery accompanied by surging, symphonic underscoring (for *Alexander Nevsky* and *Ivan the Terrible* the composer was Williams's essential model, Sergei Prokofiev).

Spielberg's strong commercial sense led to his production (by his company named after his first film, *Amblin'*) of a new crew of Warner Brothers cartoon characters (apparently Bugs Bunny and Daffy Duck have nephews and nieces), newly beloved by youngsters, as well as science-fiction television shows unfortunately weakened by his failure to direct them.

His films display the cinematography of a virtuoso. Spielberg is among the greatest technicians in movie history. He always seems to find the camera angle, focus, coloring, and framing best suited for the emotion or characterization desired. More often than not, his films have a freshness that derives not simply from magical special effects. The films are repositories of cinematic devices and techniques sure to influence young movie-makers for generations.

Spielberg's stories often seem to be told through a child's eyes (whether or not the protagonist is young). In *Empire of the Sun,* the horrors of war in the Pacific during the Second World War are retold through the saga of a young boy separated from his parents under Japanese occupation. Indiana may have a young boy as his sidekick in the second of his thrillers, but then, no kid ever had as much fun as Dr. Jones. The perspectives in *E.T.* are mostly kid level, the strange world of suburban America viewed by the alien not much higher than three feet.

Spielberg apparently had a great deal of fun as a kid, making home movies and being dubbed his family's official photographer. After studies in English at California State College at Long Beach, he produced a series of vaguely artistic films, culminating when he was twenty-three with the commercially viable *Amblin'* (paired with the sickly *Love Story* in national distribution). Spielberg's work on television dramas honed his technical skills on weak scripts. The made-for-television film *Duel* and his first feature-length presentation, *The Sugarland Express,* gave him an early reputation as a specially gifted craftsman. When Universal movie executives gambled on the young director to direct *Jaws,* a show-business legend was born (along with immense profits).

Spielberg has used his influence, gathered in the glowing afterburn of huge corporate bottom lines, to help younger directors find their voice (such as Robert Zameckis, director of the *Back to the Future* series), largely independent of the pressures of big studio executives. Whether Spielberg's films themselves have lasting influence, it is still much too early to predict. No other director has had more blockbuster films. Few other creative artists have left so large a mark on popular culture.

Only Steven Spielberg could have made *Schindler's List.* To most people, *Gone With The Wind* represents the American Civil War. Next to the remembrances of Primo Levi and Elie Wiesel and the opera and chamber music of the composer of the "model Ghetto" Terezin, Viktor Ullmann (who died in Auschwitz), Spielberg's Oscar-winning *Schindler's List* will remain a vital testament of and most people's link to the Shoah. With virtuoso camera work not seen since the silent era (only the work of D.W. Griffith is comparable), an unparalleled ease with a talented actors' ensemble, and a refusal to sentimentalize or shield the audience from the darkest reality, Spielberg created the greatest film about the worst catastrophe in Jewish history.

96

Marc Chagall

(1887–1985)

And God spoke all these words, saying:
I am the LORD thy God, who brought thee out of the
land of Egypt, out of the house of bondage.
Thou shall have no other gods before Me. Thou shall
not make unto thee a graven image, nor any manner
of likeness, of any thing that is in heaven above, or
that is in the earth beneath, or that is in the water
under the earth...

—Exodus 20:1

Until Camille Pissarro, Chaïm Soutine, Jacques Lipchitz, Amedeo Modigliani, and Marc Chagall, there were no great Jewish painters. Biblical prohibitions of representational art stifled any creative impulses to express images in living pigments. Jewish artisans may have carved lions out of wood to adorn sacred arks or stained glass in dull colors, but no portraits of nobles or pastoral scenes were permitted, no classical nudes lounging in the grass ever imagined.

Pissarro, one of the grand old men of Impressionism, surely influenced his great successors, Paul Gauguin and Paul Cézanne. But Pissarro's output was too large, not consistently fine, and in later years often formulaic and repetitive.

Some critics characterize Chagall's work similarly, yet his early period was truly extraordinarily expressive, unique in inspiration, and something more than just art. Chagall's oeuvre captured in oils the irreplaceable culture of Eastern European shtetl (village) life, its purest essence. In his pictures, blue, bloated smiling cows fly eternally over thatched cottage rooftops. Villagers celebrate a wedding, forever massed together in a bonfire of celebration while bride and groom standing together under the huppah or canopy almost rise up out of the picture. Chagall's art preserved for all time a world now vanished without a trace.

In his gentle way, Chagall symbolized the individual artist's resistance not only to political oppression (the Bolsheviks) but also against the domination of art by so-called avant-garde movements. He did not consider scientific approaches to art a good thing. Impressionism and rigidly geometric Cubism were "foreign" to him.

During the early years of Israeli independence, Chagall also became an international symbol of the flowering of Jewish artistic creativity. Unlike Pissarro or Modigliani, who never consciously drew on Jewish subject matter, Chagall clearly sought to create out of the experiences of his youth in Russia a Jewish art, sparkling new and modern. (The only other artists comparable to Chagall in this respect were the Swiss-born Ernest Bloch, composer of among many works, a great cello rhapsody about King Solomon called *Schelomo,* and a moving *Sacred Service;* the short story writer and playwright, Sholem Aleichem; and the Nobel

Prize–winning novelist Isaac Bashevis Singer). Chagall's murals and glass panels on biblical themes for churches in France, Switzerland, Pocantico Hills, New York, and at the Hadassah Medical Center and the Israeli Knesset in Jerusalem, the Vatican, New York's Metropolitan Opera House and the United Nations Secretariat provided public displays of his humane, loving, and healing message.

Born in Liozno, Vitebsk, in tsarist Russia, Chagall's real last name was Segal (the great American composer Aaron Copland also traced his roots to Vitebsk). Chagall's father worked for over thirty years as a common laborer in a herring warehouse. He never fully appreciated his son's remarkable talents. Marc first entered heder, a primitive religious education usually conducted in a study house, then public school. When a friend admired his work, Chagall convinced his mother to support lessons with a local portrait painter.

In 1906, Chagall ventured to St. Petersburg for study at the Imperial Society for the Furtherance of the Arts. Later, he met and briefly studied with Léon Bakst, the Jewish designer for Diaghilev's Ballet Russe (next to Chagall in Bakst's class stood the great dancer Vaslav Nijinsky, somehow assuming he too could paint). With a stipend from a lawyer, Chagall was able to leave Russia for four years of productive work in Paris. Exposure to the vibrant art scene of pre–First World War France and the treasures of the Louvre Museum, Chagall felt liberated. Back in Russia, as he recalled in his autobiography, "at every step" Chagall felt, or rather people made him feel, that he "was a Jew." In France, Chagall became a great artist of Russian Jewish origin. His special brand of Expressionism—lyrical, fantastic, born out of the fertile soil of Vitebsk—resulted in ecstatic, brightly colored canvases. Without question, Chagall became one of the greatest and most influential colorists of the twentieth century.

After a one-man show in Berlin in 1914, he went back to Vitebsk, was drafted into the imperial army, and like countless Russian soldiers in the massed evacuation at the end of the war, simply got up from his government desk job and left. When Lenin seized power in 1917, Chagall was named commissar and director of fine arts in Vitebsk. His works were put on exhibit in the Winter Palace in Leningrad. He was publicized as the great painter of a Soviet New Age. But his individualism proved too warm and humane for the cold conformity of developing Socialist Realism, and he was deposed as commissar.

After innovative work for the stage at the Jewish State Theater in Moscow, Chagall fled Russia with his wife and daughter in 1922. He had already become a well-known name in Western Europe and was honored by the sponsorship of the influential Jewish dealer Paul Cassirer and the Frenchman Ambroise Vollard, who both commissioned etchings based on biblical stories. By the 1930s, Chagall was recognized in Europe as one of the greatest modern painters. In 1937 the Nazis banned his work, destroying some paintings and including others in their infamous exhibition on "Degenerate Art" (which also ridiculed the music of Kut Weill) in Munich. At the invitation of the Museum of Modern Art in New York in 1941, the Chagalls, fearing the approaching Nazi menace, fled to America.

After the Second World War, especialy through his remarkable stained-glass windows and much sought-after lithographs, Chagall became one of the most famous painters in the world. However, through the many remaining years of his long life he remained unaffected by the postwar movements from Abstract Expressionism to pop and photo realism and did not in any meaningful way change the direction or philosophy of art (except perhaps in his use of color). It can never be said that Chagall influenced whole generations of artists in the way Picasso did. Neither did Sholem Aleichem or Isaac Bashevis Singer change the art of fiction writing inthe way Kafka and Gertrude Stein did. Yet, Chagall's masterpieces touched his people with a deep religiosity, sense of fun and magic, and an almost Hasidic passion for ecstasy. He enriched and marked world culture permanently with visions of his Vitebsk, a phantasmagoric yet universally recognizable village located at the core of the Jewish soul.

97

Bob Dylan

(b. 1941)

Beatty and Abe Zimmerman's son Robert Allen was born in Duluth, Minnesota just before America's entry into the Second World War. Bobby grew up in nearby Hibbing, a largely Christian and plain Midwest small town among other small towns. As in most of America at the time, people were exposed to culture through the radio, early television, and in movies. James Dean's film *Rebel Without a Cause* and Marlon Brando's *The Wild One* swayed the impressionable young Zimmerman into modifying his dress and attitude toward society. Always intensely creative, writing poems, teaching himself piano, guitar, and harmonica, Bobby was attracted to 1950s rock and roll, reveling in and imitating the late-night broadcasts of Johnny Cash, Jerry Lee Lewis, and Little Richard.

Hearing rock and roll these first times changed his life. All he wanted to be was a rock and roll star. During high school and later while briefly at the University of Minnesota, Bob tried out his act at small clubs and coffeehouses. Even then he produced music that was raw, not the coaxing, bland diet of Tab Hunter and Fabian, but elemental and searching, unstructured but sharp. On his way to college, this son of Abraham "killed him a son" and changed his last name to Dylan after the rebellious great Welsh poet Dylan Thomas. The Jewish-born Zimmerman had become a Celtic Dylan. Bob also soon recognized that first, only through folk music, not rock and roll, could he find his true musical and artistic voice and complete the personal transformation he so desired.

Never a "pretty face" like so many of the rock stars of his generation, Dylan was particularly drawn to the rough-hewn folk songs of Woody Guthrie. Transforming himself into a kind of teenage Woody, bound for glory, Dylan sang in scratchy, harsh sounds, uncompromising in his inattention to sweet timbre. In a uniquely American *Sprechstimme* or speech-song, he reinterpreted the almost classic folk music of Guthrie, Pete Seeger, and others with almost alarming inventiveness. Dylan in his late teens and early twenties began to compose, his first accomplished work the paean *Song to Woody*.

He began to perform at the now mythical Gerdes Folk City club in New York City's Greenwich Village. Folk City was a hothouse of postwar popular music, with the likes of Judy Collins, Peter Yarrow, Paul Stookey, Mary Travers, Richie Havens, Tom Paxton, Phil Ochs, and Buffy Saint-Marie jamming together nightly. Most of them lived at the time in great poverty, always in search of a hot meal. Dylan's appearances at Folk City brought him to the attention of the great record producer (and brother-in-law of Benny Goodman) John Hammond. Hammond's important role in the development of American popular music is well-known from his work with artists such as Billie Holiday and Bruce Springsteen. Hammond produced Dylan's first album with Columbia Records in 1962. One year later, at age twenty-three,

Bob Dylan composed *Blowin' in the Wind*, which when popularized by the group Peter, Paul and Mary became the theme song of a generation.

During these years of the early 1960s, Dylan was the nation's singing poet laureate of protest, establishing his reputation for topical and bardic commentary on the state of our lives. His 1963 composition *The Times They Are A-Changin'* echoed the great strides in human freedom made and the loss of innocence felt during those turbulent days when John Kennedy was still president and Vietnam was a country known mainly to geographers.

Dylan shocked folk music aficionados when he performed at the Newport Folk Festival in 1965 with electric guitar accompanied by a rock band. His *Mr. Tambourine Man* and *Like a Rolling Stone* heralded a fusion of folk and rock. Restless throughout his career, never holding for long one homogeneous style, Dylan (after a near-fatal motorcycle accident incapacitated him for nearly two years in the late 1960s) changed his style again, merging country and western music with folk and rock. This style mellowed in the '70s when Dylan's music became more personal and introverted. Yet he never ceased to explore other influences, exposing his unique brew to Latino, soul, and Caribbean music.

Dylan's private life mirrored his creative pursuits. Born a Jew, he flirted with born-again fundamentalist Christianity in the early 1980s, only to return later to Orthodox Judaism (he was linked, for example, to the Lubavitcher Hasidic movement and its charismatic grand rabbi, Menachem Schneerson).

Dylan's willingness to combine various styles has influenced many popular music stars. Like John Cage in classical music and jazzman Dizzy Gillespie, Dylan did not let himself be restricted by norms, but searched in a personal (and sometimes quixotic) way to express the rages and hates, the melancholy, hopes, and desires, of modern life.

98

Sandy Koufax

(b. 1935)

Somehow I believe the baseball stars of my youth were greater than the highly paid executives of today's national conference rooms. My father, Sam, took my brother, Barry, and me to Ebbets Field in 1955. I remember men sitting around us wearing ties, some sporting summer hats, much more formal than today's careless hordes. Jackie Robinson hit a shot, jumped on first, and when the next batter came up, started to rock to and fro. The place exploded. The opposing pitcher was careless, Jackie took advantage, bolted, and stole second with unforgettable style.

366

When the Phillies later scored, Roy Campanella threw down his catcher's mask, stood up behind home plate, a look on his sweet, beautiful face so doleful and upset that I still mourn for the run let in, the loss suffered. Although the four-year-old me got bored by the seventh inning and asked my father to tell the cop to stop the game, I was a made Dodger fan, and I would forgive them Walter O'Malley's treachery when Brooklyn's heart was ripped out of Flatbush for the charms of California and Chavez Ravine.

Upon reaching eight years of age, American boys dream baseball. When I was eight in 1959, out on the West Coast another, older Jewish boy from Brooklyn began to assert his mastery over that most difficult of all baseball skills, pitching. His name was Sanford (Sandy) Koufax, he came from my borough, he was a Dodger, he was Jewish, and I adored him.

Even as a young boy in the city's sandlot leagues, he was a legend. His fastball as a teenager was clocked in the nineties but he had next to no control. Until Koufax was in his mid-twenties, a batter's hard skull and swiftness in ducking were little protection for those balls whizzing past like bullets.

Sandy had tremendous control, however, on the Lafayette High School and University of Cincinnati basketball squads. He was an outstanding six-foot-two forward with an accurate one-handed jump shot and an average ten points per game. Also, Koufax secured a place on the freshman baseball team roster as an incredibly precocious cannonballer. The college student struck out fifty-one batters in thirty-two innings, thirty-four of those strikeouts in consecutive games.

The next summer, he tried out for the New York Giants, was passed over, but then sought out by the Pirates and the Braves. The Dodgers organization beat out Pittsburgh and Milwaukee by appealing to his family's Kings County loyalty and offering a larger signing bonus.

Koufax joined the Brooklyn Dodger team during the spring training of 1955, the year "dose bums" would finally grab their World Series rings. He was still unable to throw precisely, had limited experience, was literally all over the lot, and to compensate for his nervousness, he threw faster and still more wildly. Due to the rule mandating that a "bonus baby" should not be sent for seasoning in the minors, but slowly ripen or rot on the bench in the big leagues, Koufax observed Don Newcombe, Johnny

Podres, Sal Maglie, and Clem Labine mow down the National League, and then, blessedly, beat those "damn" New York Yankees for Brooklyn's first (and last) world championship.

Finally, in 1959, after four years of benchwarming, Koufax became what field manager Walter Alston had so patiently expected—a great pitcher. In just 153 innings, Koufax struck out 173 (eighteen in one game to set a record—after thirteen in the previous outing for another record of thirty-one strikeouts in two straight), helping to propel the now Los Angeles Dodgers to a pennant and World Series championship over Chicago's White Sox.

He was nearly traded to the Yankees during the off-season, but the Dodgers kept the faith and him. A disastrous 1960 season followed, his 1959 won-lost record of 8–6 plummeting to 8–13 due to an unnatural rush in his pitching gait and a "silent temper" (in general manager Buzzie Bavasi's words).

When the Jewish second-string catcher Norm Sherry advised Koufax to "just try to get the ball over," he began to throw more easily, naturally. And woe to National League hitters, for Koufax began to juxtapose his brutal fastball with a winding curve more accurate than a Cruise missile. Koufax kind of gave away his curveball with a unique twist of his elbow when he threw, but batters were lost when it fell off the table crossing the plate.

Sandy Koufax pitching in the 1963 World Series.

No-hitters followed in each of years 1962 through 1965, including a perfect, no-runners-on-base game thrown against the Chicago Cubs. In a first inning of what would be nine innings of wondrous no-hit perfection against the New York Mets, three batters struck out on nine straight pitches. Star hitter Richie Ashburn, a skilled man with the bat, was said to have stood amazed, laughing as the strikes flew irresistibly by.

A very private man, Koufax was called by the press "The Man with the Goldern Arm," and for five seasons that is what he was. Not since Lefty Grove had there been such a southpaw. Before Koufax retired after the 1966 season due to an arthritic elbow, he had led the league in earned run average for five consecutive seasons, complete games for two, most strikeouts and innings pitched for four out of six, and virtuosic twenty-six- and twenty-seven-win seasons back to back to conclude.

Perhaps his most famous outing to the mound, surely his most influential, was the day on Yom Kippur, 1965 when Koufax refused to pitch in the first game of the World Series against the Minnesota Twins. Preferring to attend synagogue with his parents rather than disobey religious proscription against work on the holiest of Jewish holidays, Koufax became a world figure. (His beloved comrade, ace Don Drysdale, substituted, was shelled by Minnesota after two and a half innings, and when yanked in the third inning quipped to manager Alston, "Bet you wish I was Jewish, too!") When Koufax returned after the holiday to pitch shutouts in the fifth and seventh games, clinching the series for the Dodgers, a divine inspiration for his miraculous skills was commonly implied.

For post-Holocaust Jewry and to millions of non-Jews glued to their television sets, Sandy Koufax's genius pitching (even more than the exploits of trailblazers slugger Hank Greenberg, basketball's Nat Holman, and quarterback Sid Luckman before the war) confirmed that great Jewish athletes could compete and triumph in America's sports with exemplary talent, integrity, and fierce pride. Before Koufax, Jews had excelled in nearly every field but never had there been a Jewish athlete quite like him. Koufax was the greatest southpaw in modern baseball history (sorry, Lefty Grove fans!), quite simply the best, the dominant pitcher of his era, and forever a hero to Jewish kids who cannot get enough of baseball.

99

Bernard Berenson

(1865–1959)

Perhaps the greatest art critic in history, certainly the most important in awakening public awareness of the Italian Renaissance, Bernard Berenson began his life a poor boy in Eastern Europe and ended his many years in a palazzo near Florence, Italy, the most renowned connoisseur in the world. His texts, *The Venetian Painters of the Renaissance, Aesthetics and History, Drawings of the Florentine Painters,* and the magnum opus *The Italian Painters of the Renaissance* not only identified the greatest masterworks of the greatest masters, but also their styles of composition and the historical context surrounding their work. Paid lavish sums by

American and English collectors to locate and then authenticate important works of art, Berenson was his own greatest creation, the ultimate civilized man. With his business partner, the British art dealer Joseph Duveen, Berenson made huge sums certifying the validity of artworks to interested but untutored buyers.

Berenson's saga began in a small town outside Vilna in Lithuania. Butrimonys was an Eastern European shtetl much like countless other villages in the Pale of Settlement. Young boys took their Hebrew lessons, reveling in the intricacies of the Talmud, largely oblivious of the outside world. In 1875, Berenson emigrated to Boston with his family. Out of a humble background, he rose in a few years, largely self-taught from long hours of study in the public library, to Boston Latin School, Boston University, and then scholastic fame at Harvard.

Liberal wealthy Bostonians were charmed by Berenson's brilliance and spirituality. Sent to Europe on a traveling fellowship funded by the patron Isabella Stewart Gardner, he came under the influence of Giovanni Morelli, a Florentine who preached a new canon of art criticism based on scientific methods. Berenson visited every church and museum he could find in Italy, systematically noting in his encyclopedic mind the works of the great and lesser *maestri*.

His choice of a mate, a married woman named Mary Costelloe, also changed his life. Overwhelmed by Berenson's wit and intellect, Mary left her husband, a lawyer and the father of her two children. Berenson educated her about art, and she reciprocated by organizing their family unit into the most sought-after art specialists in Europe. Berenson's old benefactor, Gardner, called upon their services in building up a wondrous private collection of Renaissance paintings.

The Berensons also began to work for others of similar wealth and lavish spending habits, intent on owning that most highly regarded of all possessions of the time, the private art collection. Cheated by deceitful art dealers not constrained by ethical concerns, wealthy collectors and institutions came to view the Berensons as their only reliable source of expert advice. Although he was repulsed all his life by the commercial art world (his biographer Ernest Samuels recalls Berenson calling it the "pig trade"), enormous profits were made from fees collected in the service of confused patrons. Through his association with the art dealer Duveen, Berenson assembled many of the great private collections that later found their way into the major American art museums.

With their newfound wealth, the Berensons purchased a villa outside Florence named I Tatti. The formal house became the center of international art commerce. Berenson, an avid collector of books, devoted great energy to amassing a library of tens of thousands of volumes. The library was bequeathed to Harvard University and became the cornerstone of I Tatti Institute, known also as The Center for Italian Renaissance Studies.

Berenson lived in I Tatti like a Renaissance prince. His palatial home became a center of European culture, attracting disciples (such as future great art historians Kenneth Clark and Meyer Schapiro), literary greats (Somerset Maugham, John Steinbeck, Mary McCarthy, and Edith Wharton), and public figures (Harry Truman, Walter Lippmann, Judge Learned Hand) to his influence. Surrounded by fascist and then deadly Nazi persecution, he remained in Italy for the duration of the war, somehow surviving the Holocaust (unlike the fictional character Aaron Jastrow, whom Herman Wouk in his *The Winds of War* and *War and Remembrance* loosely based on Berenson and had murdered in the flames of Auschwitz). Berenson lived for another fourteen years after the war, a true esthete, resplendent in the glory of his intellect and culture, his scholarly methods the prime model for generations of art historians.

100

Jerry Siegel
(1914–1996)

Joe Shuster
(1914–1992)

LOOK—UP IN THE SKY! IT'S A BIRD! IT'S A PLANE!
IT'S—SUPERMAN

In 1933, nineteen-year-olds Jerry Siegel and Joe Shuster, two childhood friends living twelve blocks apart in Cleveland, Ohio, created a fictional character who would become more famous than Sherlock Holmes or Tarzan and the force behind the launching of a new industry based on a new literary genre—the comic book. Their character was a man "more powerful than a locomotive, faster than a speeding bullet, able to leap tall buildings in a single bound!"

Superman was the first and the most American (although literally out of this world) of all the superheroes. Modeled after Edgar Rice Burroughs's John Carter of Mars, intellectual, muscle-bound Doc Savage, and the Saturday matinee serial spaceman Flash Gordon, his tale adapted from the science-fiction novel *When Worlds Collide*, Superman was conceived during the darkest days of the Depression and European fascism. Born Kal-El (a curiously Hebraic-sounding alien) on the immense planet Krypton, "whose inhabitants had evolved, after millions of years, to physical perfection" (from early DC Comics' explanations of his amazing strength), the first *Action Comics* featuring Superman (1938) was a spectacular hit, 200,000 copies selling out in days.

Siegel and Shuster had met through Jerry's cousin, who was the editor of their school newspaper at Glenville High. Siegel was a fanatic science-fiction fan, while Shuster enjoyed the study of art and drawing. Jerry was already publishing his own science-fiction magazine off a mimeograph machine. Siegel and Shuster began to collaborate, producing a bald-headed villainous super-man who bore a strange resemblance to Superman's future nemesis, Lex Luthor.

Reacting to the horrible news from Europe and the spreading blight of Depression in America, Siegel gradually formed the idea of another superman who would help the downtrodden, stand tall for justice, and defeat the bad guys. This superhero would be an alien from a much larger planet than Earth, warmed by a red sun. Unlike Flash Gordon, who rocketed to the planet Mongo to fight a fascist-style dictator named Ming, Superman was launched toward Earth in an experimental rocket ship just as his doomed planet, Krypton, exploded into fragments. Reversing the science-fiction plot typical of the day of the good space cowboy rescuing fair alien maidens from evil tyranny, Superman had journeyed to our planet to rescue us from ourselves.

Rising like a phoenix from the ashes in an interstellar resurrection, Superman arrived on our planet to be raised in the Midwest and become a real American. Fearing that people would be scared of him, his foster parents taught him to hide his true identity. Ma and Pa Kent raised their Clark to use his great strength to "assist humanity." Siegel found in Clark Kent's personality a soulmate. Hiding behind glasses, an able but shy writer, clumsy with the girls, was a superhero (and ladies' man—Lois and Lana could not get enough of him). Siegel had also adapted the device of the secret identity then common in pulp fiction. It would become a requirement for all superheroes to come.

Jerry and Joe tried to sell their character to newspapers for five years as a comic strip. Rejection followed rejection. They secured a job with what would become Detective Comics (DC), producing words and pictures for such unforgettable titles as *Dr. Occult, Slam Bradley, Spy, Radio Squad,* and *Federal Men.* When printer-publisher Harry Donenfeld needed material for his new *Action Comics,* they were in the right place at the right time. Superman was not even on the cover of the first issue, but became the first comic book superhero to carry his own magazine successfully. Readers could not have enough of him. Within a year Siegel and Shuster were celebrities and had their own *Superman* magazine along with the *Action* series to tell the tales of America's greatest hero (and later the *World's Finest* comics, originally called *New York World's Fair*). The Superman series inspired DC to commission the creation of other superheroes, resulting most prominently in the creation of Batman and Robin (by Jewish cartoonist Bob Kane). Much later, Superman would inspire another Jewish marvel, Stan Lee, to create Spider-Man and a legion of other superstars.

The early Superman stories (now available in a splendidly bound DC Archives edition) were written and drawn out of Siegel and Shuster's Cleveland studios. For ten years they enjoyed moderate financial success as employees of DC Comics.

The Superman character was licensed out and became an incredible moneymaker. *The Adventures of Superman Collecting* by Harry and Amanda Murrah Matetsky lists the incredible amount of "Super Stuff" marketed under the Superman logo. Prize collectibles, jigsaw puzzles, Krypto-Rayguns, dolls, adventure cutouts, bubble gum, valentines, big bread, fan clubs, pinball machines, and filmstrips were but some of the merchandising. Color cartoons of the Man of Steel were produced by Fleischer Studios at great expense for the early 1940s ($100,000). Patriotic posters and war bond ads proclaimed Superman's support of the war effort against Nazi "supermen."

After the war a popular duo of movie serials were produced starring Kirk Alyn. Siegel and Shuster attempted in 1948 to regain full rights to the Superman character and enjoy the full fruits of their creative genius. Donenfeld fired them after their unsuccessful lawsuit. Years of struggle and hardship followed. Shuster's sight failed him. For a time the talented artist who had drawn ecstatic visions of leaps and flowing capes worked in the Post Office to support his family. Siegel briefly worked for DC again in the 1960s. Recognition again and some financial support from a more benevolent corporate regime came only late in life (and largely, not soon enough for Shuster).

The Superman character, however, continued to flourish through the 1940s and 1950s in popular radio and television shows starring respectively Bud Collyer (later of *Beat the Clock* and *To Tell the Truth* fame) and George Reeves (late of *Gone With the Wind*). The immense success of the films with Christopher Reeve (no relation to George Reeves) confirmed the appeal of Superman across generations and led to the blockbuster success of the Batman films.

The comic book and superhero industry has expanded through what their creators would only have viewed as cosmic explosions. Wonder women, barbarians, hulksters, and mutant amphibians have enthralled youngsters now for over fifty years. Yet despite all the commercialism, Superman remains an enduring symbol of America's finest values.

ACKNOWLEDGMENTS

First, my thanks for a lunch at Runyon's to my publisher and friend Steven Schragis and our colleague, the esteemed writer and all-around raconteur, Bert Randolph Sugar, at which the idea for this book (over Philly steak sandwiches) was surprisingly conceived (as well as Sugar's *The Hundred Greatest Athletes of All Time*). Editor Kevin McDonough's smart queries and able assistance helped clarify my thought and toughen my language.

I owe how I think to my teachers Carl Bamberger, Consuelo Elsa Clark, Sidney I. Fetner, Stanley J. Friedman, Wallace Gray, Renee Longy, Joel Newman, Melville Dewey Nussbaum, Vincent Persichetti, Karl-Ludwig Selig, and Elie Siegmeister.

To sources—William Rosenwald and Alex Anagnos for essential background information on Julius Rosenwald; Paul Levitz and Len Schafer of DC Comics; Abraham Peck of the American Jewish Archives at Hebrew Union College; David Clough and Barbara Haws of the New York Philharmonic; Franklin Levy and A. Peter Lubitz for their unique perspectives; research librarian Carolyn Reznick of the Chappaqua Library; Suzanne Hutchinson of *Time* magazine; Robert Freedman and Leon Manoff of Williams Real Estate; Faith Popcorn of BrainReserve; and Ken Cramer, Egon Dumler, and Mark Gittelson, learned soldiers and menschen—my gratitude for your ideas and patience with all my questions.

The Angelus, Berkman, Cohen, Cole, Collas-Lolis, Davis-Israel, Feldman, Flaum, Goodman, Harris, Hilberg, Kaufman, Kempner, Kombert-Rosenblatt, Leiva, Levitt, Manzino, Mason, McAdams, Mc-Comas-Mueller, Meisel, Moak, Nitkin, Poor, Poretsky, Prol-Sexton, Rose, Simon, Spitalny, and Zachary families dealt graciously with my preoccupation with this large task, blessing me with their sweet friendship.

Drs. Marvin Chinitz, Teresa Montague Devins, Jeffrey Gurian, Helene Kaminski, and Michael Wolff not only showed the way toward improved health but inspired by their examples of kind service.

I am especially appreciative of the guidance of Rabbi David Greenberg of Temple Shaaray Tefila of Bedford, New York and Dr. Gottfried H. Wagner, for their unique insights and vision.

My everlasting love to my immediate family, my favorite aunt, Jean Millman; erudite cousin, the photographer John Morrin; heartfelt thanks to my brilliant cousin Dr. Arthur Millman for the use of his large library of Judaica and his wonderful Felella, Ariel, Ilana, and Noah; the Hon. Laura Millman; beloved pethera Mary Vorgia; dearest sisters Marjorie Shapiro, Catherine Esche, and Tina M. Vorgia; brother-in-law Carl Esche; greatest nephews and neighborhood guys Andrew M. and Daniel E. Shapiro; and my best brother, Barry Robert Shapiro.

PICTURE ACKNOWLEDGMENTS

All photographs and illustrations not otherwise credited below are reprinted with permission of the New York Public Library Picture Collection. The author also wishes to thank the following for permission to reprint:

American Jewish Archives: Albert Einstein, pp. 12 and 14; Sigmund Freud, p. 17; Theodore Herzl, p. 35; Moses Mendelssohn, p. 75; David Ben-Gurion, p. 93; Samuel Gompers, p. 159; Gertrude Stein, p. 162; Albert Michelson, p. 165; Golda Meir, p. 171; Felix Mendelssohn, p. 185; Louis B. Mayer, p. 189; Haym Salomon, p. 195; David Sarnoff, p. 212; Julius Rosenwald, p. 220; George Gershwin, p. 228; Chaim Weizmann, p. 233; Franz Boas, p. 236; Leonard Bernstein, p. 243; Louis Brandeis, p. 254; Emile Berliner, p. 258; Sarah Bernhardt, p. 261; Levi Strauss, p. 265; Martin Buber, p. 282; Emma Goldman, p. 314; Sir Moses Montefiore, p. 317; Harry Houdini, p. 329; Henrietta Szold, p. 348.

The Bettmann Archive: Karl Marx, p. 30; Franz Kafka, p. 90; Ferdinand Cohn, p. 156; Jerome Kern, pp. 321 and 324; Leopold Auer, p. 336.

UPI/Bettmann: Mark Rothko, pp. 151 and 154; Arthur Miller, p. 302; Edward Bernays, p. 333; Joe Shuster and Jerry Seigel, p. 373.

Reuters/Bettmann Newsphotos: Arthur Miller, p. 304.

Judaic Heritage Society: Rashi, p. 82; Hillel, p. 98; Issac Luria, p. 130; Philo Judaeus, p. 168.

YIVO Institute for Jewish Research: The Vilna Goan, p. 176; Queen Esther, p. 279.

Fotofolio: Walter Benjamin, p. 251.

Israel Museum, Jerusalem: Baruch de Spinoza, p. 44; Nahmanides, p. 268.

JNUL Schwadron Collection: David Ricardo, p. 139.

Teddy Kolleck Collection: Shabbeti Zevi, p. 239.

Wingate Institute: Simon Bar Kokhba, p. 104.

INDEX

Pissarro, Camille, 360
Pius IX, Pope, 319
Planck, Max, 15
Plato, 169, 180
Plautus (Roman humorist), 312
Pollock, Jackson, 151–52, 153, 155
Porgy and Bess (Gershwin), 231, 313, 322
Porter, Cole, 229
Prince, Harold (Hal), 292, 311, 313
Prince, Rabbi Judah, 107
*Principles of Political Economy and Taxation,
    The* (Ricardo), 139, 140–41
Prokofiev, Sergei, 232, 357
Prophets (biblical), 57–59
Proudhon, Pierre Joseph, 31
Proust, Dr. Adrien, 109
Proust, Marcel, 108–11, 179, 193, 252, 253,
    264
Proust, Robert, 110
Puccini, Giacomo, 66, 264

Rabin, Yitzhak, 274, 275, 321–24
Rabinow, Jacob, 260
Rabinowitz, Harry and Lena (Rips), 289, 290
Rachmaninoff, Sergei, 326
Racine, Jean Baptiste, 263
Rashi (Rabbi Shlomo Itzhaki), 68, 82–84, 281
Ravel, Maurice, 231
RCA (Radio Corp. of America), 212–15
Reeve, Christopher, 376
Reeves, George, 376
Reiner, Fritz, 101, 244
Reinhardt, Ad, 152, 153
Reitman, Ben, 316
*Remembrance of Things Past (A la recherche
    du temps perdu)* (Proust), 108–11, 264
Reveltuas, Silvestre, 232
Rhapsody in Blue (Gershwin), 230
Ricardo, Abraham, 139–40
Ricardo, David, 139–41
Rilke, Rainer Maria, 326
Ritchard, Cyril, 291
Robbins (Rabinowitz), Jerome, 245, 289–93,
    311
Robinson, Jackie, 366
Rockefeller, John D., 223, 335
Rockefeller, Nelson, 296
Rodgers, Richard, 291, 312, 322, 324
Rodin, Auguste, 345
Rodzinski, Artur, 244
Rogers, Ginger, 352
Roller, Alfred, 65
Rooney, Mickey, 190
Roosevelt, Franklin D., 16, 148, 150, 153,
    215, 221, 255
Roosevelt, Theodore, 165
Rosen, Harold, 260
Rosenbloom, "Slapsie" Maxie, 308

Rostand, Edmond, 261, 263
Rothko, Mark (Marcus Rothkovich;
    Rothkowitz), 151–55
Rothschild, Amschel, 113, 115
Rothschild, Lionel de, 86, 116
Rothschild, (Lord) Mayer (Amschel), 62,
    112–16, 234
Rothschild, Nathan, 113, 115, 318
Rothschild, Solomon, 113, 115
Rothschilds, the, 88, 113–16, 318
Rubin, Jerry, 343
Rubinstein, Akiba, 299
Rubinstein, Anton, 187, 326, 337
Russell, Bertrand, 47
Rutherford, Ernest, 73
Ryskind, Morrie, 231, 340

Sabbatai Zevi (Mehmet Effendi), 132, 183,
    239–42
Sabin, Albert, 286, 287
Sadat, el-, Anwar, 175, 272, 274
Sahlein, William, 266
Saint-Simon, Comte Claude de, 122
Saladin, 67, 69
Salieri, Antonio, 128, 218
Salk, Jonas, 286–88
Salomon, Haym, 195–97, 294
Salomon, Haym Moses, 195
Salvador, Francis, 196
Salvarsan (drug), 79, 81
Samuel, Herbert, 234
Samuels, Ernest, 371
Sand, George, 31, 122, 262
Sandherr (colonel), 144, 147
Sanger, Margaret, 134, 135, 316
Sanhedrin (high court), 99–100
Sardou (playwright), 261, 264
Sarnoff, David, 212–15, 334
Sartre, Jean-Paul, 92, 179–80
Saul (warrior), 49, 50
Saul of Tarsus, 25–29
    See also Paul
Scheurer-Kestner, Auguste, 146
Schiff, Jacob, 223, 257
Schiller, Johann von, 54, 78
Schindler's List (film), 53, 358
Schmidt, Karl Ludwig, 270
Schnapper, Gutele, 114
Schneerson, Menachem, 365
Schnitzler, Arthur, 36, 201
Schoenberg, Arnold, 15, 64, 200–204, 231,
    311, 330
Scholem, Gershom (Gerhard), 130, 131,
    132, 253
Schonberg, Harold C., 301
Schubert, Franz, 121, 201, 232
Schumann, Clara, 188
Schumann, Robert, 121, 187, 188